ZOMBIE SCIENCE

ZOMBIE SCIENCE

MORE ICONS OF EVOLUTION

JONATHAN WELLS

SEATTLE   DISCOVERY INSTITUTE PRESS   2017

Description

In 2000, biologist Jonathan Wells took the science world by storm with *Icons of Evolution*, a book showing how biology textbooks routinely promote Darwinism using bogus evidence—icons of evolution like Ernst Haeckel's faked embryo drawings and peppered moths glued to tree trunks. Critics of the book complained that Wells had merely gathered up a handful of innocent textbook errors and blown them out of proportion. Now, in *Zombie Science*, Wells asks a simple question: If the icons of evolution were just innocent textbook errors, why do so many of them still persist? Science has enriched our lives and led to countless discoveries, but now, Wells argues, it's being corrupted. Empirical science is devolving into zombie science, shuffling along unfazed by opposing evidence. Discredited icons of evolution rise from the dead while more icons—equally bogus—join their ranks. Like a B horror movie, they just keep coming! Zombies are make-believe, but zombie science is real—and it threatens not just science, but our whole culture. Is there a solution? Wells is sure of it, and points the way.

Library Cataloging Data

Zombie Science: More Icons of Evolution by Jonathan Wells

Illustrations (unless otherwise noted) by Brian Gage and Anca Sandu

238 pages, 6 x 9 x 0.5 in. & 0.72 lb, 229 x 152 x 13 mm & x 325 g

Library of Congress Control Number: 2017936551

SCI027000 SCIENCE / Life Sciences / Evolution

SCI008000 SCIENCE / Life Sciences / Biology

SCI075000 SCIENCE / Philosophy & Social Aspects

ISBN-13: 978-1-936599-44-8 (paperback), 978-1-936599-46-2 (Kindle), 978-1-936599-45-5 (EPUB)

Publisher Information

Discovery Institute Press, 208 Columbia Street, Seattle, WA 98104

Internet: http://www. discoveryinstitutepress.org/

Published in the United States of America on acid-free paper.

First Edition: April 2017.

*Dedicated to the students who will need
to discern the truth for themselves*

Want to dig deeper?

Visit www.IconsofEvolution.com.

Your one-stop location for additional information about
biologist Jonathan Wells and the "icons of evolution," including
articles, responses to critics, podcasts, and more.

Praise for *Zombie Science*

"In *Zombie Science*, Jonathan Wells gives both a very informative and entertaining account of the problems surrounding Darwinian evolution. He makes a compelling argument that the case in favor of evolution is being driven by a commitment to materialistic philosophy and not by scientific evidence. In fact, Wells convincingly shows that the 'icons' used to support evolution continue to be taught in spite of the increasing evidence against them. Whether a person is convinced of the truth of evolutionary theory, a skeptic, or convinced of the design argument, a clearer and greater understanding of the evolution/design debate will be gained by reading this book."

Russell W. Carlson, Ph.D., Professor Emeritus,
Dept. of Biochemistry & Molecular Biology and the Complex
Carbohydrate Research Center, University of Georgia

"On TV and at the movies, zombies are simultaneously scary and comedic. Zombie science is even more frightening and, at times, even more laughable— and worthy of the exposure and ridicule Dr. Jonathan Wells delivers here with his customary gusto and clarity. This important new book makes a persuasive case that the most radical, least rational and tolerant of all contemporary religious faiths is the fundamentalist belief in materialism."

Michael Medved, nationally syndicated talk radio host
and author of *The American Miracle*

"*Zombie Science* poses a crucial question: If it's true that 'Nothing in biology makes sense except in the light of evolution,' as Darwinists often claim, why do textbooks continue to tout trivial, misleading, or downright fake illustrations fifteen years after Jonathan Wells first exposed many of them? If these are the best examples, the theory itself is extinct."

Michael Behe, Ph.D., , Professor of Biological Sciences, Lehigh University,
and author of *Darwin's Black Box* and *The Edge of Evolution*

"Evolutionary biologists provide contradictory hypotheses of the tree of life and mistaken answers on walking whales, junk DNA, the human eye, the origin of life, and many other captivating topics. To be up to date and informed on the many falsehoods dominating contemporary science and biology textbooks, I strongly recommend *Zombie Science*, the latest 'politically incorrect' book by Jonathan Wells."

Wolf-Ekkehard Lönnig, Ph.D., Senior Scientist,
Dept. of Molecular Genetics, Max Planck Institute of
Plant Breeding Research, Cologne (retired)

"When I read *Zombie Science*, the old phrase 'My mind is made up, don't confuse me with the facts' kept coming to mind. Against the facts, Establishment Science continues to push a materialist narrative with religious zeal. Dr. Wells provides a very readable account of Establishment Science's efforts to shore up a failed theory. Like zombies, neo-Darwinism just refuses to die. But readers will come away with good protection from the zombie arguments that keep appearing."

Ralph Seelke, Ph.D., Professor Emeritus, Dept. of Natural Sciences
(Microbiology, Cell Biology, Genetics), University of Wisconsin-Superior

"In this sequel to his seminal book *Icons of Evolution*, molecular biologist Jonathan Wells not only responds to his critics, but reveals even more examples of dubious and overrated scientific evidence for evolution. He shows that the theory of macroevolution still lacks empirical support, and that the materialist dogma has corrupted modern science, which desperately tries to close the door for any alternative explanations like Intelligent Design. Wells' book represents an important contribution for a paradigm change that is long overdue. It is easy to understand even for laymen, and an enjoyable read as well."

Günter Bechly, Ph.D., Paleontologist and Former Curator
for Amber and Fossil Insects, Dept. of Paleontology, State
Museum of Natural History, Stuttgart, Germany

"*Icons of Evolution* proved the emperor has no clothes. Now *Zombie Science* shows that it doesn't even have a pulse. In this lucid and highly readable sequel, Jonathan Wells again turns the tables on the Darwinists, documenting how their supposedly overwhelming evidence for unguided evolution is 'one long bluff.'"

Tom Bethell , author of *Darwin's House of Cards*
and *The Politically Incorrect Guide to Science*

"Seventeen years ago Jonathan Wells exposed ten 'icons of evolution' that had wide acceptance but that didn't fit the evidence. Now he demonstrates that these 'icons' not only continue to haunt the popular media and remain in commonly distributed textbooks, but that at least six more can be added to the list. Their persistence and proliferation suggest that these icons are now the substance of what he calls 'zombie science,' the promotion of dead ideas as if they were living facts. Wells' strategy is to treat these dead icons like you would all zombies that prefer the cover of darkness: He removes the darkness, shedding revealing light on the 'central dogma' that DNA = RNA = Us, the myth of 'walking whales,' the notion of vestigial organs and other evolutionary 'junk,' the eye as an evolutionary icon, and the boasts of Darwinian medicine in 'explaining' antibiotic resistance and cancer. Told with a scathing wit that would have made Thomas Henry Huxley envious, *Zombie Science* is bound to be next on every Darwinian's growing *Index Librorum Prohibitorium*. To conceal this contraband, Wells even includes instructions for making a plain brown cover for the book. I'm marking mine *Pride and Prejudice*, which may best describe the sources of this 'zombie' phenomenon. A fascinating, lively book that should be on everyone's reading list."

Michael A. Flannery
Professor Emeritus, University of Alabama at Birmingham,
and author of *Alfred Russel Wallace: A Rediscovered Life*

"I could not put this book down; every page has mind-opening information that exposes errors, misinterpretations and even fraud from the hard-line Darwinian evolution proponents. Dr. Jonathan Wells has married his sharp wit and extensive research to deliver an exciting look at the flaws of Darwinian evolution that just keep popping up. If science educators were confident that the current teaching of Darwinian evolution could stand up to scientific criticism, then Dr. Wells' work would be included in school and university syllabi; thus I don't expect to see it in any biology textbook soon. There is a battle for the minds and culture of our future generations, but Dr. Wells shows good reason for optimism as more recent advances in biology come to light and an increasing body of the scientific community are realizing that the current teaching of evolution cannot stand up to recent discoveries."

Dr. Philip Anderson, M.B., Ch.B. D.A. (South Africa) FRCA

"Dr. Wells once again demonstrates his unique ability to bring clarity to the many misrepresentations of the evidence for Darwinian evolution that clutter biology textbooks today. This is the most comprehensive critique I have seen. It is a must read for truth-seeking biology students and their parents."

Roger DeHart, M.A., high school biology teacher for forty years

"In his much anticipated encore to *Icons of Evolution*, Jonathan Wells delivers a 1–2 punch to those who refuse to see that the Darwinian head-lock on 'science' is nothing more than a desperate attempt by the reigning materialist junta to block the search for truth in origins science. A great read."

William S. Harris, Ph.D., medical researcher and
President, OmegaQuant Analytics

CONTENTS

ACKNOWLEDGMENTS

I ALONE AM RESPONSIBLE FOR THE CONTENTS OF THIS BOOK, BUT I would like to thank Laszlo Bencze for suggesting its title. I also gratefully acknowledge the years of support and encouragement I have received from my wife, Lucy, and my children; Phillip and Kathie Johnson; and my colleagues at the Discovery Institute, including Bruce Chapman, Steve Meyer, John West, Steve Buri, Doug Axe, and Ann Gauger, among many others. I am especially grateful for comments on the manuscript by Paul Nelson, Rick Sternberg, David Berlinski, and Jonathan and Amanda Witt.

For making embarrassingly candid or unwittingly humorous statements, I would like to thank (in alphabetical order) David Barash, Jerry Coyne, Richard Dawkins, Daniel Dennett, W. Ford Doolittle, Niles Eldredge, Douglas Futuyma, Karl Giberson, Dan Graur, Richard Lewontin, Geoffrey Miller, Kenneth R. Miller, Randy Olson, Kevin Padian, Massimo Pigliucci, Donald Prothero, Eugenie Scott, and Michael Shermer.

I also gratefully acknowledge help from several students who must remain anonymous lest enforcers of the scientific consensus destroy their very promising careers.

JONATHAN WELLS

SEATTLE 2017

1. WHO LET THE ZOMBIES OUT?

ZOMBIES ARE THE WALKING DEAD. IN SCIENCE, A THEORY OR IMAGE is dead when it doesn't fit the evidence. I wrote a book in 2000 about ten images, ten "icons of evolution," that did not fit the evidence and were empirically dead. They should have been buried, but they are still with us, haunting our science classrooms and stalking our children. They are part of what I call zombie science.

Egg on Their Face

I LIKE eggs for breakfast. In fact, I've been eating eggs for years. I knew I was not supposed to, because some scientists and the U. S. government said they were bad for me. According to the American Heart Association (AHA) and the United States Department of Agriculture (USDA), science had proven that eggs—especially egg yolks—contained too much cholesterol and were thus bad for my heart. But I liked them, and my heart was fine, so I ate them anyway.

It had all started in the early 1950s, when scientist John Gofman and his colleagues concluded that the risk of heart disease could be lowered by reducing the intake of dietary fat.[1] Another scientist, Ancel Keys, had come to the same conclusion.[2] In 1957 two other scientists demonstrated that Keys had actually manipulated his evidence by "cherry-picking" (relying only on data that fit his hypothesis while ignoring the rest).[3,4] No matter; in 1961 an AHA committee with Keys as a member recommended that people should reduce their consumption of meat, eggs, and dairy products to lower their risk of heart disease.[5]

In 1977 a U. S. Senate committee endorsed the AHA's recommendations,[6] and in 1992 the USDA published its famous Food Pyramid. It depicts in cartoon form that carbohydrates (the wide bottom of the pyramid) should be the major component of our diet, and that eggs (just below the point at the top) should be relegated to a minor role.[7,8]

I ate eggs anyway.

Imagine my relief when, in February 2015, the U. S. government called off its decades-long War On Eggs by announcing, "Cholesterol is not considered a nutrient of concern for overconsumption."[9,10] Although there is a correlation between heart disease and the levels of various forms of cholesterol in our bodies, there is no significant correlation between our cholesterol levels and what we eat. Eggs were never bad for us. Indeed, whole eggs are close to being a perfect food.

"But science said..."

Yes, and now "science says" something else. What should we make of this? Obviously, we cannot always trust what "science says," and an endorsement by the government doesn't make it any more trustworthy.

In fact, we are told many things by "science" that are not true. The misguided War On Eggs was a relatively benign instance of this. Eggs were not declared unconstitutional, and people who ate them were not publicly ridiculed or driven from their jobs. But "science says" is not always so benign.

WARNING: This book is politically incorrect, even dangerous. If you are seen reading it on a college campus, your career could suffer. So you may want to disguise it with a different cover. The Supplement on page 189 shows how to make a plain paper cover.

How can you know whether something "science says" is true? Ultimately, you will have to discern the truth for yourself. This doesn't mean there is no objective truth and everything is subjective. But sometimes people—even decent, intelligent people—commit themselves to an idea that seems reasonable yet distorts the objective truth. When it comes to science, you will be told one thing by our enormously powerful and wealthy scientific and educational institutions, as well as by the mainstream news media that serve as their mouthpiece. But you may learn something else if you look at the actual evidence—that is, the objective truth.

Before we go any further, let's look at some of the ways people use the word "science."

What Is Science?

MANY PEOPLE are inclined to respect science and trust its authority. But science can mean different things. In one sense, science is the enterprise of seeking truth by formulating hypotheses and testing them against the evidence. If a hypothesis is repeatedly tested and found to be consistent with the evidence, we may tentatively regard it as true. If it is repeatedly found to be *inconsistent* with the evidence, we should revise it or reject it as false. We call this enterprise *empirical science*. At some level we are all scientists in this sense, because in our daily lives we compare our ideas with our experiences and revise them when necessary, often without a second thought.

In another sense, people think of science as the modern advances in medicine and technology that have enriched our lives. Those advances originate in human creativity and design, but their practical application involves testing them against the evidence to find out if they work. So advances in medicine and technology have an empirical aspect as well as a creative one. Let's call this *technological science*.

In a third sense, science refers to the scientific establishment, which consists of people who are trained and employed to conduct research in various areas. Let's call this *establishment science*, or just Science. The majority opinion of this group is sometimes referred to as "the scientific consensus," which is at times expressed as "All scientists agree..." (even though usually some don't), or as "Science Says..."

Throughout history, the scientific consensus has often proven to be unreliable. In 1500, the scientific consensus held that the sun revolves around the Earth, a view that was overturned by Nicolaus Copernicus and Galileo Galilei. In 1750, the consensus held that some living things (such as maggots) originate by spontaneous generation, a view that was overturned by Francesco Redi and Louis Pasteur. There are many such examples in the history of science.

In a fourth sense, some people define science as the enterprise of providing natural explanations for everything—that is, accounting for all phenomena in terms of material objects and the physical forces among them. This is sometimes called "methodological naturalism," the view that science is limited to materialistic explanations because repeatable experiments can be done only on material objects and physical forces.

In principle, methodological naturalism is not a claim about reality, but a limitation on method. It does not rule out the existence of a non-material realm. But in practice many scientists assume that if they search long enough they will find a materialistic explanation for whatever they are investigating. This assumption that there are materialistic explanations for everything is not just a statement about method. It is equivalent to materialistic philosophy, which regards material objects and physical forces as the only realities.[11,12] Mind, free will, spirit, and God are considered illusions. Intelligent design (ID), the view that some features of the world are due to an intelligent cause rather than to unguided natural processes, is also regarded as an illusion.

Not all scientists today are materialists, and indeed modern science was launched primarily by European Christian theists. Nevertheless, science today is dominated by materialistic philosophy. Priority is given to proposing and defending materialistic explanations rather than to following the evidence wherever it leads. This is materialistic philosophy masquerading as empirical science, and I call it *zombie science*.

I am not calling scientists (or any other real people) zombies. But whenever people persist in defending a materialistic explanation after it has been shown to be inconsistent with the evidence, and is thus empirically dead, they are practicing zombie science.

We find the most prominent displays of zombie science in evolutionary biology.

What is "Evolution"?

EVOLUTION IS another term that can mean different things: simple change over time; the history of the cosmos; the progress of technology; the development of culture; or the fact that many plants and animals now living are different from those that lived in the past. In these general senses, evolution is uncontroversial.

Evolution can also mean minor changes within existing species from generation to generation. There is abundant evidence for such changes; they are obvious in our own families. People have also been observing such changes in other species for thousands of years—certainly since the domestication of plants and animals. So evolution in this sense is also uncontroversial.

In 1859, Charles Darwin proposed that minor variations within existing species are preserved or eliminated by natural selection (survival of the fittest), and that given enough time this process generates new species, organs, and body plans. Darwin argued that variations and selection are unguided, so the results of evolution are left to the working out of what he called chance. "There seems to be no more design in the variability of organic beings, and in the action of natural selection," he once wrote, "than in the course which the wind blows."[13]

Evolution as Materialistic Science

DARWIN DESCRIBED his most famous book, *The Origin of Species*, as "one long argument."[14] It was basically an argument *against* creation by design, and it took the following form: The facts of biology are "inexplicable on the theory of creation" but make sense on his theory of descent with modification.[15] Starting with the fourth edition of his book, Darwin went further and argued that the idea that living things were created according to a plan "is not a scientific explanation."[16] Design was, as it were, ruled out of court by definition.

It is often claimed that people in the nineteenth century were converted to Darwin's theory because he provided so much evidence for it, but this is not true. For one thing, Darwin could offer no evidence for natural selection, only "one or two imaginary illustrations."[17] And despite the title of his most famous book, he failed to explain the origin of species. People were converted to Darwin's theory mainly because it fit the increasingly materialistic tenor of the times.

Historian Neal C. Gillespie wrote that "it is sometimes said that Darwin converted the scientific world to evolution by showing them the process by which it had occurred. Yet the uneasy reservations about natural selection among Darwin's contemporaries and the widespread rejection of it from the 1890s to the 1930s suggest that this is too simple a view of the matter. It was more Darwin's insistence on totally natural explanations than on natural selection that won their adherence."[18]

This explains why we hear little about the co-discoverer of natural selection, Alfred Russel Wallace. Although the theories of both men were first publicly presented on the same day in 1858, Wallace was skeptical that unguided variation and survival of the fittest could account for things such as "the brain, the organs of speech, the hand, and the external form of man." He concluded instead that evolution must have been directed by an "Overruling Intelligence."[19]

Darwin was horrified by this idea. As historian Michael Flannery has pointed out, Wallace's idea challenged Darwin's entire framework, "a framework that served not only to bolster a materialistic metaphysic but, in effect, proposed to become its operative manifesto." The "inescapable conclusion," according to Flannery, is "that Darwinian evolution, far from being a scientific [i.e., empirical] theory, is 'one long argument' in favor of an *a priori* metaphysic."[20]

So the "Darwinian revolution" was a triumph of materialistic philosophy.[21] Even so, Darwin's theory did not rise to prominence in biology until the 1930s, when it hitched a ride with a theory of genetics that was empirically much better supported. (See Chapter 4.) The combination of the two became known as "the modern synthesis" or "neo-Darwinism."

Microevolution and Macroevolution

IN THE 1930s, neo-Darwinian biologist Theodosius Dobzhansky used the word "microevolution" to refer to minor changes within existing species, and the word "macroevolution" to refer to the origin of new species, organs, and body plans. "There is no way toward an understanding of the mechanisms of macroevolutionary changes," he wrote, "which require time on a geological scale, other than through a full comprehension of the microevolutionary processes observable within the span of a human lifetime and often controlled by man's will. For this reason we are compelled at the present level of knowledge reluctantly to put a sign of equality between the mechanisms of macro- and microevolution, and proceeding on this assumption, to push our investigations as far ahead as this working hypothesis will permit."[22]

As we saw above, microevolution is not controversial. But Darwin did not write a book titled *How Existing Species Change Over Time*. He wrote a book titled *The Origin of Species by Means of Natural Selection*. And while he didn't use Dobzhansky's words (which came later), Darwin's theory was that microevolution—given enough time—produces macroevolution. Yet despite an enormous amount of biological research since the 1930s, the "sign of equality" between microevolution and macroevolution remains nothing more than what Dobzhansky called it: a hypothesis. And indeed, it remains a hypothesis starving for lack of evidence.

People speaking for the current scientific consensus often lump microevolution and macroevolution together and refer to them simply as evolution—a verbal sleight of hand in place of evidence for Dobzhansky's hoped-for "sign of equality" between the two. Such confusion is regrettable, but common.

The scientific consensus also follows Darwin in insisting that evolution is unguided, though its adherents can be evasive about this point when it suits their rhetorical purposes. I want to dispel as much fog as possible in these pages, but I also want to avoid cumbersome language, so I will use "evolution" throughout the book to refer to "unguided macroevolution" except where I specify otherwise.

Nothing in Biology

IN 1973, Dobzhansky wrote an article titled "Nothing in Biology Makes Sense Except in the Light of Evolution."[23] And by evolution Dobzhansky meant neo-Darwinian evolution. His statement has become a guiding principle in the lives of most modern biologists. It is now a fundamental assumption underlying most research and writing in the discipline.

People who believe Dobzhansky's statement insist that they do so because of the evidence, but what follows below will show that this is not the case.[24] A person does not have to believe in materialism to believe in evolution, but evolution is a materialistic story. And since the materialistic story trumps the evidence, it is zombie science.

Icons of Evolution

ACCORDING TO the current scientific consensus, there is "overwhelming evidence" for evolution. The evidence is typically represented by images that have been used so often they have achieved the status of "icons." In 2000, I wrote a book analyzing ten of them:[25]

The Miller-Urey Experiment: A 1953 experiment that supposedly showed how the chemical building blocks of life could have formed spontaneously on the early Earth;

Darwin's Tree of Life: A branching tree diagram used to illustrate the notion of descent with modification of all living things from common ancestors;

Homology in Vertebrate Limbs: Similarities in limb bones used as evidence that vertebrates (animals with backbones) are all descended from a common ancestor;

Haeckel's Embryos: Drawings of similarities in early embryos used as evidence that all vertebrates (including humans) evolved from fish-like animals;

Archaeopteryx: A fossil bird with teeth in its mouth and claws on its wings, often cited as the missing link between ancient reptiles and modern birds;

Peppered Moths: Photos of moths resting on tree trunks, supposedly providing evidence for evolution by natural selection;

Darwin's Finches: Thirteen species of finches on the Galápagos Islands that are used as evidence for the origin of species by natural selection;

Four-Winged Fruit Flies: Fruit flies with an extra pair of wings that supposedly provide evidence that DNA mutations provide the raw materials for macroevolution;

Fossil Horses: Fossils once used to show that evolution proceeds in a straight line and later used to show that it doesn't; and

The Ultimate Icon: Drawings of ape-like creatures gradually evolving into humans, used to show that we are just animals produced by purposeless natural causes.

All these "icons of evolution" misrepresent the evidence, and as we shall see, many biologists have known this for decades. So by the year 2000 the icons should have been removed from biology textbooks. Yet they were, and still are, used to convince students that evolution is a fact.

Chapter 2 looks at the icon at the center of evolutionary theory, Darwin's tree of life. The chapter also examines how evolution has corrupted the concept of homology. Chapter 3 summarizes why the other eight icons were dead in 2000 and documents how they are nevertheless still being used today. Chapters 4 through 8 introduce six additional icons of evolution that—like the ten icons listed above—are used to mislead and indoctrinate people about evolution. Chapter 9 describes how zombie science has spread beyond science to religion and education, and how it continues to corrupt science generally.

Yet, as I will also show, there are some rays of hope.

2. The Tree of Life

O F ALL THE MISLEADING ICONS OF EVOLUTION, NONE IS MORE foundational than the tree of life.

We know intuitively that a robin and a finch are more similar to each other than either is to a frog; that these three vertebrates are more similar to each other than they are to an oyster; that these four animals are more similar to each other than they are to a daffodil; and that these five living things are more similar to each other than they are to a chunk of iron.

So far, so good.

People have been classifying organisms like this for centuries, and the result is a nested hierarchy: Daffodils and animals are nested in the set of living things; oysters and vertebrates are nested in the set of animals; frogs and birds are nested in the set of vertebrates; and robins and finches are nested in the set of birds. Over the centuries, most people have believed that this nested hierarchy reflects a divine plan of creation. Swedish biologist Carl von Linné (Latinized version: Linnaeus), who in the eighteenth century founded the modern science of taxonomy by naming and classifying plants and animals according to genus and species, believed this.

The similarities we use to classify living things are called "homologies," sometimes defined as features that are similar in structure and/or position but which may perform different functions. In the nineteenth century, British biologist Richard Owen distinguished homologies from "analogies," features that use different structures to perform similar functions. For example, a bat's wing and a bird's wing contain bones of similar structure and position, so their wings are homologous. An insect wing performs the same function, but it has a totally different structure, so its wing is analogous to that of a bat or a bird (See Figure 2-1). Owen and others reasoned that analogy suggests independent adaptation to external conditions, while homology suggests deeper morphological (anatomical) affinities, so homology is a better guide to classification than analogy. Bats and birds are nested in the vertebrates, but insects are not.

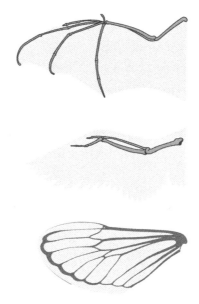

FIGURE 2-I. HOMOLOGY AND ANALOGY: (Top) Bat wing. (Middle) Bird wing. (Bottom) Insect wing. Homology: The bat and the bird have a single bone on the right, two bones in the middle, and several digits on the left (the bird has fewer digits than the bat, but they are similar in structure and position). Analogy: The insect wing has no bones at all, but a network of veins.

Owen attributed homology to construction on a common plan, but Charles Darwin argued that the best explanation for homology is descent from a common ancestor. In *The Origin of Species* he wrote that genealogy is "the only known cause of the similarity of organic beings."[1] Thus "I view all beings not as special creations, but as the lineal descendants of some few beings" that lived in the distant past.[2] Although Darwin was ambivalent about whether there were separate ancestors for "each great class" or a single common ancestor for all living things, he leaned toward the latter. Indeed, he wrote that "probably all the organic beings which have ever lived on this earth have descended from some one primordial form."[3]

So Darwin conceived of a "great Tree of Life," with the common ancestor as the trunk, intermediate forms as the branches, and modern species as "green and budding twigs"[4] (See Figure 2-2).

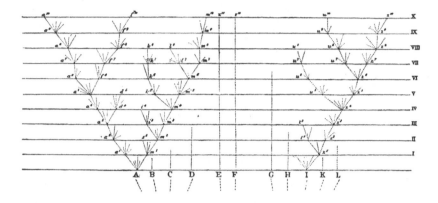

FIGURE 2-2. DARWIN'S TREE OF LIFE: The only illustration in *The Origin of Species*. The letters A through L represent species. The horizontal lines mark times, with the oldest at the bottom and the most recent at the top. Darwin wrote that the intervals between them "may represent each a thousand or more generations." The first lines radiating upwards from A represent varieties, and by the end of the first interval two of those varieties have become separate species, a and m. After many more generations, additional species have branched off from a and m, but all have gone extinct except species f. The horizontal distances between a, f, and m represent the differences among them, which increase over time. Of the original eleven species, only A and I have given rise to new species; the others have remained unchanged and in most cases have gone extinct. The dashed lines at the bottom reflect Darwin's ambivalence about whether all classes of living things shared a common ancestor, though he reasoned that they probably did. From *The Origin of Species*, Charles Darwin (London: John Murray, 1859).[5]

For Darwin, evolution was completely materialistic. All living things after the first resulted from descent with modification by natural selection, and there could be no discontinuities in the subsequent history of life. In 1859 he wrote to geologist Charles Lyell, "I would give absolutely nothing for [my] theory of nat. selection, if it require miraculous additions at any one stage of descent."[6]

Darwin spelled it out this way in *The Origin of Species*:

By the theory of natural selection all living species have been connected with the parent-species of each genus, by differences not greater than we see between the varieties of the same species at the present day; and these parent-species, now generally extinct, have in their turn been similarly connected with more ancient species; and so on backwards, always converging to the common ancestor of each great class. So that the number of intermediate and transitional links, between all living and extinct species, must have been inconceivably great.[7]

It's a magnificent image, but it doesn't fit the facts.

Fossils

THE "INCONCEIVABLY great" numbers of transitional links postulated by Darwin have never been found. Indeed, one of the most prominent features of the fossil record is the Cambrian explosion, in which the major groups of animals (called "phyla") appeared around the same time in a geological period called the Cambrian, abruptly and without fossil evidence that they diverged from a common ancestor.

Darwin knew about this in 1859, and he acknowledged it to be a serious problem that "may be truly urged as a valid argument" against his theory.[8] He attributed the problem to the imperfection of the fossil record, and he hoped future fossil discoveries would help to fill in many of the blanks. But more than a century of additional fossil collecting has only made the problem worse. In 1991, a team of paleontologists (people who study fossils) concluded that the Cambrian explosion "was even more abrupt and extensive than previously envisioned."[9]

One of the authors of the 1991 paper, James Valentine, published a book in 2004 with the University of Chicago Press titled *On the Origin of Phyla*. Valentine believes in evolution and states in the book's preface, "Darwin was correct in his conclusions that all living things have descended from a common ancestor and can be placed within a tree of life."[10] But later in the book Valentine concedes that "organisms with the characteristic body plans that we identify as living phyla appear abruptly in the fossil record, many within a narrow window of geologic time.... It is consistent with the fossil record that all of the characteristic animal body plans had evolved by the close of this period, but none of them can be traced through fossil intermediates to an ancestral group."[11]

In 2013, Valentine and Douglas Erwin published another book on the Cambrian explosion. Like Valentine, Erwin believes in evolution, and most of their book consists of evolutionary hypotheses woven into a story about what they think happened before and during the explosion. In the process they employ "ghost lineages"—hypothetical links that left no fossil record but whose existence is required by the assumption of common ancestry. Erwin and Valentine even refer tongue-in-cheek to their hypotheses as "exercises in evolutionary séances."[12]

But what if the Cambrian explosion cannot be explained by evolution? What if the animal phyla did not descend from a common ancestor by material processes? What if the abrupt appearance of the major groups of animals required new information, which is immaterial? In his 2013 book Darwin's Doubt, philosopher of science Stephen Meyer argues that since different body plans require different information, the Cambrian explosion was an explosion of novel information. According to Meyer, the only known source of such information is intelligence, so the Cambrian explosion is evidence of intelligent design.[13]

So the evidence may say yes. But Science Says No.

Punctuated Equilibria

THE ABRUPTNESS seen in the Cambrian explosion can also be seen on smaller scales throughout the fossil record. The vast majority of species appear abruptly in the fossil record and then persist unchanged for some period of time (a phenomenon called "stasis") before they disappear. In 1972, paleontologists Niles Eldredge and Stephen Jay Gould called this pattern "punctuated equilibria."[14] According to Gould, "every paleontologist always knew" that it is the dominant pattern in the fossil record.[15]

Eldredge and Gould attributed stasis to constancy of the environment or internal constraints on embryo development, and they attributed abrupt appearances to "allopatric speciation." ("Speciation" refers to the origin of a new species.) According to the hypothesis of allopatric speciation, a small part of an existing population becomes geographically separated ("allopatric" comes from words meaning "other" and "fatherland") and thus genetically isolated from the main population. Hypothetically, genetic changes ("mutations") might then turn the isolated fragment into a new species, though because of its small size and rapid evolution it would leave no fossil record. Later, if the new species begins to leave a fossil record, it would seem to originate abruptly.

Some critics objected that this was merely an attempt to explain away the *absence* of evidence for transitional forms. Indeed, some critics even pointed out that a pattern of punctuated equilibria is more consistent with creation than with evolution. But Darwin had declared that idea unscientific.

Another criticism of punctuated equilibria was that the evolution of new morphological features by genetic mutations and natural selection would require large populations and long periods of time. Such features would not be expected to emerge in small populations in a short time, as required by Eldredge and Gould's hypothesis. Thus evolutionary biologists Brian Charlesworth, Russell Lande and Montgomery Slatkin wrote in 1982 that "some of the genetic mechanisms that have been proposed to explain the abrupt appearance and prolonged stasis of many fossil species are conspicuously lacking in empirical support."[16]

So punctuated equilibria is not an empirically supported explanation. It is really little more than a restatement of the observation that new species tend to appear abruptly in the fossil record and then remain unchanged until they disappear. Ancestors and transitional forms are missing. From time to time, fossils are discovered that have features that seem to be intermediate between older and newer species, and some people claim that these confirm the truth of evolutionary theory. These "transitional forms" or "missing links" often make headlines, but it turns out that none of them are actual ancestors. (More on this in Chapters 3 and 5.)

Why Fossils Cannot Establish Ancestor-Descendant Relationships

ACCORDING TO British biologist Ronald Jenner, without a good fossil record there is "little choice but to resort to our more-or-less informed imagination to produce the historical narratives that are the ultimate goal of our studies of animal evolution." Indeed, "our imagination is the only tool that can braid the fragmentary evidence into a seamless histori-cal narrative that relates the *what, how,* and *why*" of evolution.[17]

The situation for evolutionists is actually worse than that. Even if we *did* have a good fossil record, we would still need to use our imagination to produce narratives about ancestor-descendant relationships.

Here's why. If you found two human skeletons buried in a field, how could you know whether one was descended from the other? Without identifying marks and written records, or perhaps in some cases DNA, it would be impossible to know. Yet you would be dealing with two skel-etons from the same recent, living species. With two different, ancient, extinct species—often far removed from each other in time and space—there would be no way to demonstrate an ancestor-descendant relation-ship.

Decades ago, American Museum of Natural History paleontologist Gareth Nelson wrote, "The idea that one can go to the fossil record and expect to empirically recover an ancestor-descendant sequence, be it of species, genera, families, or whatever, has been, and continues to be, a pernicious illusion."[18] In 1999, *Nature* editor Henry Gee wrote that "it is effectively impossible to link fossils into chains of cause and effect in any valid way." He concluded: "To take a line of fossils and claim that they represent a lineage is not a scientific hypothesis that can be tested, but an assertion that carries the same validity as a bedtime story—amusing, perhaps even instructive, but not scientific."[19] Gee (like Valentine and Erwin) believes in evolution, but his belief (like theirs) is clearly not based on fossil evidence.

Phylogenetic Trees

DESPITE THE fact that ancestor-descendant relationships cannot be empirically recovered from fossils, the modern biological literature is full of evolutionary trees—called "phylogenetic" trees—that supposedly show such relationships. The trees are typically accompanied by stories of how earlier organisms evolved into later ones. But phylogenetic trees don't require ancestors. In fact, they don't even require organisms.

In 2013, a science education group produced a lesson plan for teaching high school and college students how to construct a phylogenetic tree with differently shaped metal fasteners, pastas, or cookies. Even though the objects are artificial, "the problems faced and the questions posed are similar to those addressed by paleontologists using specimens of fossils."[20]

The first guiding principle is: "Organisms that resemble each other in many ways are probably more closely related than are organisms that resemble each other only slightly. That is, the greater the similarity in structure (the more features in common), the closer the probable relationship between two forms." Students are instructed "to choose the smallest, simplest form as the probable common ancestor for the group and then try to arrange the others as branches of a tree derived from this ancestor."[21]

Obviously, nothing about these forms requires or implies common ancestry. And in fact, we all know that the metal fasteners, pasta, and cookies were products of intelligent design. So what we have is merely an exercise in choosing what features to compare and deciding on degrees of relationship. But "relationship" is ambiguous. In one sense it can refer to genealogy, as in "Charles Darwin was more closely related to Erasmus Darwin (his grandfather) than either was to Geronimo." In another sense it can refer to similarity, as in "iron is more closely related to aluminum than either is to a daffodil." In the case of fossil species, relationships are unknowable in the first sense, so phylogenetic trees are constructed using relationships in the latter sense. But many evolutionists then equivocate, suggesting that they have demonstrated relationships in the genealogical sense.

Cladistics

IN 1950, German biologist Willi Hennig pioneered the field of phylogenetic systematics, later called cladistics. ("Clade" comes from the Greek word meaning "branch," and in biology it refers to a branch of the tree of life.) Hennig believed that evolution is a fact, but he disliked unconstrained evolutionary storytelling, and he sought a more rigorously empirical way to establish relationships among living things.[22]

In cladistics, a "cladogram" is a diagram made by comparing characteristics shared by certain taxa (groups of organisms such as species, genera, families, etc.) but not by another taxon (singular of taxa). The former are designated the "ingroup." The latter, the "outgroup." Characteristics found in the ingroup but not the outgroup are said to be "derived," and a cladogram is based on "shared derived characteristics." The result is a nested hierarchy (See Figure 2-3). Cladists view this approach as more precise and testable than simply counting resemblances.

There is no element of time or ancestral relationship in a cladogram. An evolutionary biologist may assert that the outgroup and ingroup are related through ancestry and descent, but there is nothing in a cladogram itself that requires such a relationship. Ancestors and transitional forms are left to the imagination. Berkeley paleontologist Kevin Padian acknowledges this even though he believes in evolution. (Indeed, he aggressively defends it.) As he explains, in a properly drawn phylogeny "extinct animals are no longer seen as direct ancestors of each other ('missing links'), but rather as representatives of a tree of life that help us to read the sequence of evolution of major features (not 'transitional forms')." Since Padian considers it important to convince students of evolution, however, he recommends supplementing cladograms to make "evograms."[23] In other words, ancestral relationships are asserted despite the lack of evidence.

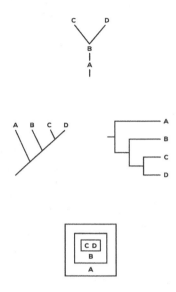

FIGURE 2-3. A TREE, CLADOGRAMS, AND A NESTED HIERARCHY: (Top) A diagram showing species A evolving into species B, and species B splitting into C and D. (Middle) Two ways of representing with cladograms the relationships among the four species; note that all four are now on the same line, and none is represented as the ancestor of another. (Bottom) A nested hierarchy that contains the same information as the cladograms above it, namely that A and B share some characteristics but B has at least one characteristic that is derived (not found in A), while C and D share some characteristics with B but also have at least one characteristic that is not found in B. Note that the top figure includes the time dimension (A comes before B and B comes before C and D), but the cladograms and nested hierarchy do not.

The old-fashioned evolutionary trees that used to adorn biology textbooks have now been largely replaced by cladograms. Nevertheless, most textbooks still mislead students into believing that cladograms are ancestor-descendant diagrams. For example, Kenneth Miller and Joseph Levine's 2014 *Biology*, a widely used high school biology textbook, states that "a cladogram links groups of organisms by showing how evolutionary lines, or lineages, branched off from common ancestors."[24] But the common ancestors are nowhere to be seen.

Molecular Phylogeny

SINCE THE rise of molecular biology in the mid-twentieth century, biologists have increasingly used comparisons of sequences in DNA, RNA and protein to construct phylogenetic trees. For example, a particular DNA sequence might be present in different species, though with minor variations. Comparing the sequence differences in species A, B, and C could lead to an inference that species A is more closely related (that is, more similar) to species B than it is to species C. The similarity between two sequences (often called homology) can be expressed as a percentage, representing how many subunits at corresponding positions are identical between them.

Similarity may be assumed to imply genealogy, but this is only an assumption. Any inference to genealogy based on sequence similarity is hypothetical. And since molecular sequences (with rare exceptions) are available only from living organisms, any inference about the evolutionary past of those organisms—including their ancestors—is even more hypothetical.

The Alignment Problem

BEFORE SEQUENCES can be compared, they have to be aligned. But molecular sequences in living things typically contain repeated and/or deleted segments. This means it is often unclear where to start aligning them. Sequences can be quite long, and since they can be aligned in more than one way the result depends heavily on what alignment the investigator chooses. And when many sequences are compared, as they are in molecular phylogenies, the problem becomes much worse.[25]

Computer programs are available to align sequences, but they depend on the parameters built into them by their programmers, and sometimes the results are biologically implausible. In 2009, biologist David Morrison surveyed the scientific literature and found that "more than one-half of evolutionary biologists intervene manually in their sequence alignments, and more than three-quarters of phylogeneticists do so."[26] In 2015, Morrison noted "a proliferation of alignment methods" that "produce detectably different multiple sequence alignments in almost all realistic cases."[27]

So even before the process of comparing sequences begins, subjective choices influence the eventual results. Similarities are supposed to be telling the investigators who might be related to whom and how closely. But as it turns out, the investigators are doing much of the telling by picking and choosing their preferred alignments.

Conflicting Trees

IT IS not surprising, then, that sequence comparisons often produce conflicting phylogenetic trees. Decades ago, it was assumed that the inclusion of more molecules in analyses would eliminate the discrepancies, but that has not happened. In 2005, evolutionary biologists Antonis Rokas, Dirk Krüger, and Sean B. Carroll analyzed fifty genes from seventeen animal groups and concluded that "different phylogenetic analyses can reach contradicting inferences with [seemingly] absolute support."[28]

In 2008, an international team of eighteen biologists used 150 genes to construct a phylogeny of animal groups. Their tree was contradicted the following year by another international team of twenty biologists using 128 genes.[29,30] In 2012, biologists Liliana Dávalos, Andrea Cirranello, Jonathan Geisler, and Nancy Simmons reported, "Incongruence between phylogenies derived from morphological *versus* molecular analyses, and between trees based on different subsets of molecular sequences has become pervasive."[31]

To eliminate conflicts among molecular phylogenies, biologists often exclude data from their analyses, justifying the practice on the grounds that not all sequences carry "strong phylogenetic signals."[32] For example, taxa are usually inferred to be closely related if their corresponding sequences are similar, but sequences can be very different even in taxa that are believed on other grounds to have diverged recently from a common ancestor. The anomalous sequences are then assumed to be "fast evolving" and are excluded from the phylogenetic tree.[33] Or corresponding sequences can be very similar in taxa that are assumed to have diverged a long time ago, in which case their similarity is attributed to having accumulated enough mutations to converge on each other (a phenomenon called "long branch attraction").[34]

Notice how much work the assumptions are doing in these arguments. All molecular sequences (with rare exceptions) are from living organisms. There is no way to look deep into the past and determine whether they diverged rapidly or converged slowly. So a phylogeneticist assumes that evolution is true and the history of life is tree-like, then chooses a particular phylogenetic tree and discards whichever sequences don't fit it (See Figure 2-4).

FIGURE 2-4. DRAWING A PHYLOGENETIC TREE.

Orphan Genes

THE PRACTICE of discarding unwanted sequences has become more prevalent because of the recent discovery that many DNA sequences are restricted to a single taxon.

According to evolutionary theory, all new sequences evolve from old ones by duplication and/or by mutation and natural selection. In 1977, French molecular biologist François Jacob wrote, "Once life had started in the form of some primitive self-reproducing organism, further evolution had to proceed mainly through alterations of already existing compounds." Therefore, the "creation of entirely new nucleotide [DNA] sequences could not be of any importance in the production of new information."[35] So a sequence in species X should resemble its ancestral sequence in species Y.

By the 1990s, however, biologists had discovered many sequences with no similarity to those in other taxa. In 1999, Daniel Fischer and David Eisenberg examined the complete DNA sequences of over a dozen species of bacteria and concluded that about a third of the protein-coding regions had "no detectable sequence similarity to proteins of other genomes." ("Genome" here refers to the whole of an organism's DNA.) This poses an uncomfortable question for evolutionary theory. "Why, if proteins in different organisms have descended from common ancestral proteins by duplication and adaptive variation," Fischer and Eisenberg asked, "do so many today show no similarity to each other?" Good question!

Since protein-coding regions are also known as "open reading frames" (ORFs), Fischer and Eisenberg called these orphan genes "ORFans."[36] The number of known ORFans has been growing ever since. They have been discovered in yeast,[37,38] fruit flies,[39,40] mice,[41,42] and humans.[43,44] A 2015 article in *Nature* reported hundreds of ORFans restricted to squids and octopuses.[45] In fact, every species whose whole genome has been studied has a significant number of ORFans. Biologists now expect to find ORFans wherever they look.

Where do orphan genes come from? German biologist Henrik Kaessmann wrote in 2010 that a gene that seems to originate "from scratch" probably arises from a "previously nonfunctional genomic sequence, unrelated to any pre-existing genic material."[46] In 2011, biologists Diethard Tautz and Tomislav Domazet-Lošo argued similarly that "many orphan genes may have arisen de novo from non-coding regions."[47] But "may have arisen de novo" isn't much better than saying orphan genes "just happen."

Aware of the problem, an international team of biologists in 2012 proposed "an evolutionary model according to which functional genes evolve de novo through transitory proto-genes."[48] Just as the evolutionary story requires "ghost lineages" to bridge the gaps between fossils, so it requires imaginary "proto-genes" to bridge the gaps between ORFans and non-coding regions.

So it's difficult to explain the origin of orphan genes. It is even more difficult to deal with them when constructing phylogenetic trees. The authors of a 2016 article about insect phylogeny decided to deal with them by ignoring them completely. They explained that "our approach eliminates any gene that is present in only a single taxon," because "such genes are phylogenetically uninformative." Uninformative, that is, if taxa are assumed to have descended from a common ancestor. Perhaps "counterinformative" would be a better word. So the authors cherry-picked data from every insect they studied, discarding forty percent of the sequences from the fruit fly and eighty percent of the sequences from the water flea, in order to produce a phylogenetic tree to their liking.[49]

The methodology of constructing phylogenetic trees can thus be summarized as follows: (1) Assume that common ancestry is true. (2) Cherry-pick the data to construct a tree that includes various organisms. (3) Conclude that those organisms are related to a common ancestor. This is not empirical science. This is more like reading tea leaves.

The Case of the Missing Trunk

IF THERE were a single tree of life, its base would have been a single "universal common ancestor." A single trunk. But discrepancies in molecular phylogenies have convinced some scientists that the history of life cannot be represented by a single tree. The evidence for a common ancestor, a common trunk in other words, is missing. And some evolutionists have decided that the evidence is missing because the trunk is a mirage.

Living cells were traditionally classified in two broad domains: prokaryotes (without membrane-bound nuclei) or eukaryotes (with nuclei). The former included bacteria, and the latter included single-celled organisms such as yeast, as well as multicellular organisms such as plants and animals. Based on molecular comparisons, however, Carl Woese and George Fox reported in 1977 that some prokaryotes are so radically different from bacteria that they should be classified in a third domain, which they called the "archaebacteria." The term was later shortened to "archaea."[50]

The archaea are very different from bacteria in the chemical make-up of their cell walls and in their DNA replication machinery. Indeed, some of the enzymes the archaea use to replicate DNA are similar to those used by eukaryotes.[51] Woese concluded that the differences between archaea and bacteria, and between them and eukaryotes, were too great to be explained by descent from a universal common ancestor, as that term is normally understood. "The ancestor cannot have been a particular organism, a single organismal lineage," Woese wrote in 1998. "It was communal, a loosely knit, diverse conglomeration of primitive cells that evolved as a unit, and it eventually developed to a stage where it broke into several distinct communities, which in their turn become the three primary lines of descent." According to Woese, the primitive cells (which he called "progenotes") were "very unlike modern cells." A progenote "was more or less a bag of semi-autonomous genetic elements" that "would come and go," so progenotes were "not 'organisms' in any conventional sense."[52]

But if our common ancestor with archaea and bacteria was not an organism, in what sense was it an ancestor? Why stop with a community of progenotes? Why not say our common ancestor was the primordial soup? Or the elements in the periodic table?

Yet evolutionary biologists—even those who share Woese's view—continue to defend the idea of universal common ancestry. For example, W. Ford Doolittle wrote in 2009 that he doubts "there ever was a single universal common ancestor," but "this does not mean that life lacks 'universal common ancestry'" because "'common ancestry' does not entail a 'common ancestor.'" Why such mental gymnastics? Doolittle freely admits that it is because "much is at stake socio-politically," namely the need to defeat "anti-evolutionists" in "the culture wars."[53]

So we can't infer ancestors from fossils, and there are no ancestors in cladograms. Molecular phylogenies—even if all their methodological problems and conflicting results could be resolved—can only suggest hypothetical ancestors. And a nondescript mish-mash of non-organisms is not an ancestor in any meaningful sense of the word. All the ancestors are missing, but zombie science goes right on insisting they *must* have existed.

Homology

As WE saw at the beginning of this chapter, we classify living things based on homology, which comes from Greek roots meaning "same" and "speak." Although we can all see—and speak of—features that appear the same (or similar) in different species, it is not always easy to define exactly why we call those features similar, though one way is to define homology as similarity of structure or position.

Darwin saw homology as evidence for his theory, listing it in *The Origin of Species* among the facts that "proclaim so plainly, that the innumerable species, genera and families of organic beings, with which this world is peopled, have all descended, each within its own class or group, from common parents."[54] But how were homologous features transmitted from ancestors to descendants? The bones in a bird's wing are not present in the egg.

According to one hypothesis, the mechanism is genetic: Structures are homologous because they are specified by similar genes. The evidence does not support this hypothesis, however, and biologists have known it for decades. In 1971, British embryologist Gavin de Beer wrote, "Characters controlled by identical genes are not necessarily homologous" and "homologous structures need not be controlled by identical genes."[55]

According to another hypothesis the mechanism is developmental: Structures are homologous because they arise from similar cells in the embryo. But again, the evidence does not support the hypothesis. As far back as 1958, de Beer noted, "Correspondence between homologous structures cannot be pressed back to similarity of position of the cells in the embryo, or of the parts of the egg out of which the structures are ultimately composed, or of developmental mechanisms by which they are formed."[56]

Homology as Common Ancestry

In the absence of a biological mechanism to generate homologies, Darwin's followers simply redefined homology to mean similarity due to common ancestry. Harvard evolutionary biologist Ernst Mayr wrote in 1982 that there is only one definition of homology that makes biological sense: "Attributes of two organisms are homologous when they are derived from an equivalent characteristic of the common ancestor."[57] Thus, according to Berkeley evolutionary biologist David Wake, "common ancestry is all there is to homology."[58]

Defining homology in terms of common ancestry, however, leads to a serious problem: Once homology is defined in terms of common ancestry it can no longer be used as *evidence* for common ancestry. To use it as evidence would be to reason in a circle: How do we know that feature B descended from feature A? Because B is homologous to A. How do we know that B is homologous to A? Because B descended from A.

A phylogenetic tree cannot be constructed without homologies, but if we define homology in terms of common ancestry we can't know whether features are homologous until we have a phylogenetic tree. So to get what we want, we need to have it already. It's like an employer telling a job applicant that to get the job she must be in the union, but she can't join the union unless she already has the job.

This logical problem with homology (defined as similarity due to common ancestry) has been known for decades, but most recent textbooks ignore it. Miller and Levine's 2014 *Biology* (mentioned above) defines homologies as features that "have been inherited from a common ancestor" and two pages later states that "homologous molecules provide evidence of common ancestry."[59] According to Sylvia Mader and Michael Windelspecht's 2016 *Biology*, "Structures that are anatomically similar because they are inherited from a common ancestor are called homologous. In contrast, analogous structures serve the same function but originated independently in different groups of organisms that do not share a common ancestor. The wings of birds and insects are analogous structures. Thus, homologous, not analogous, structures are evidence for a common ancestry of particular groups of organisms."[60]

This is circular reasoning masquerading as evidence.

A Recent Attempt to Resolve the Confusion

IN 2014, Yale biologist Günter Wagner published a book titled *Homology, Genes, and Evolutionary Innovation*. According to Wagner, "every biologist will agree that homology is a confused and confusing subject," and he wrote the book to try to reduce the confusion.[61] His starting assumption was that "homology is a hypothesis of descent from a common ancestor," and he reaffirmed de Beer's point that homologies "cannot be explained by the identity of the set of genes that directs their development."[62] Yet morphological features are not passed from one generation to the next; genes are. So Wagner attributed homologies to developmental gene regulatory networks that "underlie the evolution of developmental pathways and, thus, the evolution of morphological structures."[63] Thus, paradoxically, homology "has a genetic basis" after all.[64]

Wagner's starting assumption also led him to another paradoxical conclusion: Homology no longer means similarity. As we saw above, corresponding DNA sequences can be very different in two species believed to share a recent common ancestor. If homology is defined in terms of common ancestry, then the descendant sequences are homologous even though they are dissimilar. The same thing can happen with morphological features. "The identity of a morphological character is not tied to similarity," Wagner wrote, but rather "to historical continuity of descent."[65] Yet without employing similarities, how can evolutionary biologists construct phylogenetic trees? And without phylogenetic trees, how can they infer continuity of descent?

Wagner's book was a sincere attempt to straighten out the confusion surrounding homology. But once homology is defined in terms of common ancestry, it seems the confusion is unavoidable.

Philosopher of biology Ronald Brady wrote three decades ago, "By making our explanation [common ancestry] into the definition of the condition to be explained [homology], we express not scientific hypothesis but belief. We are so convinced that our explanation is true that we no longer see any need to distinguish it from the situation we were trying to explain. Dogmatic endeavors of this kind must eventually leave the realm of science."[66]

Of course, Brady meant empirical science. Unfortunately, dogmatic endeavors of this kind are right at home in zombie science.

Convergence

COMPLICATING THE problem is the existence of many similarities that are clearly *not* due to common ancestry. A classic example is the striking similarity between the camera eye of a vertebrate and the camera eye of a squid or octopus, which no one thinks was inherited from a common ancestor of vertebrates, squids and octopuses possessing a camera eye.

Such curious similarities were known in Darwin's time, and evolutionary biologist Ray Lankester proposed in 1870 to replace "homology" with two new terms: "homogeny," which meant similarity due to common ancestry, and "homoplasy" (hōmō-PLAY-zee), which meant similarity *not* due to common ancestry.[67] Homogeny did not catch on, and biologists continued to use homology. But homoplasy is now used to refer to similarity not due to common ancestry.

Apparently, similarity is evidence of common ancestry, except when it isn't.

Another term often used instead of homoplasy is "convergence." Two recent books have listed hundreds of examples of convergence in a wide variety of organisms: paleontologist Simon Conway Morris's *Life's Solution* (2003), and morphologist George McGhee's *Convergent Evolution* (2011). The examples of convergence are legion. Conway Morris goes so far as to say that "convergence is ubiquitous."[68]

Animal Convergence

MAMMALS HAVE three modes of giving birth. Placental mammals nourish a fetus with a placenta and give birth to a fully developed baby. Marsupial mammals give birth to fetuses that climb into a pouch where they complete fetal development. And monotremes lay eggs instead of giving birth to live young. Because the modes of giving birth are so different, evolutionary biologists believe these three groups diverged long before most of their modern characteristics evolved.

Yet modern mammals in these three groups exhibit widespread convergence. Echidnas are monotremes that live in Australia and New Guinea, but they bristle with sharp spines and look like placental porcupines that live in North America. Duck-billed platypuses are also monotremes, yet these strange mammals have bills like ducks (which are birds rather than mammals). And also like ducks, platypuses lay eggs.

Australia is also home to many marsupials that have converged on characteristics found in placental mammals. Wombats look like American groundhogs. Flying phalangers look like placental flying squirrels from North America, Europe, and Asia. Marsupial moles look like placental moles from North America, Europe, Asia, and Africa. Marsupial mice look like placental mice that inhabit every continent except Antarctica. And kangaroos are Australian marsupials that have multi-chambered ruminant stomachs like those in placental camels. In none of these cases do biologists think the striking thing in common comes from a common ancestor with that feature. So, for example, biologists do not imagine that there is a common ancestor of the kangaroo and camel with a multi-chambered ruminant stomach. They suppose instead that the multi-chambered ruminant stomach arose at least twice in the history of life.

One final example: Sharks are fish with skeletons of cartilage instead of bone, while dolphins are placental mammals. Yet sharks and dolphins both have similar-looking dorsal fins. The explanation? Convergence!

Plant Convergence

CONVERGENCE IS widespread in plants as well. Several examples occur in carnivorous plants. Pitfall plants have a pitcher with nectar deep inside and slippery walls. Insects attracted by the nectar fall into the trap and cannot get out. Flypaper plants have leaves that secrete a thick, gluelike substance that immobilizes insects. In both groups, trapped insects are then digested by plant enzymes or microorganisms, and the plants absorb the nutrients. Pitfall plants apparently originated separately six different times, and flypaper plants five different times.[69] In other words, neither pitfall plants nor flypaper plants descended from common ancestors possessing their distinctive carnivorous features.

A particularly striking case of convergence involves plants of the cactus family in the Americas and the euphorbia genus in Africa. Such plants have thickened, fleshy stems to store water and prickly spines instead of leaves, but they apparently originated separately. Cactus and euphorbia both live in drylands that are superficially similar, and evolutionary theory attributes their convergence to natural selection due to similar environmental conditions. Yet an international team of scientists pointed out in 2013 that previous studies "included only qualitative descriptions of the environment or coarse climatic measurements," but "they have left untested the crucial assumption of similar environmental pressures." Accordingly, the team made a detailed study of the environments of cactus and euphorbia. Their study showed that these plants "occur in areas with different climates," which "differ in major details of their rainfall and temperature regimes." Indeed, "points of similarity were fewer than the differences."[70] Why, then, did the plants converge to become so similar?

What Causes Convergence?

GEORGE McGHEE argues that "the view that evolution is entirely historically contingent, and thus unpredictable (and nonrepeating), is demonstrably false." He concludes, "The phenomenon of convergent evolution demonstrates that life repeatedly evolves in a finite number of preferred directions."[71] If this is true, and if convergence is not due to natural selection in similar climates, what does cause it?

For Simon Conway Morris, convergence is due to biological constraints that guide embryo development down specified pathways. "The constraints of life make the emergence of the various biological properties very probable, if not inevitable,"[72] he argues. Thus, widespread convergence is to be expected. Then he goes a step further. "Not only is the Universe strangely fit to purpose," he writes, "but so, too... is life's ability to navigate to its solutions."[73] Purpose? Sounds suspiciously like design.

A Concept Masquerading as a Fact

IRONICALLY, AS evolutionary biology has become more scientific (in the empirical sense), the tree of life has become more illusory. Yet in mainstream biology textbooks, and in popular television shows and science magazines, the tree of life is presented as an unquestionable fact. Why?

One reason is that, as far as we can tell, all living things are descended from other living things. Spontaneous generation has never been observed, and we see descent only within existing species. Since all living things apparently come from other living things, it is not unreasonable to think that perhaps some species might be descended from other species. But why all?

The reason Science Says that *all* species must have descended from common ancestors is that materialistic science abhors the idea that any of them were created. According to materialistic science, creation is ruled out from the start. If (as Darwin thought) the only alternative to the tree of life is separate acts of creation, and if creation is not allowed, then the tree of life wins by default, whatever the evidence.

Notice that such reasoning cannot be defended on the grounds of methodological naturalism. Someone operating within the framework of methodological naturalism could decide that the true history of life is beyond the reach of empirical science and move on to more tractable problems. But nothing forces such a person to assume a materialistic conclusion that has been refuted by the evidence. Evolutionists who insist there *must* be a materialistic tree of life—regardless of the fact that fossils cannot provide evidence of ancestry and descent, regardless of the persistent inconsistencies in the molecular evidence, and regardless of the evidence against materialistic explanations for homology—are practicing not methodological naturalism but philosophical naturalism. And worse, they are dressing it up as empirical science, when it is really zombie science.

The tree of life is an illustration of an idea, though in the hands of materialistic science it has become more than that. It is an icon that has been used—and continues to be used—to indoctrinate people into the dogma of evolution. Although Stephen Jay Gould believed in evolution, he wrote insightfully in 1989, "The iconography of persuasion strikes even closer than words to the core of our being.... But many of our pictures are incarnations of concepts masquerading as neutral descriptions of nature. These are the most potent sources of conformity."[74]

3. Survival of the Fakest

After it was published in 2000, my book *Icons of Evolution* got rave reviews—filled, not with lavish praise, but with furious denunciations.[1,2]

Several critics wrote that I was stupidly trying to discredit evolution just because of a few textbook mistakes. According to evolutionary biologist Jerry Coyne, "Wells's book rests entirely on a flawed syllogism: hence, textbooks illustrate evolution with examples; these examples are sometimes presented in incorrect or misleading ways; therefore evolution is a fiction."[3]

Biologist and philosopher Massimo Pigliucci wrote, "Because there are omissions, simplifications, and inaccuracies in some general biology textbooks, obviously the modern theory of evolution must be wrong. This is the astounding line of reasoning that is the backbone of Jonathan Wells's *Icons of Evolution*."[4] Kevin Padian and Alan Gishlick of the militantly pro-evolution National Center for Science Education made the same point, heavily seasoned with scorn: "The Whine Expert: Wells reminds us of those kids who used to write to the letters page of Superman comics many years ago. 'Dear Editor,' they would write, 'you made a boo-boo! On page 6 you colored Superman's cape green, but it should be red!' Okay, kid, mistakes happen, but did it really affect the story? Wells cannot hurt the story of evolution; like a petulant child, he can only throw tantrums."[5]

But if the icons of evolution were really just a few textbook "boo-boos," biologists would have quickly corrected them. This point can be illustrated with an actual example from a physics textbook. The 1997 edition of Prentice-Hall's *Exploring Physical Science* contained a photograph of singer Linda Ronstadt holding a microphone, and the caption identified her as a silicon crystal doped with arsenic. The following page had a drawing of a silicon crystal doped with arsenic, accompanied by a caption about the usefulness of solid-state microphones. Obviously, the captions had been inadvertently switched. John L. Hubisz pointed this out in a Packard Foundation report on mistakes in physical science textbooks.[6] Of course, the publisher corrected the mistake in subsequent editions.

Imagine, though, the following scenario: The identification of Ronstadt as a silicon crystal appears year after year in almost *all* science textbooks. The caption is consistent with other materials in the textbooks promoting the theory that human life is based on silicon rather than carbon. And the theory is vigorously defended by establishment science, even to the point of vilifying its critics. Obviously, we would no longer be dealing with a mistake, but with a deliberate campaign to convince people that life is silicon-based.

If the icons of evolution were just innocent mistakes, as Coyne, Pigliucci, Padian, and Gishlick claimed, then the icons would have been corrected in subsequent textbooks, just as the Ronstadt-as-a-silicon-crystal error was quickly corrected in the physical sciences textbook. Let's see what actually happened.

The Miller-Urey Experiment

AFTER THE first edition of *The Origin of Species* appeared in 1859, Darwin concluded later editions with the statement that life had been "originally breathed by the Creator into a few forms or into one." A few years later, Darwin wrote to his friend Joseph Hooker, "I have long regretted that I truckled to public opinion" by using the biblical term, when what he really meant was "appeared by some wholly unknown process."[7]

In 1871, Darwin wrote to Hooker again and outlined his true thinking about the origin of life: "If (& oh what a big if) we could conceive in some warm little pond with all sorts of ammonia & phosphoric salts,—

light, heat, electricity &c present, that a protein compound was chemically formed, ready to undergo still more complex changes."[8]

Maybe the first cells actually did live in a warm little pond, but Darwin clearly believed that they were not *created* there. Instead, he believed they formed by some material process involving the spontaneous self-assembly of various chemicals.

In the 1920s, Russian scientist A. I. Oparin and British scientist J. B. S. Haldane suggested that the Earth's primitive atmosphere consisted mainly of methane, ammonia, hydrogen, and water vapor.[9,10] The first three are what chemists call "reducing" gases, as opposed to neutral gases such as carbon dioxide and nitrogen, or oxidizing gases such as oxygen. In a reducing atmosphere, according to Oparin and Haldane, natural energy sources such as lightning could have produced the chemical building blocks of life, which could have then dissolved in the ocean to form a primordial "soup" from which the first living cells emerged.

An interesting idea, but could it be tested?

In 1953, University of Chicago graduate student Stanley Miller announced that he had shown experimentally (in the laboratory of his Ph.D. adviser, Harold Urey) that lightning in the Earth's primitive atmosphere could have produced amino acids, the chemical building blocks of proteins.[11] Miller used a closed glass apparatus in which he boiled water, circulated the steam with a mixture of methane, ammonia, and hydrogen past a spark discharge, and then collected the products in a container at the bottom. After a week he analyzed the result (a brown tarry mixture) and detected some of the amino acids that occur in living cells. The experiment was widely advertised as evidence that scientists had demonstrated the first step in the origin of life.

By 1980, however, most geochemists had concluded that the Earth's early atmosphere probably wasn't a reducing atmosphere, as Oparin and Haldane had supposed, and as Miller had assumed when constructing his experiment. Instead, the early atmosphere likely consisted of neutral gases like those emitted from modern volcanoes—mostly water vapor, carbon dioxide, and nitrogen (though some carbon monoxide, a reducing gas, is also emitted). Since hydrogen is the lightest element, if there had been any in the early atmosphere it would probably have escaped into space.

In 1983, Miller reported that he and a colleague had sparked an atmosphere containing carbon monoxide and carbon dioxide instead of methane and ammonia, and they were able to produce a small amount of the simplest amino acid—but *only if the atmosphere contained more hydrogen than carbon monoxide or carbon dioxide*. In order to produce other amino acids they needed not only an excess of free hydrogen but also methane.[12] Harvard geochemist Heinrich Holland came to a similar conclusion.[13]

So the Miller-Urey experiment could not produce amino acids from a realistic mixture of gases. Furthermore, the brown tarry mixture that it produced contained not only amino acids, but also substances that would have interfered with the origin of life. For example, the mixture contained cyanide and formaldehyde, which a skilled chemist can use to synthesize biologically useful molecules, but which by themselves are extremely toxic to living cells. In 2015, an international team of scientists reported that bacteria could survive in the residue from a Miller-Urey experiment, but only after the residue had first been purified to remove these toxic substances.[14] In other words, an intelligent agent had to orchestrate matters to make the residue hospitable to life.

The Textbooks Respond

So how did the biology textbooks respond to these discoveries showing that Stanley Miller's experiment missed the mark? Many of them in 2000 persisted in using images of the Miller-Urey apparatus to convince students that scientists had demonstrated the first step in the origin of life. And many biology textbooks are still doing this. For example, Kenneth Mason, Jonathan Losos and Susan Singer's 2014 edition of Raven and Johnson's widely used *Biology* acknowledges that there is a controversy over the composition of the Earth's early atmosphere, but it proceeds to tell the standard story anyway. It concludes that Stanley Miller demonstrated that "the key molecules of life could have formed in the reducing atmosphere of the early Earth."[15]

Kenneth Miller and Joseph Levine's 2014 *Biology* includes a drawing of the Miller-Urey apparatus with the following caption: "Miller and Urey produced amino acids, which are needed to make proteins, by passing sparks through a mixture of hydrogen, methane, ammonia, and water vapor. Evidence now suggests that the composition of Earth's early atmosphere was different from their 1953 experiment. However, more recent experiments with different mixtures of gases have produced similar results."[16]

This last statement is profoundly misleading, if not downright false. As we saw above, Stanley Miller himself showed that his experiment needed excess hydrogen to produce even the simplest amino acid, and methane was necessary to produce more complex amino acids. So the "different mixtures of gases" that Kenneth Miller and Joseph Levine claim "produced similar results" must have been *very* different from the probable atmosphere of the early Earth.

According to the 2014 edition of *Campbell Biology* and the 2014 edition of Scott Freeman's *Biological Science* (both of which feature drawings of Miller's apparatus), Miller-Urey-type experiments using realistic mixtures of volcanic gases have produced organic molecules such as formaldehyde and hydrogen cyanide.[17,18] Yes, but as we saw above, these chemicals are very toxic to living cells. Life could not have emerged spontaneously from a primordial soup containing significant amounts of them.

A "Volcanic" Experiment to the Rescue?

THE 2016 edition of Mader and Windelspecht's *Biology* accompanies its drawing of the Miller-Urey apparatus with this: "In 2008, a group of scientists examined 11 vials of compounds produced from variations of the Miller-Urey experiment and found a greater variety of organic molecules than Miller reported, including all 22 amino acids."[19] True, but the additional amino acids all came from experiments that used a mixture of reducing gases, so the experiments suffered from the same flaw as the original one.

The 2014 edition of *Campbell Biology* mentions the same 2008 study: "Perhaps the first organic compounds formed near volcanoes. In a 2008 test of this hypothesis, researchers used modern equipment to reanalyze molecules that Miller had saved from one of his experiments. The 2008 study found that numerous amino acids had formed under conditions that simulated a volcanic eruption."[20]

That sounds pretty convincing, except that it's dead wrong.

In all fairness, the authors of *Campbell Biology* may have made an honest mistake in this case, misled by a 2008 article in *Science* titled "The Miller Volcanic Spark Discharge Experiment." Jeffrey Bada (who completed his Ph.D. under Stanley Miller) and five other scientists examined samples saved from a 1955 experiment in which Miller modified his apparatus by using a narrow nozzle to inject steam from the boiling water into the circulating gases. Based on a 2000 report suggesting that small water droplets in volcanic eruptions can attract lightning,[21] Bada and his colleagues claimed that this modification "possibly simulates the spark discharge synthesis by lightning in a steam-rich volcanic eruption," and they called this "the volcanic experiment."[22]

But Miller himself did not call it "volcanic," and for good reason. The only thing "volcanic" about it was that instead of passing the gases over boiling water, Miller injected steam into them. But the gases he used in 1955 were the same he had used in 1953: methane, ammonia, hydrogen, and water vapor.[23] Calling the experiment "volcanic" gave the false impression that criticisms of the 1953 experiment had been overcome in the new experiment, but they had not. Nevertheless, Bada and his colleagues are continuing to promote the Miller-Urey experiment, including what they call its "volcanic" version.[24] They have even posted online instructions on how to re-enact the experiment in a science classroom.[25]

So despite its irrelevance to the origin of life on Earth, the Miller-Urey experiment just keeps coming back. Why?

The Grand Materialistic Story

DARWIN'S THEORY of evolution by natural selection is a materialistic story about how life diversified *after* it originated, but Darwin realized that his evolutionary story is incomplete without a materialistic explanation for the origin of life. He hoped that such an origin could be shown to have been possible in some "warm little pond" on the ancient Earth, but what if the origin of life cannot be explained materialistically? What if it required the origin of new information, which is immaterial? And what if that information required an intelligence?

In his 2009 book *Signature in the Cell*, philosopher of science Stephen Meyer argues that the complex information in biological molecules cannot result from unguided natural processes such as the spontaneous aggregation of chemicals. The only known source of large amounts of complex information is intelligence. Therefore, Meyer concludes, the origin of life required intelligent design.[26]

But Science Says No, life must have originated materialistically.

So origin-of-life researchers rely more on a grand materialistic story than they do on evidence. Biologist Jack Szostak tells the story this way: "Simple chemistry in diverse environments on the early Earth led to the emergence of ever more complex chemistry and ultimately to the synthesis of the critical biological building blocks. At some point, the assembly of these materials into primitive cells enabled the emergence of Darwinian evolutionary behavior, followed by the gradual evolution of more complex life forms leading to modern life."[27]

But this story consists entirely of assumptions. If ("& oh what a big if") simple chemistry led to the synthesis of biological building blocks, and *if* these building blocks assembled themselves into primitive cells, etc., etc. None of these steps have been empirically demonstrated. In fact, origin-of-life research has been spectacularly unsuccessful. The Miller-Urey experiment is just one of its many dead ends.

Rice University synthetic organic chemist James Tour points out that the prebiotic (i.e., prior to life) synthesis of complex organic molecules remains a mystery. A chemist who wants to synthesize such molecules from scratch must start with targets in mind, then think of possible routes to reach them. "Further refinement of various routes leads to a set of desired paths; these are the routes that can be attempted in the laboratory," Tour wrote in 2016. But "finding a direct path to a target is far too complicated. Dead ends are everywhere"—even for a skilled chemist with a target in mind. But, Tour continued, "There are no targets in evolution."[28]

"Those who think scientists understand the issues of prebiotic chemistry are wholly misinformed," Tour concluded. "Nobody understands them. Maybe one day we will. But that day is far from today. It would be far more helpful (and hopeful) to expose students to the massive gaps in our understanding."[29]

And prebiotic synthesis would be just the first step. Even if we could explain how life's chemical building blocks formed on the early Earth, we would still be a very long way from explaining how they assembled themselves into a living cell.

But the grand materialistic story lumbers on.

Haeckel's Embryos

DARWIN THOUGHT that embryology provided "by far the strongest single class of facts in favor" of his theory.[30] In 1859 he wrote that we see "a close similarity in the embryos of widely different animals in the same class," and that this similarity "reveals community of descent."[31] Ten years later he wrote that "it is highly probable that with many animals the embryonic or larval stages show us, more or less completely, the state of the progenitor of the whole group in its adult condition."[32] To support his point, Darwin cited some drawings of vertebrate embryos made by German biologist Ernst Haeckel[33] (See Figure 3-1).

Haeckel's contemporaries accused him of faking his drawings to make the embryos appear more alike than they really were. Nevertheless, the drawings continued to be widely used in textbooks as evidence of common descent.

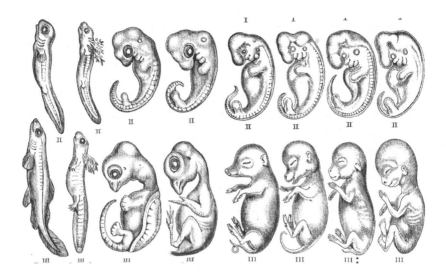

FIGURE 3-1. HAECKEL'S EMBRYOS: The top row was portrayed by Haeckel as the earliest stage in the development of these eight embryos. The embryos are (left to right): fish, salamander, turtle, chicken, hog, calf, rabbit, human. Note that the four animals on the right are all mammals. To represent amphibians, Haeckel chose a salamander instead of a frog, which looks quite different. (See Figure 3-2.) From *Darwinism Illustrated*, George J. Romanes (Chicago: The Open Court Publishing Company, 1892).[34]

Recently, the credibility of the drawings took another hit. In 1997, British embryologist Michael Richardson and an international team of biologists compared Haeckel's drawings with photographs of actual vertebrate embryos and found many discrepancies.[35] In an interview for the journal *Science*, Richardson said, "It looks like it's turning out to be one of the most famous fakes in biology."[36]

But the icon was just too good to abandon without a fight. Never mind the evidence. In 2008, University of Chicago historian Robert Richards published a book defending Haeckel against charges of fraud. According to Richards, Haeckel's drawings were no less accurate than those of his contemporaries, including the people who criticized him.[37] Cambridge historian Nick Hopwood also defended Haeckel against the fraud charge in a 2015 book that included several pages criticizing *Icons of Evolution* as a creationist "primer for textbook activism."[38]

The real issue, however, is not whether Haeckel deliberately committed fraud. The real issue is that Haeckel's drawings omitted half of the evidence—the half that doesn't fit Darwin's claim that embryos are most similar in their early stages. By the logic of Darwin's argument, the earliest stages should be the most similar, but vertebrate embryos actually start out looking very different from each other, then they converge somewhat in appearance midway through development (Haeckel's "first" stage) before diverging to their adult forms.[39] Biologist Rudolf Raff has called this pattern the "developmental hourglass"[40] (See Figure 3-2). Haeckel helped Darwin by simply omitting the top half of the hourglass.

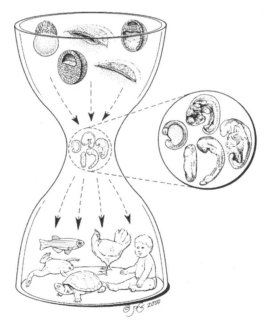

FIGURE 3-2: The Developmental Hourglass: At the top are the earliest stages of five classes of vertebrates (clockwise starting at the left: fish, bird, mammal, reptile, amphibian). Their patterns are noticeably different. Midway through development the embryos converge somewhat in appearance, though not nearly as much as Haeckel portrayed. In the circle on the right the embryos are (clockwise starting at the left): zebrafish, chicken, human, turtle, frog. This is the stage Darwin and Haeckel represented as the first. As the embryos continue to develop they become very different again (bottom). Copyright 2000 by Jody F. Sjogren; used by permission.

When Jerry Coyne reviewed *Icons of Evolution* in 2001, he criticized the book for failing to recognize that "embryos of different vertebrates tend to resemble one another in early stages, but diverge as development proceeds, with more closely related species diverging less widely," thus providing "copious evidence for evolution." Yet Coyne knew that vertebrate embryos are *not* most similar in their early stages. Indeed, in the same review he acknowledged that "the earliest vertebrate embryos (mere balls of cells) are often less similar to one another than they are at subsequent stages." But he brushed this aside. For Coyne, evolution *must* be true, whether early embryos are similar or not.[41]

Coyne followed this with a 2009 book titled *Why Evolution Is True*, which contained the following: "Each vertebrate undergoes development in a series of stages, and the sequence of those stages happens to follow the evolutionary sequence of its ancestors." Thus "all vertebrates begin development looking like embryonic fish because we all descended from a fishlike ancestor."[42]

So much for the evidence.

Textbooks Still Haunted By Haeckel's Embryos

HAECKEL'S DRAWINGS had been discredited before I ever wrote about them, and yet the drawings (or re-drawn versions of them) continued to find their way into many biology textbooks as evidence for evolution. In 2000, Stephen Jay Gould wrote that we should all be "astonished and ashamed by the century of mindless recycling that has led to the persistence of these drawings in a large number, if not a majority, of modern textbooks."[43] Haeckel's embryos, it seemed, were not just dead; they deserved to be buried face down.

Yet many textbooks published after 2000 continue to use versions of Haeckel's drawings as evidence for evolution. Donald Prothero's 2013 textbook *Bringing Fossils to Life* actually features Haeckel's original drawings, with the caption: "Embryos of different vertebrates at comparable stages of development (top row) are strikingly similar in every group."[44] Mader and Windelspecht's 2016 *Biology* uses a re-drawn version of Haeckel's embryos, accompanied by the statement, "All vertebrates inherit the same developmental pattern from their common ancestor, but each vertebrate group now has a specific set of modifications to this original ancestral pattern."[45]

Some recent textbooks don't use drawings but make essentially the same claim. The 2014 edition of Raven and Johnson's *Biology* tells students, "Some of the strongest anatomical evidence supporting evolution comes from comparisons of how organisms develop. Embryos of different types of vertebrates, for example, often are similar early on, but become more different as they develop."[46] Miller and Levine's 2014 *Biology* informs its readers that "the early developmental stages of many animals with backbones (called vertebrates) look very similar," and these similarities provide "evidence that organisms have descended from a common ancestor."[47]

So despite the evidence, Haeckel's embryos continue to stalk the halls of science education. When materials containing Haeckel-like illustrations were submitted in 2011 to the Texas State Board of Education for adoption into the science curriculum, Discovery Institute's Casey Luskin wrote, "Like a zombie that just won't die, these bogus drawings keep coming back."[48]

Flock of Dodos

IN 2007, biologist-turned-filmmaker Randy Olson released a film titled *Flock of Dodos: The Evolution-Intelligent Design Circus*. The film included an interview with John Calvert, director of the Kansas-based Intelligent Design Network and a critic of evolution, who asked Olson whether he had read *Icons of Evolution*. Olson said he had, and he acknowledged that Haeckel's embryo drawings misrepresented the truth. "Haeckel did commit scientific fraud," he said. But he insisted that Haeckel is no longer relevant to what's being taught today, and the embryo drawings are no longer used in textbooks. "There's no trace of them," Olson claimed.[49] He concluded that *Icons of Evolution* was no more reliable than a supermarket tabloid.

But Olson already knew of textbooks published after 2000 that contained such drawings.[50] In 2007 he came to Seattle for a screening of his film and (to his credit) stopped by the office of the Discovery Institute, where Casey Luskin and I showed him a stack of recent textbooks that used versions of Haeckel's embryos to teach evolution. Olson's response, in essence, was that the story he told in his film was just too good to give up. At that point, the Discovery Institute established a website to document Olson's misrepresentations.[51]

Nevertheless, the misrepresentations did not stop. On April 12, 2012, *Flock of Dodos* was shown at Villanova University, followed by a panel discussion that included Olson and Lehigh biochemist (and intelligent design advocate) Michael Behe. Behe presented photocopies of Haeckel-style embryo drawings from some recent textbooks, but Olson defended the film anyway.[52,53]

In 2015 Olson published a book titled *Houston, We Have a Narrative*, in which he wrote, "Scientists must realize that science is a narrative process, that narrative is story, therefore science needs story."[54]

Even if the story's untrue.

Archaeopteryx

Two YEARS after Darwin first published *The Origin of Species*, a fossil bird was discovered in Germany that had teeth, a long lizard-like tail, and claws on its wings. Its discoverer named it *Archaeopteryx* ("ancient wing"). Since *Archaeopteryx* had features of reptiles as well as birds, some people regarded it as the missing link between those two groups and a confirmation of Darwin's theory. In 1998, anthropologist Pat Shipman wrote that *Archaeopteryx* is "an icon, a holy relic of the past that has become a powerful symbol of the evolutionary process itself. It is the First Bird."[55]

But there are too many structural differences between *Archaeopteryx* and modern birds for the latter to be descendants of the former. In 1985, paleontologist Larry Martin wrote, "*Archaeopteryx* is not ancestral of any group of modern birds." Instead, it is "the earliest known member of a totally extinct groups of birds."[56] If animals evolved in a branching-tree pattern, as Darwin believed, then *Archaeopteryx* was at the end of a long-dead branch.

But if *Archaeopteryx* was not the ancestor of modern birds, what was? This question has generated a heated controversy among evolutionary biologists. Some (most prominently Berkeley's Kevin Padian) believe that birds evolved from dinosaurs, while others (most prominently North Carolina's Alan Feduccia) believe they evolved from a very different group of extinct reptiles. According to the "dino-bird" group, flight evolved from the ground up: Feathers developed in small dinosaurs, which then ran, jumped, glided, and eventually flew. According to the other group, the idea that theropod dinosaurs (with large hind limbs and small forelimbs) evolved into birds is contrary to common sense, and it is more likely that flight evolved from the trees down: Ancient reptiles first jumped from trees, then glided, then developed feathers and flew.

Dino-bird advocates base their view on cladistic analyses of various skeletal features shared by dinosaurs and modern birds. But as we have seen there are no ancestors in a cladogram, so the idea that birds evolved from dinosaurs is only a hypothesis. Nevertheless, the dino-bird party has declared itself to be The Scientific Consensus. As far as they are concerned, the debate is over, and Science Says birds *are* dinosaurs.

When the fossil of a dinosaur covered with tiny fibers was discovered in China in 1996, the fibers were called "protofeathers" and the animal was proclaimed a "feathered dinosaur."[57,58] Many more such fossils have been found since then, and The Scientific Consensus claims them all as evidence that birds evolved from dinosaurs. But critics disagree. According to Feduccia and his colleagues, the fossil fibers are not feather-like at all, but consist of collagen (a skin protein).[59] "Contrary to popular paleontological belief," Feduccia wrote in 2012, "there is no evidence of protofeathers from any Chinese fossils."[60] Fossils have been found of extinct terrestrial animals with true feathers, but according to Feduccia they were all secondarily flightless birds (like ostriches and kiwis, supposedly descended from birds that once flew), not feathered dinosaurs.

In 2016, a portion of a tail with true feathers was found fossilized in a piece of amber.[61] Although only two vertebrae were clearly present, the fossil's discoverers argued that it must originally have been much longer. The dino-bird party declared the two vertebrae to be part of a dinosaur tail, but critics pointed out that *Archaeopteryx* had a tail, too, and that the newly discovered fossil could have come from an extinct bird.[62]

So the controversy continues.

Where does this leave *Archaeopteryx*? In 2009, a fossil bird was discovered in China that apparently predated *Archaeopteryx*,[63] so *Archaeopteryx* is not even the oldest bird, much less the ancestor of modern birds.

Meanwhile, both sides in the dino-bird controversy must invent ghost lineages to connect the fossils with each other. Neither side has found the ancestor of modern birds. But one thing is for sure: *Archaeopteryx* is not it.

Nevertheless, the 2014 edition of Raven and Johnson's *Biology* still calls *Archaeopteryx* "the first bird,"[64] and Prothero's 2013 textbook *Bringing Fossils to Life* still calls *Archaeopteryx* "a 'missing link' between reptiles and birds."[65] Apparently, this icon of evolution—like Olson's story about Haeckel's embryos—is just too good to give up.

Peppered Moths

DARWIN WAS convinced that in the course of evolution "Natural Selection has been the main but not exclusive means of modification."[66] But (as we noted in Chapter 1) he had no evidence for this. The best he could do in *The Origin of Species* was to "give one or two imaginary illustrations."[67] It wasn't until the 1950s that British physician Bernard Kettlewell provided what seemed to be good evidence of natural selection.

During industrialization in the nineteenth century, peppered moths in England went from being mostly light-colored to being mostly dark-colored ("melanic"), a phenomenon dubbed "industrial melanism." In 1896, British biologist J. W. Tutt proposed that the change occurred because dark moths are better camouflaged on pollution-darkened tree trunks, and thus are less likely to be eaten by predatory birds. In other words, Tutt attributed industrial melanism to natural selection.[68]

Half a century later, Kettlewell tested Tutt's hypothesis by releasing marked light and dark moths onto nearby tree trunks in polluted and unpolluted woodlands. Kettlewell later recaptured some of the marked individuals and noted that the proportion of light moths had increased in the unpolluted woods and the proportion of dark moths had increased in the polluted woods, which was consistent with Tutt's hypothesis. In an article written for *Scientific American*, Kettlewell called this "Darwin's missing evidence."[69]

Peppered moths soon became the classic example of natural selection in action. The story was featured in most biology textbooks, often accompanied by photographs of light and dark moths resting on light and dark tree trunks.

It's worth pointing out that even if the classic peppered moth story were true, it would not confirm Darwin's claim that new species, organs, and body plans were produced by unguided evolution. All it would demonstrate is that natural selection produced a shift in the proportions of two existing varieties of the same species.

But as it turns out, even on this point the peppered moth story was not as good as it sounded.

Problems with the Classic Story

IN THE 1980s, researchers discovered that peppered moths don't normally rest on tree trunks. Instead, they mostly rest where they are hidden, probably in the higher branches of trees. Furthermore, peppered moths rarely fly in the daytime. So by releasing moths onto nearby tree trunks in daylight, Kettlewell had created an unnatural situation.

But now we know that the textbook photographs had been staged, often with dead moths pinned or glued in place.[70]

In 1998, British biologist Michael Majerus published a book about industrial melanism that included a table showing the resting positions of peppered moths found in the wild between 1964 and 1996. Of the many thousands of peppered moths that biologists had studied during that 32-year period, only 47 had been found resting in the wild, and of these only 6 had been found on exposed tree trunks. Majerus concluded that "peppered moths do not naturally rest in exposed positions on tree trunks."[71]

In a review of Majerus's book for *Nature*, Jerry Coyne wrote, "From time to time, evolutionists re-examine a classic experimental study and find, to their horror, that it is flawed or downright wrong." For Coyne, the mere fact that peppered moths don't normally rest on tree trunks invalidated Kettlewell's experiments. Coyne compared his reaction to "the dismay attending my discovery, at the age of six, that it was my father and not Santa who brought the presents on Christmas Eve." He also acknowledged that he was "embarrassed" at having taught the classic textbook story for many years.[72]

As empirical science, the classic story seemed as dead as the moths in the staged photographs. In 2002, *The New York Times* featured some of the photographs in an article titled, "On scientific fakery and the systems to catch it."[73] Many biology textbooks dropped the classic story. But advocates of evolution defended it anyway. Coyne even reversed himself in 2002, writing in a review of another book that "despite arguments about the precise mechanism of selection, industrial melanism still represents a splendid example of evolution in action."[74] Meanwhile, Majerus set out to find better evidence for the story.

Majerus's New Evidence

FROM 2001 TO 2006, Majerus studied peppered moths in a large, unpolluted rural garden about sixty miles north of London. He began by climbing a few trees, where he counted 135 moths resting on trunks, branches, and twigs. Of these most were on branches, but forty-eight (thirty-six percent) were on the trunks.

Majerus conceded that his "results may be somewhat biased towards lower parts of the tree, due to sampling technique."[75] Brits are known for understating things, but this deserves a place in the Understatement Hall of Fame. Since Majerus's goal was to find out where peppered moths normally rest, and biologists had already concluded that they probably rest in the higher branches of trees, Majerus should have found a way to survey those higher branches, not just the ones he could reach by climbing up a tree from the ground. He could have built some scaffolds, or he could have rented a hydraulic aerial work platform. As it is, his technique was a bit like counting fish in the ocean from the deck of a boat and concluding that most of them live within ten feet of the surface.

Over the course of six years, Majerus artificially released almost five thousand light and dark moths onto the trees. He would release a few moths each night into netting sleeves he had placed around selected branches, then he would remove the sleeves before dawn and note the branches on which moths had come to rest. Four hours later he would count those still on the branches. In four of the six years, more dark moths disappeared than light ones.[76] He concluded that those he couldn't find had been eaten by birds. Majerus did observe some moths actually being eaten by birds, but he assumed *all* moths that disappeared had been eaten by birds and that none that disappeared had simply moved to a different location.

Despite his obvious sampling bias—and his unsupported assumption that all disappearing moths had to have been eaten by birds—Majerus confidently interpreted his findings as evidence for the classic Darwinian story of evolution. Thus, when Majerus presented his results in 2007, he urged the teaching of the peppered moth story again because "It provides after all: **The Proof of Evolution**" (boldface by Majerus).

It didn't, of course, but Majerus clearly wanted it to. At one point in his presentation he revealed why, declaring out of the blue that humans invented God and that there will be "no second coming; no helping hand from on high."[77]

Apparently, what really mattered to Majerus was the grand materialistic story. This is not empirical science, but zombie science.

Darwin's Finches

WHEN CHARLES Darwin visited the Galápagos Islands aboard the British survey ship *H.M.S. Beagle* in 1835, he collected specimens of the local wildlife. These included some finches that he threw into bags, many of them mislabeled. Although the Galápagos finches had little impact on Darwin's thinking, biologists who studied them a century later called them "Darwin's finches" and invented the myth that Darwin had correlated differences in the finches' beaks with different food sources (he hadn't).[78] According to the myth, Darwin was inspired by the finches to formulate his theory of evolution, though according to historian of science Frank Sulloway "nothing could be further from the truth."[79]

In the 1970s, biologists Peter and Rosemary Grant and their colleagues camped out on one of the Galápagos islands, called Daphne Major, and studied one finch species (the medium ground finch) in great detail. In 1977, a severe drought left only hard-to-crack seeds, and about eighty-five percent of the birds died. Those that survived had beaks that were, on average, five percent bigger, and their offspring also tended to have larger beaks. The Grants had documented an example of natural selection.[80]

Of course, no individual birds had changed—only the average beak size among the survivors. Nevertheless, Peter Grant estimated that if there were more droughts and the average beak size continued to increase, natural selection could eventually produce a new species of finch. In a 1991 article in *Scientific American*, he wrote, "If droughts occur once a decade, on average, repeated directional selection at this rate with no selection in between droughts would transform one species into another within 200 years."[81]

Using the same reasoning, the authors of a 1999 pro-evolution booklet from the U.S. National Academy of Sciences called Darwin's finches "a particularly compelling example of speciation."[82] The same claim could be found in many biology textbooks at the time—along with the myth that the finches had played an important role in the formulation of Darwin's theory.

After the drought ended, however, birds with smaller beaks thrived again, and the average beak size returned to its previous level. No net evolution had occurred. And that's not the only problem with the finch icon.

Evidence for Interbreeding

THE FINCH icon is all about speciation, so it's worth considering how we distinguish one species from another. There is a good deal of debate on this subject, but animals are generally considered to belong to the same species if they can interbreed and produce robust offspring. This is why we don't regard dog breeds as distinct species, because they can effectively interbreed.

So, what about the finches of the Galápagos islands? By the 1990s, the Grants and their colleagues had observed that several of the Galápagos finch species were interbreeding and producing offspring that were more fit than their parents.[83] Instead of diverging through natural selection, the species appeared to be merging through hybridization.

But Darwin's finches are supposed to be an icon of "adaptive radiation," in which species first split from a common ancestor and then become increasingly different over time (See Figure 2-2). According to neo-Darwinian theory, new species diverge because they no longer exchange genes; they are reproductively isolated from each other. If they continue to interbreed and exchange genes, they are usually regarded as varieties of the same species, even if they are morphologically different (as is the case with dog breeds).

In 1981, a large male finch arrived on Daphne Major from a nearby island. The Grants nicknamed it "Big Bird," and genetic testing showed that it was a hybrid. It mated with several medium ground finch females and produced fertile offspring that were larger than other medium ground finches, had a distinctive song, and kept to themselves. In 2009, the Grants reported that this hybrid population was reproductively isolated from the other finches on the island and therefore supported "some expectations" of a particular theory of speciation.[84]

They weren't quite ready to call the population of Big Bird's descendants a new species, but "for the present it is functioning as a [separate] species because its members are breeding only with each other."[85] In a 2014 interview, Peter Grant said, "We are reluctant to name the lineage as a new species when it has been in existence for only a few generations and may be short-lived."[86]

In 2015, the Grants and a team of scientists reported that they had sequenced the genomes of all the species of Darwin's finches. Although they continued to call the finches "an iconic model for studies of speciation and adaptive radiation," they found "extensive evidence for interspecific gene flow throughout the radiation."[87] Apparently, the Galápagos finches had been interbreeding ever since they arrived there. The team even cited several examples in which species A and species B on island X are genetically more similar to each other than species A on island X is to species A on island Y.

All this evidence of extensive hybridization among various "species" of Galápagos finches hardly makes them a "compelling example of speciation." Indeed, it is far from obvious why we should consider them separate species at all. The Ainu people of northern Japan and the !Kung people of southern Africa are separated not only physically and linguistically, but also (for all practical purposes) reproductively. Are they therefore separate species? Or are they all human beings? Of course the Ainu and the !Kung are all members of the same species.

Since the Galápagos finches regularly interbreed, why should we call them separate species, other than to make them appear to be evidence for evolution?

Sisyphean Evolution

In Greek mythology, Sisyphus was a king noted for his greediness and deceitfulness. He also considered himself cleverer than the gods, so when he died he was condemned to spend eternity rolling a huge boulder up a steep hill. Every time he approaches the top, the boulder escapes his grip and rolls back down the hill, and Sisyphus has to start over.

In 2015, biologists Bailey McKay and Robert Zink wrote that ground finches on the Galápagos Islands "cycle between stages of differentiation and never attain species status, a process we refer to as Sisyphean evolution," which "has been confused with the standard model of speciation." According to McKay and Zink, instead of being an icon of "speciation and adaptive radiation, which is featured in nearly every textbook on evolutionary biology," the finches are "trapped in an unpredictable cycle of Sisyphean evolution."[88]

So this "particularly compelling example of speciation" is not so compelling after all.

The Textbooks

DESPITE ALL these problems, many biology textbooks still feature Darwin's finches as an icon of evolution. After describing the Grants' research, Miller and Levine's 2014 *Biology* concludes that "average beak size in this finch population has increased dramatically.… Changes in food supply created selection pressure that caused finch populations to evolve within decades."[89] Not a word about how the increase in average beak size disappeared after the drought ended. And not a word about evidence that the different finch "species" interbreed to produce robust hybrids.

The 2014 edition of Raven and Johnson's 2014 *Biology* describes the Grants' research and acknowledges that average beak size went back to normal after the drought ended, but the textbook retells the myth that Darwin observed finches with different beaks eating different foods on different islands and claims that this was one of the "phenomena that were of central importance to his reaching his ultimate conclusion."[90]

The Galápagos finches have provided evidence for differential survival correlated with environmental changes—that is, for natural selection. But the finches do not provide evidence for the origin of new species, organs or body plans—that is, for evolution. Nevertheless, Miller and Levine conclude from their misleading description of the Grants' research that "evolution is the key to understanding the natural world."[91]

Once again, it is not the evidence but the materialistic story that matters.

Four-Winged Fruit Flies

NORMAL FRUIT flies have two wings. Behind each wing is a tiny "balancer" that vibrates rapidly during flight to stabilize the fly's movements. In the 1970s, geneticist Edward Lewis discovered that by artificially combining three separate DNA mutations in a fruit fly embryo he could transform the balancers into a second pair of normal-looking wings.[92,93] To some people, Lewis's discovery seemed to corroborate the neo-Darwinian theory that DNA mutations provide the raw materials for evolution, and biology textbooks started using photos of a four-winged fruit fly to show students what mutations can accomplish.

But the mutant four-winged fruit fly lost its balancers in the bargain. Worse, the mutant wings do not have any flight muscles. So the four-winged fly has great difficulty flying and mating, and it cannot survive for long outside the laboratory.[94,95] It is a sideshow freak, an evolutionary dead end.

Yet some textbooks in 2000 featured photos of four-winged fruit flies, and some continue to do so. For example, Freeman's 2014 *Biological Science* includes a photo of the four-winged fly, accompanied by text stating that mutations "can turn a segment in the middle part of the body into a segment just like the one that lies in front of it." So instead of having balancers "the transformed segment now bears a pair of wings." No mention of the fact that the mutant wings are effectively dead, or that the fly is severely handicapped.[96]

Turning a Shrimp into a Fly

THE GENE Lewis mutated to make four-winged fruit flies was *Ultrabithorax* (abbreviated *Ubx*). In 2002, a press release from the University of California at San Diego announced that biologist William McGinnis and his colleagues had discovered how *Ubx* mutations supposedly allowed aquatic shrimp-like animals, "with limbs on every segment of their bodies, to evolve 400 million years ago into a radically different body plan: the terrestrial six-legged insects."

The news release boasted that this was "a landmark in evolutionary biology, not only because it shows how new animal body plans could arise from a simple genetic mutation, but because it effectively answers a major criticism creationists had long leveled against evolution—the absence of a genetic mechanism that could permit animals to introduce radical new body designs."[97]

But what did McGinnis and his colleagues actually show? Shrimp embryos contain a version of the Ubx protein that does not inhibit leg formation, while a fruit fly embryo contains no Ubx protein in its thorax (from which its legs and wings develop), but does contain a version of the Ubx protein in its abdomen that inhibits leg formation there. (Gene names are italicized, but the protein names are not.) McGinnis and his colleagues showed that when Ubx from the abdomen of a fruit fly is inserted into the thorax of a fruit fly embryo, leg development is inhibited; but when Ubx from a shrimp abdomen is inserted into the same location, a fruit fly embryo develops fruit fly leg rudiments. They speculated that the Ubx gene in a shrimp-like ancestor might have mutated into the fruit fly version that now suppresses leg development but is not expressed in the thorax.[98]

Yet McGinnis and his colleagues did not reduce the number of legs in a shrimp, which is what supposedly happened in the course of evolution. And of course it would have taken a lot more than the loss of some legs to change a shrimp into a fruit fly. So despite the hype, the experiment did not come close to showing "how new animal body plans could arise from a simple genetic mutation."

Eighteen-Winged Dragonflies.

Ubx is one of a family of genes called "Hox genes," which affect head-to-tail development. In 2007, Donald Prothero published a book defending evolution. The book included a photo of a four-winged fruit fly to illustrate how "big developmental changes can result from small genetic mutations."[99] The book also claimed that modern four-winged dragonflies evolved from ancient dragonflies that had more wings, and it featured a drawing of an eighteen-winged dragonfly together with a four-winged dragonfly. According to its caption, the drawing illustrated "the evolutionary mechanism by which *Hox* genes allow arthropods to make drastic changes in their number and arrangements of segments and appendages, producing macroevolutionary changes with a few simple mutations."[100]

In November 2009, Prothero (together with *Skeptic* magazine editor Michael Shermer) debated Discovery Institute senior fellows Stephen Meyer and Richard Sternberg. During the debate, Sternberg pointed out that eighteen-winged dragonflies never existed.[101] A few days later, Prothero responded in a blog post that Meyer and Sternberg had "completely missed the point" of the illustration. According to Prothero (apparently having forgotten the number of wings in his drawing), "the text clearly points out that the twelve-winged dragonfly is a thought experiment, an illustration to show that a simple change in *Hox* genes allows the arthropods… to make huge evolutionary changes by simple modifications of regulatory genes."[102]

But the text in Prothero's book did *not* identify the eighteen-winged dragonfly as a "thought experiment." Instead, it stated, "Experiments have shown that a few *Hox* genes cause arthropods to add or subtract segments, and other *Hox* genes can produce whatever appendage is needed." Thus the "macroevolutionary transition from one body form to another with a completely different number of segments and appendages is a very easy process."[103]

In 2013 Prothero published another book, *Bringing Fossils to Life*, which claimed that "a tiny change in *Hox* genes can make a big evolutionary difference." Indeed, "the fossil record confirms this idea that simply switching on or off *Hox* genes allows abrupt changes not only in appendages and wings, but even in the number of body segments."[104]

Two pages later the book reproduced the 2007 drawing of an eighteen-winged dragonfly, with a caption that stated, "Fossils demonstrate that many early arthropods were capable of adding or losing wings or other appendages.... This cartoon of real fossils shows how this multiplication or reduction process can rapidly produce entirely new body forms from a single [Hox] mutant."[105]

So in 2009 the eighteen-winged dragonfly was an imaginary thought experiment, but in four years it evolved into a real fossil! Isn't zombie science amazing?

Fossil Horses

THREE YEARS before Charles Darwin's death in 1882, American paleontologist Othniel Marsh published a drawing of horse fossils to illustrate the evolution of modern one-toed horses from a small four-toed animal. Some people took this to indicate that horse evolution had taken a straight path to the modern horse, and Marsh's drawing became an icon of evolution. But additional discoveries showed that the fossil record of horses is much more complicated, with many side branches and dead ends. Thereafter, fossil horses were used to show that evolution does *not* take straight paths.

In any case, the pride of place once held by fossil horses is now held by fossil whales, which we shall examine in Chapter 5.

Ape-to-Human

DARWIN DID not deal with human evolution in *The Origin of Species*, other than to predict that on the foundation of his theory "light will be thrown on the origin of man and his history."[106] Twelve years later, in *The Descent of Man*, he wrote that "man is descended from some lower form" by the same materialistic process of variation and natural selection that gave rise to all other forms of life.[107] Although Neanderthal fossils had already been discovered, they were not thought to represent intermediates between lower forms and humans (*Homo sapiens*), so Darwin based his argument on homology and embryology rather than on fossil evidence.

Since Darwin's time, many more fossils have been discovered, and the term "hominid" was coined to include all living and extinct apes, humans, and extinct ape-like animals believed to be ancestral to humans. But no consistent picture of human evolution has emerged. In 1982, paleontologists Niles Eldredge and Ian Tattersall noted that it is a "myth that the evolutionary histories of living beings are essentially a matter of discovery." If this were really true, they wrote, "one could confidently expect that as more hominid fossils were found the story of human evolution would become clearer. Whereas if anything, the opposite has occurred."[108]

What Eldredge and Tattersall wrote in 1982 is still true.

In 1991, paleoanthropologist Misia Landau concluded that "themes found in recent paleoanthropological writing... far exceed what can be inferred from the study of fossils alone and in fact place a heavy burden of interpretation on the fossil record—a burden which is relieved by placing fossils into pre-existing narrative structures."[109] The framework for these pre-existing narratives is the grand materialistic story, starting with the spontaneous origin of life from inanimate chemicals and culminating in the evolution of humans from other animals by unguided natural processes.

Using Fossils to Illustrate the Story

SEVERAL FOSSILS reported since 2000 have been proclaimed to be ancestors of humans. In May 2009, a team of scientists published an article describing a primate fossil named (in honor of Charles Darwin) *Darwinius masillae*.[110] One member of the team, Norwegian paleontologist Jørn Hurum, nicknamed the fossil "Ida" after his daughter. Ida was advertised as the "missing link" between humans and other mammals, and its announcement was accompanied by a two-hour television documentary that had been produced beforehand. According to Hurum, Ida represented "the closest thing we can get to a direct ancestor."[111] In a newspaper interview, he called the fossil "our Mona Lisa," and another member of the team called it "the eighth wonder of the world."[112]

Questioned about the hype, Hurum defended himself in *The New York Times*. "Any pop band is doing the same thing," he said. "We have to start thinking the same way in science."[113] But the hype turned out to be completely unjustified. Other paleontologists began studying Ida, and a few months later an article in *Nature* declared that it was "related to lemurs, not humans."[114,115] The following year another study concluded the same thing.[116] So Ida was not the eighth wonder of the world after all.

Another fossil was described in 2009, without quite so much hype. *Ardipithecus ramidus*, nicknamed "Ardi," had first been found in 1992, but it was in very poor condition.[117] The fossil's discoverer, Tim White, called it road kill. The skull is "squished," he said, "and the bone is so chalky that when I clean an edge it erodes, so I have to mold every one of the broken pieces to reconstruct it."[118]

After many years, White and his colleagues finally described the fossil in detail. They concluded that it was older than *Australopithecus afarensis*, the famous "Lucy" fossil that had been hyped as our ancestor since its discovery in 1974. White argued that Ardi walked on two feet, but although the expectation was that fossils older than Lucy would be more like chimpanzees, Ardi was not. Indeed, White wrote in 2009 that Ardi "indicates that the last common ancestors of humans and African apes were not chimpanzee-like."[119] So the common ancestor of apes and humans, if there was one, remained a mystery.

In 2010, paleontologist Lee Berger and his colleagues reported the discovery of an *Australopithecus* fossil that they described as more recent and more human-like than Lucy.[120] Berger and his colleagues called it *Australopithecus sediba*, and they argued that the new species may be the best candidate yet for our immediate ancestor.[121] But other paleontologists disagreed, arguing that there are human-like fossils older than *sediba*. According to Tim White, "Given its late age and *Australopithecus*-grade anatomy, it contributes little to the understanding of the origin of genus *Homo*."[122]

In 2013, Berger and his colleagues published some more details of *sediba* in *Science*.[123] According to an accompanying analysis, Berger was still arguing that it "could be the long-sought species that gave rise to *Homo*," but (the analysis added) "few paleoanthropologists agree."[124]

Berger reported another fossil find in 2015: *Homo naledi*.[125] He and his co-workers discovered the bones of what appeared to be at least fifteen individuals in a cave in South Africa, though the bones' age remains unknown. The fossils have a strange combination of features: ape-like hands, human-like feet, and chimp-sized skulls. Berger and his colleagues believe they are all members of one species, though evolutionary biologist Jeffrey Schwartz thinks that the material is too varied to represent a single species.[126] Indeed, Schwartz and Tattersall argue that it is now time to "scrap the iconic list of names in which hominin fossil specimens have historically been trapped, and start from the beginning" by formulating new hypotheses and rethinking genera and species.[127] ("Hominin" refers to the subset of hominids that includes human and extinct ape-like animals believed to be ancestral to humans.)

So with every fossil find, it seems, the paleoanthropological fossil record becomes more confused. Although we have fossils of extinct animals with some ape features and some human features, we still don't have a coherent story to connect them.[128] No doubt there's a story to be told, but why should it be the materialistic story?

Ninety-Nine Percent Chimp?

WHEN THE *Homo naledi* fossils were discovered, a writer for *National Geographic* magazine asked, "Why are scientists certain that human evolution happened?" The first reason she gave was that "we share nearly 99% of our genetic sequence with chimpanzees."[129] But do we?

In 1975, biochemists Mary-Claire King and Allan Wilson compared several dozen proteins from chimps and humans and reported that their amino acid sequences were "on the average, more than 99 percent identical."[130] By 2000, chimp and human DNA sequences were being compared, and in 2005 the Chimpanzee Sequencing and Analysis Consortium published a draft sequence of the chimp genome and compared it with the human genome. The Consortium found that at the level of single subunits the two genomes were 98.77 percent similar, though that figure excluded many deleted or inserted sequences.[131,132]

But looking at single subunits is only one way to compare DNA sequences. For example, scientists who compared chimp and human DNA at the level of protein-coding sequences instead of single subunits concluded that the two genomes are no more than 93.6 percent similar.[133,134]

How much do DNA comparisons tell us, anyway?

In a book titled *What Does It Mean To Be 98% Chimpanzee?*, anthropologist Jonathan Marks pointed out that the similarity of DNA sequences in chimps and humans doesn't carry the significance many people attach to it. First, people recognized the anatomical similarity of chimps and humans long before anyone had compared their protein or DNA sequences. According to Marks, "genetic data tell us precisely what we already knew," namely that there are striking similarities between chimps and humans.[135] Second, since there are only four subunits in DNA, any two sequences will be, on average, about twenty-five percent similar. So at the DNA level we are at least twenty-five percent similar to daffodils. Third, in addition to anatomical similarities there are significant anatomical *differences* between chimps and humans—not to mention enormous behavioral differences. And everyone can see them.

Finally, there is a lot more to us than our DNA. In fact, there is even a lot more biological information in us than just our DNA and proteins, as we shall see in Chapter 4. The hype over the whatever-the-percent-is similarity between chimp and human DNA is just another chapter in the grand materialistic story.

Multiplying Zombies

ALL of the icons of evolution misrepresent the truth. The evidence does not justify the sweeping claims that are made in their name. They should be empirically dead to any informed, rational observer, but they keep coming anyway. Textbooks still carry them, but textbooks are not the main problem. The main problem is the scientific establishment's determination to promote evolution in spite of the evidence. Thanks to zombie science the ranks of the icons are swelling. If one icon of evolution is discredited, others shuffle forward to take its place.

The following five chapters describe six more icons of evolution that, like the first ten, have been used for years to support evolution. Some are old, some relatively new; but as I will show, all six—like the first ten icons—misrepresent the evidence. In the process, they have seriously compromised the scientific enterprise in its search for truth.

4. DNA—The Secret of Life

Drawings of the DNA molecule have become a familiar part of our culture, and not just in science textbooks. Like photos of *Archaeopteryx* fossils, the DNA drawings depict real evidence. But zombie science attributes far more significance to the DNA molecule than the evidence justifies. Like *Archaeopteryx*, DNA has become yet another illustration in the grand materialistic story, another icon of evolution.

On February 28, 1953, after months of work at the Cavendish Laboratory in Cambridge, England, James Watson and Francis Crick finally figured out the molecular structure of deoxyribonucleic acid (DNA). It was shaped like a winding ladder, a double helix. Watson and Crick were convinced they had solved a deep mystery, and they went to celebrate over drinks at a local pub. There Crick announced, "We have discovered the secret of life!"[1]

From Darwin to DNA

Charles Darwin's theory needed a mechanism of heredity. In order for evolution to occur, changes in one generation must be passed down to subsequent generations. In *The Origin of Species* Darwin wrote, "There can be little doubt that use... strengthens and enlarges certain parts, and disuse diminishes them; and that such modifications are inherited."[2] But how? In *The Variation of Animals and Plants Under Domestication* (1868), Darwin proposed that various tissues in the body "throw off minute granules which are dispersed throughout the whole system.... These granules may be called gemmules. They are collected from all parts of the system to constitute the sexual elements, and their development in the next generation forms the new being." Darwin called this "pangenesis."[3]

The idea that acquired characteristics can be inherited had a long history, but it is commonly associated with Darwin's predecessor, French biologist Jean-Baptiste Lamarck. Almost two decades after Darwin adopted the idea, however, German biologist August Weismann conducted experiments in which he cut off the tails of laboratory mice for several generations and noted that all of their offspring had normal tails. He concluded that "we must completely abandon the Lamarckian principle" of the inheritance of acquired characteristics.[4] Although Weismann embraced Darwin's theory of evolution, he rejected pangenesis, arguing that hereditary factors are transmitted only by the germ cells (sperm and egg), not the somatic cells (all the other cells in the body). According to Weismann, the "germ plasm" is unaffected by acquired characteristics.[5]

Genes and Chromosomes

DECADES EARLIER, Roman Catholic friar Gregor Mendel had hybridized pea plants and tracked the inheritance of seven of their traits. Mendel distinguished two forms of each trait (for example, green and yellow seed color), and he inferred from the patterns of their inheritance that one form of each trait segregates into the male germ cell (pollen) and the other form into the female germ cell (ovule), so they are inherited separately. He also inferred that each trait (for example, seed color) is inherited independently of other traits (for example, pod color). In 1865, Mendel announced his results to the Natural History Society of Brünn, in what is now the Czech Republic.[6]

Biologists ignored Mendel's work at first, but it was rediscovered around the turn of the century, and English biologist William Bateson named the study of inheritance "genetics."[7] In 1909, Danish botanist Wilhelm Johannsen distinguished between "phenotype" (the observable properties of an individual organism, which arise during development) and "genotype" (the stable underlying biological type, which is inherited and carries the information that specifies the phenotype). Johannsen also proposed the word "gene" (signifying discrete inheritance) to replace Darwin's "pangene" (which implied blending inheritance).[8–10]

American biologist Walter Sutton and German biologist Theodor Boveri noticed that during the cell divisions that produce the sperm and the egg, the behavior of chromosomes (tiny thread-like structures in the nucleus) paralleled the patterns Mendel had observed. Indeed, Sutton wrote in 1902 that chromosomes "may constitute the physical basis of the Mendelian law of heredity."[11] American biologists Thomas Hunt Morgan, Alfred Sturtevant, Hermann Muller, and Calvin Bridges studied spontaneous changes ("mutations") in the hereditary factors of fruit flies, and in 1915 they concluded that the "chromosomes furnish exactly the kind of mechanism" called for by Mendel's theory.[12]

Mendel had described heredity in terms of mathematical ratios; he did not try to explain it in material terms. Bateson and Johannsen did not think that genes could be reduced to material entities such as chromosomes. Nevertheless, the materialistic view prevailed, and most biologists soon embraced the chromosomal theory of inheritance. But materialism demanded that inheritance be reduced even further, to molecules. What molecules in chromosomes might be the actual hereditary material?

And the Winner Is...

By 1900, chromosomes were known to contain two kinds of molecules: protein and DNA. Since proteins contain more than twenty subunits and DNA contains only four, biologists assumed that DNA was too simple to be the hereditary material and that genes were made of protein.

In 1928, British bacteriologist Frederick Griffith experimented with two strains of pneumonia bacteria, one that actually causes the disease and another that doesn't. He discovered that a substance from the former could turn the latter into the disease-causing strain, and he called this substance the "transforming principle."[13] In 1944, geneticists Oswald Avery, Colin MacLeod and Maclyn McCarty demonstrated experimentally that the transforming principle was DNA rather than protein.[14] It seemed that DNA might be the material basis of heredity after all, and the race was on to discover its molecular structure.

It was already known that DNA consists of "nucleotides," and each nucleotide consists of a phosphate molecule bonded to one of four sugars. So DNA contains four "bases" abbreviated A, T, C, and G (after the names of the four sugars). The phosphate molecules bind to each other, producing a long chain. At the California Institute of Technology (Caltech) late in 1952, Linus Pauling modeled DNA as a triple helix (three linear molecules winding around each other in a spiral pattern) with the phosphate chains on the inside.

Watson and Crick, however, were convinced that Pauling's model was incorrect. Relying on data from the laboratory of Rosalind Franklin and Maurice Wilkins at King's College, London, Watson and Crick modeled DNA as a double helix with the phosphate chains on the outside and the four bases on the inside. The characteristics of the four bases suggested that an A on one chain would pair preferentially with a T on the other chain, while a C on one chain would pair with a G on the other (See Figure 4-1).

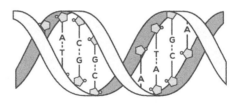

FIGURE 4-1. THE DNA DOUBLE HELIX: The winding ribbons represent the phosphate chains. The pentagons attached to A, T, C, or G are the sugars. Note that As pair with Ts, and Cs pair with Gs.

Watson and Crick published their model in April 1953, noting that it "suggests a possible copying mechanism for the genetic material."[15] A month later they wrote, "Our model for deoxyribonucleic acid is, in effect, a *pair* of templates, each of which is complementary to the other. We imagine that prior to duplication... the two chains unwind and separate. Each chain then acts as a template for the formation on to itself for a new companion chain, so that eventually we shall have *two* pairs of chains, where we only had one before. Moreover, the sequence of the pairs of bases will have been duplicated exactly."[16]

Five years later, Caltech scientists Matthew Meselson and Franklin Stahl published evidence that DNA duplicates just as Watson and Crick had suggested.

From DNA to Us

IN THE 1940s, geneticists George Beadle and Edward Tatum had performed experiments showing a correlation between DNA sequences and particular proteins. Their work suggested that genes are DNA sequences, and that each gene specifies one protein. In 1956, Elliot Volkin and Lazarus Astrachan discovered what they called "DNA-like" ribonucleic acid (RNA), which serves as an intermediate between DNA and protein synthesis.[17]

In 1958, Francis Crick proposed that the specificity of a DNA segment lies solely in its nucleotide sequence, which encodes the nucleotide sequence of a molecule of RNA, which in turn serves as a template for the amino acid sequence of a protein. Crick also proposed that the information encoded in DNA sequences can be transferred from DNA to protein, but not back again. He called the former the "sequence hypothesis" and the latter the "central dogma" of molecular biology,[18] but "central dogma" is now commonly used to refer to the sequence hypothesis as well.

In 1961, French molecular biologists François Jacob and Jacques Monod described a mechanism by which bacteria turn protein synthesis on and off, and they suggested that "messenger RNA" (which turned out to be the DNA-like RNA discovered by Volkin and Astrachan) served as an intermediate in the process.[19]

So DNA carries information that is encoded in sequences of its four-letter alphabet, the four bases. That information is "transcribed" into messenger RNAs, and those messenger RNAs are then "translated" into proteins by complex assemblies of proteins and RNAs called "ribosomes." From a materialistic point of view, organisms are reducible to molecules, so the central dogma can be summarized as "DNA makes RNA makes protein makes us." In 1970, Jacob wrote that an organism is the realization of a "genetic program" written in DNA sequences.[20] The same year, Monod said that with the central dogma "and the understanding of the random physical basis of mutation that molecular biology has also provided, the mechanism of Darwinism is at last securely founded. And man has to understand that he is a mere accident."[21]

So information seemed reducible to matter, and the central dogma became the material basis of inheritance, development, and evolution.

The most extreme interpretation of the central dogma is that of British biologist Richard Dawkins. In 1976, Dawkins wrote that "we, and all other animals, are machines created by our genes." DNA, he continued, is "a set of instructions for how to make a body," and it makes a body in order to ensure its own survival. So the body is a "survival machine" for "selfish genes." It is "the genes' way of preserving the genes."[22] Dawkins went on to trace all human qualities—including altruism and religious belief—to DNA. This is materialism with a vengeance.

From Pop-Gen to Evo-Devo and Epigenetics

IN THE 1930s, evolutionary theory was wedded to a new discipline called "population genetics," or pop-gen. Assuming that genes on chromosomes specify traits such as those studied by Mendel, the alternative forms of a gene that specify different forms of the same trait were called "alleles." Population genetics studies the distribution of variant alleles in a group of organisms.

In the early twentieth century, British geneticists J. B. S. Haldane and Ronald Fisher and American geneticist Sewall Wright pioneered methods for calculating the effects of natural selection, mutation, and other factors on the distribution of alleles in populations. As allele distributions changed, so did the "gene pool" of the population. Changes in the gene pool were assumed to cause microevolution and, eventually, macroevolution.

Many people concluded that evolution could be reduced to population genetics. One biology textbook went so far as to say that "evolution can be precisely defined as any change in the frequency of alleles within a gene pool from one generation to the next."[23]

But not every evolutionist agreed. In 1963, Ernst Mayr called the approach of Haldane, Fisher, and Wright "beanbag genetics" because it treated genes as unconnected rather than interacting.[24] "Beanbag genetics is in many ways misleading," Mayr wrote, because "an individual, the target of selection, is not a mosaic of characters each of which is the product of a given gene. Rather genes are merely the units of the genetic program that governs the complicated process of development."[25]

In 2005 Sean B. Carroll echoed Mayr's criticism. "Millions of biology students have been taught the view (from population genetics) that 'evolution is change in gene frequencies,'" he wrote, but "the evolution of form is the main drama of life's story, both as found in the fossil record and in the diversity of living species. So, let's teach that story. Instead of 'change in gene frequencies,' let's try 'evolution of form is change in development.'"[26]

In 1992 Australian-born Canadian biologist Brian K. Hall had written that despite the "domination of evolution by population genetics," it "is neither sufficient nor inclusive." In particular, population genetics ignores embryo development. To remedy this deficiency, Hall proposed a new discipline he called evolutionary developmental biology, now informally known as evo-devo (pronounced EE-vo DEE-vo).[27]

Evo-Devo to the Rescue?

EVO-DEVO SUPPLEMENTS evolutionary biology with developmental genetics. Starting with the fruit fly *Drosophila melanogaster* in the 1970s and 1980s, biologists had made great progress in understanding the genetics of embryo development. One of the most important (and surprising) discoveries was that very different organisms have similar developmental genes. For example, we saw in Chapter 3 that shrimp and fruit flies possess similar *Hox* genes (which affect development along the head-to-tail body axis). Similar *Hox* genes are also found in many other animals, including humans, mice, chicks, frogs, fish, sea urchins, octopuses, snails, earthworms, and roundworms.

If animals have similar developmental genes, why do they develop so differently? In 1990, developmental biologist Eric Davidson used the term "gene regulatory networks" to refer to sets of interacting DNA sequences, RNAs, and proteins that regulate transcription, and he argued that "the significant features" of early development "have to do directly with the distribution in embryonic space of gene regulatory molecules."[28] In other words, animals with similar underlying genes develop differently because of differences in where and when those genes are transcribed.

According to Sean B. Carroll, animals that share similar "tool kit genes" have different "genetic switches" elsewhere in their DNA. Carroll wrote in 2005 (with considerable exaggeration) that "we now have a very firm grasp of how development is controlled. We can explain how tool kit proteins shape form, that tool kit genes are shared by all animals, and that differences in form arise from changing the way they are used."[29]

Interesting ideas, but how radical are they really? Davidson's "gene regulatory networks" and Carroll's "genetic switches" are encoded in DNA. According to Carroll, "in the entire complement of DNA of a species (the genome), there exists the information for building that animal.... Evolution of form is ultimately then a question of genetics."[30] And in 2006, Davidson wrote, "Since the morphological features of an animal are the product of its developmental process, and since the developmental process in each animal is encoded in its species-specific regulatory genome, then change in animal form during evolution is the consequence of change in genomic regulatory programs for development."[31] So Davidson and Carroll actually remained wedded to the central dogma. For them, development and evolution are ultimately still all about the DNA.

Yet when Brian Hall proposed the term "evolutionary developmental biology" in 1992, he wrote that "understanding the control of development and evolution will require determining how genetic, epigenetic and environmental factors are integrated into a hierarchical set of unified controls. An understanding of the genome, important as that is, alone will not provide the explanations that we seek."[32]

Epigenetics

IN GREEK, "epi" means "above," "on," or "in addition to." In 1942, British biologist Conrad Waddington introduced the word "epigenetics" to mean the study of "the processes involved in the mechanism by which the genes of the genotype bring about phenotypic effects."[33] Three years earlier, however, Waddington had coined the word "epigenotype" to refer more broadly to "the set of organizers and organizing relations to which a certain piece of tissue will be subject during its development."[34] From the beginning, then, epigenetics had more than one meaning. In a narrow sense, it referred to the mechanisms by which genes produce phenotypic effects. In a broad sense, it referred to all of the factors involved in development, only one of which is the genome.

Most biologists now use epigenetics in its narrow sense to refer to heritable changes in the structure of a chromosome that do not change the underlying DNA sequence. In 2007, biologist Julie Kiefer wrote, "Epigenetics is the study of heritable changes in gene function that occur independently of alterations to primary DNA sequence."[35] These "epigenetic" changes in turn affect when and where specific parts of a DNA sequence are transcribed into RNA. Epigenetics in this narrow sense—like Davidson's gene regulatory networks and Carroll's genetic switches—leaves the central dogma essentially intact.

But some biologists understand epigenetics more broadly. In 1993, Susan Herring wrote, "Broadly speaking, 'epigenetics' refers to the entire series of interactions among cells and cell products" leading to embryo development.[36] In 2002, Eva Jablonka and Marion Lamb wrote that epigenetics is "primarily concerned with the mechanisms through which cells become committed to a particular form or function... Recognizing that there are epigenetic inheritance systems through which non-DNA variations can be transmitted in cell and organismal lineages broadens the concept of heredity and challenges the widely accepted gene-centered neo-Darwinian version of Darwinism."[37]

Epigenetics in this broader sense implies that there is much more to inheritance and development than DNA. Where does that leave the central dogma?

The Central Dogma is Dead

HISTORIAN OF biology Jan Sapp has documented how gene-centered thinking became the dominant viewpoint in biology during the twentieth century.[38] But evidence has accumulated that such a narrow view distorts reality. If "makes" is taken to mean "fully specifies," then it turns out that DNA does not make RNA, RNA does not make protein, and protein does not make us.

After DNA sequences are transcribed into RNAs, many RNAs are modified so they do not match the original transcript. One way this happens is "alternative splicing."

In plant and animal cells, most DNA sequences that code for proteins are interrupted by non-protein-coding segments called "introns." When DNA is transcribed, introns are included in messenger RNAs but are then cut out, and the protein-coding regions are spliced back together. The splicing can be done in various alternative ways, so many of the final messenger RNAs have sequences that no longer correspond to DNA sequences. For example, RNAs from one DNA sequence in fruit flies generate more than 18,000 different proteins through alternative splicing.[39] Alternative splicing is common in humans, too.[40]

In addition to alternative splicing, many animal transcripts undergo RNA editing, which can alter the amino acid sequence (and thus the function) of the final protein. In one example, a species of octopus living in the Antarctic and another octopus species in the Caribbean have very similar DNA sequences for a particular protein in their cell membranes, but the Antarctic octopus uses RNA editing to change the protein so it can function better in the extreme cold.[41] Recent studies have also revealed extensive RNA editing in humans.[42]

Thus it often happens that the sequence of amino acids in a protein no longer corresponds to a sequence in DNA.

Furthermore, although the function of a protein depends on its three-dimensional shape, its shape is not always specified by its amino acid sequence. Some proteins adopt similar folded forms despite having very different amino acid sequences.[43] Others assume different forms despite having the same or very similar amino acid sequences. The latter are known as "metamorphic" proteins.[44]

Finally, most plant and animal proteins are chemically modified by the addition of sugar molecules, and the modifications can change over time according to the needs of the organism. As various biochemists have put it, the result is a level of complexity "that reaches beyond the genome"[45] and "provides an additional level of information content in biological systems."[46]

So the claim that "DNA makes RNA makes protein" is false. But it is in the central dogma's final step—making us—that it fails most dramatically.

The Need for Spatial Information

IN MOST cases, after RNAs and proteins are synthesized they must be transported to specific locations in a cell in order for them to function properly. In addition to their protein-coding regions, some messenger RNAs have a sequence called a "zipcode" that specifies the "address" in the cell where they are to be transported.[47] But an RNA zipcode, like a postal zip code, is meaningless unless it matches a pre-existing address.

Cells with nuclei contain microscopic fibers called "microtubules." Molecular motors travel along the microtubules, transporting various cargoes throughout the cell.

In the postal metaphor, the molecular motors would be like delivery trucks and the microtubules would be like a highway system. But destinations for intracellular transport—like the geographical addresses in a postal system—must be specified independently of the cargoes.

Some destinations are specified by proteins embedded in the cell membrane. Scientists used to think that proteins could diffuse randomly in a membrane, like corks bobbing in water. It is now known, however, that many membrane proteins are arranged in stable, non-random patterns.[48] In many cases, membrane patterns are templated by the membranes from which they are derived in the course of cell division, with new proteins from the cell interior being incorporated into the existing pattern during membrane growth.[49] So even if the individual molecules in a membrane pattern were completely specified by DNA, their spatial arrangement would not be. In other words, biological membranes carry essential spatial information—a "membrane code"—that cannot be reduced to information in DNA sequences.[50]

According to British biologist Thomas Cavalier-Smith, the idea that the genome contains all the information needed to make an organism "is simply false." Membrane patterns play "a key role in the mechanisms that convert the linear information of DNA into the three-dimensional shapes of single cells and multicellular organisms. Animal development creates a complex three-dimensional multicellular organism not by starting from the linear information in DNA… but always starting from an already highly complex three-dimensional unicellular organism, the fertilized egg."[51]

Other Critics of the Central Dogma

MANY BIOLOGISTS have criticized the central dogma, and their number is growing. Canadian embryologist Brian C. Goodwin spent his career trying to understand the generation of form ("morphogenesis"). In 1985 he wrote that invoking a genetic program in DNA "fails to address the basic problems posed by morphogenesis, namely, how distinctive spatial order arises in embryos."[52] In 1996, Goodwin wrote, "It is clear that the specification of form requires more than the specification of the genotype, thus falsifying genetic determinism."[53]

In 1999 Italian geneticist Giuseppe Sermonti published the book *Dimenticare Darwin*, which was translated into English in 2005 under the title *Why Is a Fly Not a Horse?*[54] In the book Sermonti challenged the central dogma, asking why, if radically different animals have similar developmental genes, are the animals so different?

In 2003, cell biologist and philosopher Lenny Moss noted that "biological order is distributed over several parallel and mutually dependent systems such that no one system, and certainly no one molecule, could reasonably be accorded the status of being a program, blueprint, set of instructions, and so forth, for the remainder."[55] Noting that similar developmental genes "are common throughout the living world with no species-specific stamp on them," Moss argued that "the onus of explaining where evolutionary innovation is to be found weighs even more heavily on the 'gene-speakers.' If indeed genes are basically interchangeable across kingdoms and phyla, as a surfeit of empirical findings attests to, then surely the specificity of organisms must be determined at a higher level of organization."[56]

In her 2000 Harvard University Press book *The Century of the Gene*, MIT professor Evelyn Fox Keller had written, "For almost fifty years, we lulled ourselves into believing that, in discovering the molecular basis of genetic information, we had found the 'secret of life.'" But "the primacy of the gene as the core explanatory concept of biological structure and function is more a feature of the twentieth century than it will be of the twenty-first."[57]

This is so, she argued, because it has become clear that the program for living things "consists of, and lives in, the interactive complex made up of genomic structures and the vast network of cellular machinery in which these structures are embedded. It may even be that this program is irreducible—in the sense, that is, that nothing less complex than the organism itself is able to do the job."[58]

But if this fantastically sophisticated program is irreducible, if nothing less complex could do the job, then how could it have evolved to its present state by one mutation at a time—genetic or otherwise? Zombie science lumbers past this question without taking it seriously.

Fruit flies with useless extra wings or missing legs have taught us something about developmental genetics, but nothing about how evolution might build new form and function. All of the evidence points to one conclusion: No matter what we do to the DNA of a fruit fly embryo, there are only three possible outcomes: a normal fruit fly, a defective fruit fly, or a dead fruit fly. Not even a horse fly, much less a horse.

British biologist Denis Noble put the matter this way: "At fine enough resolution, the egg cell must contain even more information than the genome. If it needed to be coded digitally to enable us to 'store' all the information necessary to recreate life in, say, some distant extra-solar system by sending it out in an 'Earth-life' information capsule, I strongly suspect that most of that information would be non-genomic."[59]

In the same 2008 article Noble wrote, "We talk of gene networks, master genes and gene switches. These metaphors have also fuelled the idea of genetic (DNA) determinism. But there are no purely gene networks!" Every network, at the very least, "is a gene–protein–lipid–cell network. It does not really make sense to view the gene as operating without the rest of the cellular machinery. So, if this network is part of a 'genetic program,' then the genetic program is not a DNA program."[60]

Criticizing the idea that DNA is the secret of life, American cell biologist Stuart Newman wrote in 2013, "The reason genes were elevated to this status in the first place was based more on a mechanistic ideology that was already on the wane in the physical sciences than on any evidence for their generative powers." But now, "gene-determinist views have gone into a sharp decline in the basic biological sciences."[61]

Apparently, however, many people in the news media and popular culture—and even some scientists!—have not gotten the memo.

Long Live the Central Dogma!

DESPITE THE evidence against it, the central dogma lives on. American biologist Michael Lynch, while acknowledging that organisms are more than the sum of their parts, wrote in 2007 (echoing Dobzhansky) that since nothing in biology makes sense except in the light of evolution, "nothing in evolution makes sense except in the light of population genetics."[62] Not surprisingly, most biology textbooks continue to teach students that population genetics is the basis for evolution.

In 2016, Richard Dawkins reaffirmed his belief in the centrality of genes. "If you ask what is this adaptation good for," Dawkins said in an interview, "the answer is always, for the good of the genes that made it. That is the central message of *The Selfish Gene* and that remains true, and reinforced." According to Dawkins, the idea that there is something more to heredity and development than DNA sequences is a flash in the pan. "Obviously we've long known that some genes are turned on, and other genes are not turned on, in different tissues," he said. This is the "trendy thing" that "gets all the hype and doesn't deserve to."[63]

In this case, however, the "trend" is following the evidence.

And yet, despite the evidence, some research in developmental biology is still publicized as though it confirms the central dogma. A press release accompanying one 2015 study announced, "Master orchestrator of the genome is discovered, stem cell scientists report.... New research shows how a single growth factor receptor protein programs the entire genome."[64] According to the paper itself, published in a scientific journal, the growth factor receptor protein is "a global genomic programmer of cell, neural and muscle development."[65] The paper's senior author also commented in the press release that the growth factor receptor protein "occupies a position at the top of the gene hierarchy that directs the development of multicellular animals."[66]

An institute where another 2015 study was done announced its results with this headline: "Scientists uncover gene architects responsible for body's blueprint." The announcement went on to say that "researchers have identified two key proteins that act as genetic 'architects,' creating the blueprint needed by embryos during the earliest stages of their development." The published paper itself was more modest, though one of its co-authors said in an interview that the two proteins activated "the blueprint the developing organism needs for proper development."[67,68]

The "Gene for" X

FAITH IN the central dogma has misled many people into believing that we have "genes for" things such as specific anatomical features, diseases, and even behaviors. Of course, it's mutations in genes that cause some diseases, not the genes themselves. Yet single-gene diseases such as Huntington's (which killed folksinger Woody Guthrie), cystic fibrosis, and hemophilia affect relatively few people. Most diseases cannot be traced to mutations in a single gene.

The so-called breast cancer genes (*BRCA1* and *BRCA2*) have received a lot of attention because many women suffer from this disease at some point in their lives. According to the U. S. National Cancer Institute, "*BRCA1* and *BRCA2* mutations account for about 20 to 25 percent of hereditary breast cancers and about 5 to 10 percent of all breast cancers."[69] So women with a family history of the disease are encouraged to get tested for the mutations. But the vast majority of breast cancer cases have no connection to *BRCA1* or *BRCA2*, and a woman with mutations in them may never have the disease.

Some of the silliest manifestations of DNA-centrism have come from people who claim to have found the "gene for" some behavior. In 1993, geneticist Dean Hamer and his colleagues claimed to have discovered the gene for male homosexuality.[70] Hamer called it the "gay gene."[71] The same year, three geneticists wrote to *Science* that Hamer's results were statistically insignificant and in any case were "not consistent with any genetic model."[72] A 1999 study published in *Science* did not support Hamer's claim,[73] while a 2014 study published in *Psychological Medicine* did.[74] When a researcher from the University of California at Los Angeles reported in 2015 that certain chromosomal patterns were seventy percent correlated with sexual orientation in male twins,[75,76] geneticist John Greally criticized the researcher's methods and called the results "uninterpretable."[77] Science writer Ed Yong wrote in *The Atlantic* that the research was "fatally weak" and emphasized that "scientists have not found the 'gay gene.'"[78]

Other researchers have claimed to find "genes for" alcoholism, violence, IQ, schizophrenia, gambling, sadness, and political views (among other things). In 2004, Hamer published a book titled *The God Gene: How Faith Is Hardwired into Our Genes.*[79] John Horgan, formerly a senior writer for *Scientific American*, has called this "gene-whiz science." Gene-whizzers periodically announce that they have found a gene for some behavior, and the media and the public then exclaim, "Gee whiz!"

But Horgan explains that "the methodology of behavioral geneticists is highly susceptible to false positives. Researchers select a group of people who share a trait and then start searching for a gene that occurs not universally and exclusively but simply more often in this group than in a control group. If you look at enough genes, you will almost inevitably find one that meets these criteria simply through chance." Yet "follow-up studies that fail to corroborate the initial claim receive much less or no attention, leaving the public with the mistaken impression that the initial report was accurate—and, more broadly, that genes determine who we are."[80]

So the central dogma continues to mislead scientists and non-scientists alike. True, some DNA sequences encode some RNAs, and some RNA sequences encode proteins, but in general the central dogma is false. DNA does not contain the genetic program for an organism, and DNA is far from being the secret of life. Continued faith in it is rooted in materialism.

The fault doesn't lie with our genes, but with zombie science.

5. WALKING WHALES

DARWIN WROTE IN THE FIRST EDITION OF *THE ORIGIN OF SPECIES* that North American black bears had been seen "swimming for hours with widely open mouth, thus catching, like a whale, insects in the water." What did this have to do with the subject of his book? "Even in so extreme a case as this," Darwin continued, "if the supply of insects were constant, and if better adapted competitors did not already exist in the country, I can see no difficulty in a race of bears being rendered, by natural selection, more and more aquatic in their structure and habits, with larger and larger mouths, till a creature was produced as monstrous as a whale."[1]

Critics poked fun at this, and Darwin removed it from later editions, but he defended it privately. "The bear case has been well laughed at, and disingenuously distorted by some into my saying that a bear could be converted into a whale," he wrote in an 1860 letter. "As it offended persons, I struck it out in the second edition; but I still maintain that there is no especial difficulty in a bear's mouth being enlarged to any degree useful to its changing habits,—no more difficulty than man has found in increasing the crop of the pigeon, by continued selection, until it is literally as big as the whole rest of the body."[2]

But of course bears with large mouths are a very long way from being whales. The evolution of whales long remained a problem for Darwin and his followers, until some fossils were discovered in the 1990s and strung together into a new icon of evolution.

The Fossil Record

LAND MAMMALS occur in the fossil record before whales. By 1859, fossils of two extinct whales had been found: *Dorudon* (a dolphin-like mammal about sixteen feet long) and *Basilosaurus* (a serpent-like mammal about sixty-five feet long). But *Dorudon* and *Basilosaurus* were both fully aquatic: Although (like other mammals) they had to breathe air, they spent their entire lives in the sea. So there were no fossil intermediates to justify a belief that land animals had evolved into whales.

In the early 1980s, the fossil of an extinct land animal the size of a wolf was discovered in Pakistan. Judging from the rocks in which it was found, it was older than *Dorudon* or *Basilosaurus*. Although the animal looked nothing like a whale, a bone in its middle ear resembled something that had previously been found only in whales, dolphins, and porpoises: a bone called an "involucrum." Whales, dolphins and porpoises are collectively called "cetaceans" (sĕ-TAY-shuns), from the Latin word "cetus," meaning whale. Although "whale" is traditionally defined as a large, fully aquatic mammal, the small fossilized land animal was named *Pakicetus*, or Pakistani whale, because of its involucrum.[3]

The possibility that the involucrum had originated more than once was not considered. The evolutionary story about whales needed an ancestor, and *Pakicetus* was the best candidate on hand. But *Pakicetus* was fully terrestrial, so merely calling it a whale did not fill the chasm between land animals and whales. Not surprisingly, critics of evolution continued to point to that chasm as a problem for Darwin's theory. As recently as 1993, a book critical of evolution stated that "there are no clear transitional fossils linking land mammals to whales."[4]

Walking Whales?

THE VERY next year, however, paleontologist Hans Thewissen and his colleagues reported the discovery in Pakistan of a fossil older than *Dorudon* or *Basilosaurus* but younger than *Pakicetus*. The animal had legs that would have enabled it to walk on land like a modern sea lion, but it also had a long tail that would have enabled it to swim like a sea otter.

Thewissen and his colleagues interpreted the fossil to be intermediate between land animals and whales, and they named it *Ambulocetus natans*, or "swimming walking whale."[5] A few months later, paleontologist Philip Gingerich and his colleagues discovered a slightly younger fossil in Pakistan they interpreted to be intermediate between *Ambulocetus* and modern whales. They called their discovery *Rodhocetus*.[6]

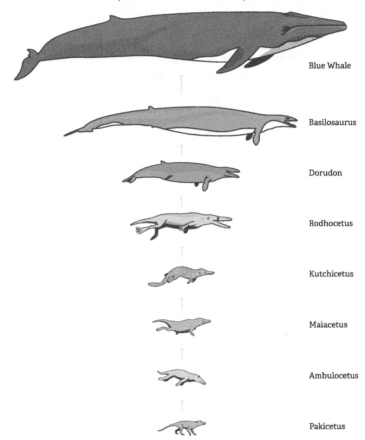

FIGURE 5-1. THE TEXTBOOK STORY OF WHALE EVOLUTION: Artists' conceptions are arranged in roughly chronological order, based on positions in the fossil record.

"The embarrassment of past absence has been replaced by a bounty of new evidence," announced Stephen Jay Gould, "—and by the sweetest series of transitional fossils an evolutionist could ever hope to find."

According to Gould, "this sequential discovery of picture-perfect intermediacy in the evolution of whales stands as a triumph in the history of paleontology. I cannot imagine a better tale for popular presentation of science or a more satisfying, and intellectually based, political victory over lingering creationist opposition."[7]

So "walking whales" became an icon of evolution.

More fossils of mammals supposedly ancestral to modern cetaceans have subsequently been reported, including *Kutchicetus* in 2000,[8] *Indohyus* in 2007,[9] and *Maiacetus* in 2009.[10] Many textbooks use artists' conceptions of these animals to illustrate the evolutionary story of whales.

Like the textbook illustrations, Figure 5-1 distorts some things to fit the evolutionary story. *Basilosaurus* and *Dorudon* were contemporaries, and the fossil records of some of the others overlapped each other. All of the "walking whales" (those whose names end in *cetus*) are reconstructed from incomplete skeletons (*Pakicetus* was known only from a skull), and *Kutchicetus* was actually smaller than *Maiacetus* or *Ambulocetus*.

In any case, none of the fossils in Figure 5-1 were ancestors or descendants of the others. According to paleontologist Kevin Padian, this is because "*Ambulocetus, Rodhocetus, Pakicetus*, and other forms each have their own... distinguishing characteristics, which they would have to lose in order to be considered direct ancestors of other known forms."[11] So if there were animals ancestral to modern whales, these fossils would not represent them. The arrows in Figure 5-1 are not just imaginary; they are misleading.

Were They Really Whales?

As IN textbook illustrations, the forms in Figure 5-1 between *Pakicetus* and *Dorudon* are drawn to show they were swimming, but they actually lived mainly on land. The *Maiacetus* that was described in 2009 by Gingerich and his colleagues was a pregnant female with a fetus inside it, and "the fetal skeleton is positioned for head-first birth, a universal birthing posture in large-bodied land mammals, but one that is anomalous in fully aquatic marine mammals."[12] In other words, the animal gave birth on land. According to Thewissen, *Maiacetus* was "most similar in skeletal proportions" to a "giant freshwater otter."[13]

So *Maiacetus*, like *Ambulocetus* and *Pakicetus*, lived primarily on land. *Kutchicetus* looked a bit like a long-snouted crocodile with short, weight-bearing legs.[14] *Rodhocetus* had smaller hind limbs; it may have moved like a sea lion on land, swum with a dog paddle on the surface of the water, and moved like an otter underwater.[15] None of these animals were really whales, or even close. Otters and sea lions are amphibious land animals that spend some of their lives in the water, but whales, dolphins and porpoises spend *all* of their lives in the water. Coming onto land is not a natural act for cetaceans; beached whales die if they are not quickly helped back into the water. Clearly, there are important differences between fully aquatic cetaceans and amphibious mammals such as otters and sea lions.

Pakicetus, the first "walking whale" to be discovered, was classified as a cetacean because it possessed an involucrum. Yet it turns out that *Indohyus* also possessed an involucrum, but it is not considered a cetacean. Instead, it is classified in the order of mammals that includes pigs, hippopotamuses, giraffes, antelopes, sheep, and cattle. Thewissen and his colleagues, who described *Indohyus*, wrote in 2007, "Until now, the involucrum was the only character occurring in all fossil and recent cetaceans but in no other mammals. Identification of the involucrum in *Indohyus* calls into question what it is to be a cetacean: It requires either that the concept of Cetacea be expanded to include *Indohyus* or that the involucrum cease to characterize cetaceans."[16] The authors argued for the latter—that the involucrum should no longer be used to characterize cetaceans.

In other words, the involucrum is diagnostic of cetaceans, except when it isn't. So why should we call *Pakicetus* a cetacean? Why not just call it what it was: a land mammal. And why should we call *Ambulocetus*, *Maiacetus*, *Kutchicetus*, and *Rodhocetus* cetaceans? Why not just call them what they were: amphibious mammals that spent part of their lives on land and part of their lives in water?

In other words, Gould's "sweetest series of transitional fossils" is missing the most important transition of all: the transition from living primarily on land to living entirely in the water.

What Does It Take to Make a Whale?

FOSSILS OF the fully aquatic whales *Dorudon* and *Basilosaurus* appeared in a geological period called the Eocene, in rocks that geologists have dated to about forty million years ago. *Maiacetus*, *Kutchicetus*, and *Rodhocetus* were found in Eocene rocks dated between two and eight million years before that. So based on this fossil evidence, the transition from land mammals to fully aquatic mammals occurred in eight million years or less.

What changes would mammals have to undergo in those eight million years to transform them from terrestrial or amphibious mammals into fully aquatic ones? Quite a few. Many features of cetaceans differ dramatically from the features of terrestrial mammals. What follows is just a small sampling of them.

Features Needed for Swimming: A cetacean propels itself through the water primarily by the up-and-down movements of large projections at the end of its tail called "flukes." Except for tail vertebrae running down their centers, flukes contain no bones; they are made of fibrous connective tissue. Yet cetacean flukes are not passive flippers like those used by human scuba divers. Instead, their movements are coordinated by a complex system of long, powerful tendons connecting them to specialized muscles in the tail.

In the blue whale in Figure 5-1, the tail begins between the small dorsal fin and the flukes. The tail can be flexed up and down relative to the body, but the flukes can be moved independently of the tail. According to Everhard Slijper's classic book on cetaceans, the flukes "can be moved with respect to the other sections, so that the fact that, during motion, the flukes make an angle with the rest of the tail is not due to their passive reaction to the pressure of the water, as it is in the fish, but to an active muscular exertion." In the 1880s anatomists already knew "how complicated and how ingenious the structure of these organs really is."[17]

Flukes are shaped like airplane wings (called "foils"), with a rounded leading edge and long tapering trailing edge. Biologists who analyzed flukes in 2007 reported that "the relatively large leading edge radius allows greater lift generation and delays stall." In fact, calculations showed that "flukes were generally comparable or better for lift generation than engineered foils."[18]

Cetaceans also have dorsal fins, which stabilize them against roll. Like flukes, dorsal fins are among the features that distinguish cetaceans from terrestrial and amphibious mammals.

Features Needed for Breathing: A cetacean breathes by means of nostrils on top of its head, called "blowholes" because when the animal surfaces it blows moisture-laden air out of them. All living cetaceans have blowholes on the tops of their heads, though in a sperm whale the blowholes are situated farther forward than in other whales.

So for a land animal to have evolved into a cetacean, its nostrils would have had to relocate to the top of its head.

A blowhole is surrounded by thick "lips" consisting of highly elastic tissue. According to Slijper, this tissue "normally keeps the blowhole closed by tension even when the whale is at the surface. To open it during breathing, the whale has numerous muscles which run from the 'lips' to the skull below. Obviously, this method of closing the blowhole is much more effective" at keeping out water than the method found in seals, sealions and land mammals, whose nostrils are normally open and must be closed underwater by an active contraction of muscles.[19]

Although they breathe at the surface, cetaceans are famous for their deep dives. (Sea lions and seals, though not fully aquatic, are also famous for their deep dives.) Dolphins and porpoises can dive to depths of 300 meters; Weddell seals can dive to 600 meters; sperm whales can dive to 2,000 meters; and beaked whales can dive to almost 3,000 meters (over 9,800 feet).[20]

The pressure on an animal at the surface of the water is one atmosphere; the pressure on an animal ten meters below the surface is about two atmospheres; and the pressure increases about one atmosphere for every additional ten meters. So a sperm whale at 2,000 meters experiences about 200 times the pressure it experiences at the surface. Bones are not strong enough to protect lungs from such high pressure, so deep-diving mammals have collapsible rib cages and collapsible lungs.

The rib cages of cetaceans have a lot of "floating ribs," ones not attached to the sternum. These floating ribs greatly enhance the flexibility of the chest wall.[21] Cetaceans and other diving mammals also have diaphragms that are oriented nearly parallel to the spine rather than perpendicular to it. Anesthesiologist Richard Brown and physiologist James Butler explain that "the large area of contact between lung and diaphragm in cetaceans allows for the diaphragm to smoothly collapse the lung along the lungs' shortest dimension" (belly to back).[22]

Chest collapse has been directly observed in a dolphin at a depth of fifty meters, and observed by underwater television at a depth of 300 meters.[23] Blood tests have shown that seal lungs collapse by the time the animals reach a depth of fifty meters.[24] Those same tests, and similar tests in sea lions, reveal one reason why lung collapse is physiologically essential: By collapsing the tiny air sacs where gases are normally exchanged with blood, the diving mammal is protected from taking in too much nitrogen. Nitrogen absorbed under pressure causes a dangerously altered mental state called "narcosis." Even worse, nitrogen absorbed under pressure can produce bubbles in the body when the pressure is reduced, causing potentially fatal decompression sickness ("the bends").[25] By collapsing their lungs, deep-diving mammals avoid these problems.

A typical sperm whale dive lasts about an hour. A beaked whale dive may last more than two hours. How can cetaceans stay under water so long? It's thanks to yet another metabolic-engineering marvel.

Cetaceans have far more myoglobin (an oxygen-storage molecule) in their muscles than land mammals.[26] Nevertheless, as Slijper pointed out, "not even the large quantities of myoglobin they have provide an adequate explanation for their long stay under water... During diving, basic changes in the metabolism must occur."[27] The blood supply is re-distributed to the brain and heart, the heart slows down, and muscles switch to anaerobic metabolism. All vertebrates do this to some extent when they are deprived of air, but deep-diving mammals do it more completely and efficiently.[28]

Deep, long dives pose a challenge, but so too does surfacing afterwards. When a cetacean surfaces after a dive, it must re-inflate its lungs quickly in order to breathe. Lungs contain fluids called "surfactants" that coat the linings of tiny air sacs to aid in gas exchange between the air and blood. Experimental results published in 2004 showed that lung surfactants in sea lions and seals have "a composition that is distinct from that of terrestrial mammals and may be uniquely suited to repetitive collapse and expansion of the lung."[29] The same is probably true of cetaceans. Other evidence published in 2006 showed that such surfactants have "primarily an anti-adhesive function to meet the challenges of regularly collapsing lungs."[30]

Some of the breathing features described above are not unique to cetaceans. Other deep-diving mammals have them, too. But blowholes are present only in cetaceans.

Features Needed for Reproduction: In most mammals, sperm production requires a temperature several degrees below normal body temperature. Thus the testicles of most terrestrial mammals are held outside the body, but male cetaceans have internal testicles, which must be cooled below body temperature despite the fact that they are surrounded by heat-generating muscles.

The cooling is accomplished with a counter-current heat exchanger. Blood that has been cooled in the dorsal fin and flukes is carried to a region near the testicles, where it flows through a network of veins that pass between arteries carrying warm blood in the opposite direction. The arterial blood is thereby cooled before it reaches the testicles[31,32] (See Figure 5-2).

FIGURE 5-2. SIMPLIFIED DIAGRAM OF BLOOD CIRCULATION AROUND A DOLPHIN TESTICLE: In the body silhouette at the top, the white lines are veins. In the expanded view below, the black lines are arteries that carry warm blood from the heart. The gray lines are veins that carry cooled blood from the dorsal fin and the tail flukes. As the warm arterial blood flows down to the testicle, cool venous blood flows up between the arteries.

If this engineering arrangement were due to evolution, the relocation of cetacean testicles to the inside could not have preceded the counter-current heat exchange system. Otherwise, the whale would have been sterile, an evolutionary dead end. Yet there is no adaptive advantage to developing a counter-current heat exchange system around the testicles unless they are inside the body. One would not come before the other, yet the probability that both would evolve simultaneously is effectively zero.

Also, after birth, cetacean calves must be nursed underwater. But young calves cannot stay underwater as long as adults; they have to surface frequently to breathe. So nursing in cetaceans is very different from nursing in terrestrial mammals.

A cetacean mother's nipples are recessed in two slits on either side of the genital opening. According to Slijper, "While suckling their young, cetaceans move very slowly; the calf follows behind and approaches the nipple from the back. The cow then turns a little to the side, so that the calf has easier access to the nipple, which has meanwhile emerged from its slit. Since the calf lacks proper lips, it has to seize the nipple between the tongue and the tip of its palate."[33] (Even sperm whales suckle this way, though because of their unusual head anatomy calves must position themselves upside-down under their mothers.)[34]

The mother then forcefully squirts milk into the calf. Even after the calf lets go, milk can often be seen squirting from the nipple. The milk is three to four times as concentrated as the milk of cows and goats; it has the consistency of condensed milk or liquid yogurt. The calf thereby receives much more nourishment in a much shorter time.[35]

Thus many features would have had to originate in the eight million years or less between the so-called "walking whales" and fully aquatic whales, including flukes (along with fluke tendons and specialized tail muscles); blowholes (with elastic tissues to keep them closed and specialized muscles to open them); internal testicles (with a countercurrent heat exchange system to cool them); specialized features for nursing (including forceful delivery and concentrated milk); and many other features not listed here.

This is a tall order. Indeed, a growing body of evidence suggests that for evolution it's an insurmountably tall order.

Neo-Darwinism assumes that anatomical changes originate in DNA mutations. As we saw in Chapter 4, this assumption is false. Decades of experiments have shown that DNA mutations do not produce beneficial new anatomical features. But for the sake of argument, let's ignore that fact and proceed as though the standard evolutionary theory might be true. Let's also ignore, for now, the criticisms in Chapter 4 of the modern use of the word "gene." Ignore all that and evolutionary theory still faces a big problem.

Whale Genes?

SOME GENES have larger effects than others because they regulate other genes. According to Thewissen, hind limbs disappeared in cetaceans because of changes in regulatory genes, and "the same regulatory genes may also have effects on other parts of the dolphin's anatomy, and possibly those same genes were involved in shaping the other parts of the anatomy of the Eocene cetaceans."[36] But what genes might they have been?

Cetaceans are divided into two sub-orders: toothed and baleen. The first sub-order includes dolphins, porpoises, and sperm whales (among others). The second sub-order includes gray whales, right whales and blue whales (among others). Baleen is made of keratin, the same protein found in human hair and nails, but in baleen whales (which lack teeth) it forms large comb-like structures in the mouth used to strain food from the water the whales take in.

As we saw in Chapter 4, *Hox* genes are involved in specifying the locations of structures along the head-to-tail axis of animals, and similar *Hox* genes are found in many kinds of animals. In 1998, a team of scientists found that a gene affecting limb development in chicks and mice also occurs in baleen whales, but the whale version was missing some nucleotides. When they inserted the whale version of the gene into a mouse embryo, they found that it was not expressed in the place where mouse hind limbs would normally form.[37,38]

It might be tempting to argue that the missing nucleotides explain why whales lack hind limbs, though the authors of the 1998 studies did not argue that, and Lars Bejder and Brian Hall pointed out in 2002 that the missing nucleotides are *not* missing in other whales (all of which lack hind limbs). Bejder and Hall concluded, "A simple evolutionary change in *Hox* gene expression or *Hox* gene regulation is unlikely to have driven loss of the hind limbs in cetaceans."[39]

A genetic analysis published in 2011 concluded that baleen whales have genes for several proteins contained in enamel, but the genes have been inactivated by mutations.[40] This might help explain why baleen whales lack teeth, but clearly it does not explain why they have baleen.

Another genetic analysis published in 2014 concluded that various taste receptor genes in both toothed and baleen cetaceans had been inactivated by mutations.[41] Once again, however, the loss of features cannot explain the origin of features.

Mutations in a gene called *ASPM* cause severe reductions in brain size in humans. In 2012, a team of scientists used a molecular phylogenetic tree to infer that the sequence of *ASPM* had changed more in cetaceans and primates (both of which have large brains) than in other mammals. The scientists concluded that "positive [natural] selection at the *ASPM* gene coincides with brain size enlargements in cetaceans."[42] A 2014 study, however, pointed out that the 2012 study did not explicitly test for a connection between *ASPM* and brain size. According to the authors of the 2014 study, the conclusion of the 2012 study was "not supported."[43]

So the available evidence does not even come close to identifying genes that could turn a land mammal into a fully aquatic cetacean. In the absence of anything like direct evidence, let's consider a more indirect approach.

How Many Mutations?

As we saw above, the fossil record shows that the transition from terrestrial or amphibious mammals to fully aquatic cetaceans occurred in eight million years or less. Eight million years might seem like a long time, but if cetaceans evolved by the accumulation of accidental mutations in a land-dwelling ancestor, it might not have been long enough.

How many genes would have to change during those eight million years? Nobody really knows, of course, but a 2016 study of giraffes might provide some insight. An international team of biologists compared over 13,000 genes from giraffes and okapis. Okapis are similar to giraffes but have much shorter necks. The comparison showed that the giraffe has seventy genes that "exhibit unique genetic changes and likely contribute to giraffe's unique features."[44] According to the authors, about two-thirds of those genes have specific roles in regulating skeletal, neural, and/or cardiovascular development, and probably played a role in the evolution of the giraffe's long neck, modified nerves, and turbocharged heart (needed to pump blood to the elevated head).

The 2016 study estimated that the common ancestor of giraffes and okapis lived about eleven million years ago, so the time frame is not very different from the gap between "walking whales" and fully aquatic cetaceans. Let's begin by assuming that it took only one mutation to modify each of the giraffe's forty-six distinctive "neck genes." This is surely an underestimate, even if mutations could produce the beneficial anatomical changes needed for evolution. But for the sake of argument, let's assume that just one mutation per gene was sufficient for the evolution of the giraffe's neck—forty-six mutations in all.[45]

So now let's extrapolate from that figure to estimate how many mutations would be needed to evolve a whale from a land mammal. Lengthening the neck and modifying the heart and nerves in giraffes might be compared to lengthening the tail and modifying the muscles and nerves in cetaceans. But that does not include the origin of new features such as flukes and dorsal fins, top-of-the-head blowholes with their specialized musculature, internal testicles with their counter-current heat exchange system, or specialized features for nursing underwater. Unless we assume (quite unrealistically) that mutations in a few regulatory genes could produce all these effects, it is clear that at least hundreds or thousands of mutations would be needed to explain how "walking whales" evolved into modern cetaceans.

How long does it take for nature to generate and select that many mutations? Mutation rates have been experimentally determined for many different organisms.[46] Mutations occur in the course of reproduction, so the rate at which they occur depends on generation time (the time between birth and sexual maturity) and the effective size of the breeding population (not all animals in a population are actively breeding at any given time). Also, for a mutation to affect an entire species, it must spread from the individual in which it occurs to the entire population. In the language of population genetics, it must become "fixed."

Neo-Darwinian population geneticists have incorporated these variables into standard formulas that estimate how long it takes for mutations to become fixed. A 2008 study used those formulas to calculate that two mutations in regulatory genes could become fixed in fruit flies in a few million years. In humans, however, which have much smaller effective breeding populations and longer generation times, the process would take more than 100 million years.[47]

Biologist Richard Sternberg has applied this analysis to cetaceans. Large mammals (such as the supposed ancestors of cetaceans) tend to have effective breeding population sizes comparable to that of humans, but modern whales reach maturity much faster, so their generation times are much shorter. Assuming a generation time of twenty-five years for humans and five years for the ancestors of cetaceans, Sternberg pointed out that fixing just two mutations in the latter would take millions of years longer than the time available in the fossil record.[48] So there isn't enough time to fix even two mutations, yet we need hundreds or even thousands of new mutations. Obviously, eight million years is not long enough to accumulate enough accidental mutations to turn a "walking whale" into a real whale—even if neo-Darwinian theory were right about the power of mutations (which it isn't).

It Gets Worse

In 2016, a team of paleontologists published a report of their discovery in Antarctica of a fossilized whale similar to *Basilosaurus*. The fossil occurred in rocks previously reported to be at least forty-nine million years old—older than some of the so-called "walking whales." This would reduce the time available for land-mammal-to-whale evolution from eight million years to practically no time at all—making the problem of whale evolution even worse.

Faced with this problem, the paleontologists who reported the discovery argued that the date of forty-nine million years "might be biased." They argued instead that a date no older than forty-six million years was "more consistent" with the fossil record of other whales.[49] But adjusting the date to be more consistent with the standard story isn't how empirical science is supposed to work.[50]

So "the sweetest series of transitional fossils an evolutionist could ever hope to find" is not so sweet after all. It quickly sours with a little additional digging.

With enough imagination anyone can invent a story about how land animals evolved into whales. But an imaginative story is not empirical science. When the materialistic story of whale evolution ignores inconvenient evidence, it is zombie science.

6. The Human Appendix and Other So-called Junk

In *The Origin of Species*, Darwin discussed "rudimentary organs," which "from being useless, will be disregarded by natural selection." He argued that the existence of such features cannot be explained by a theory of creation by design: Why would a creator make useless organs? But if such features once had functions that have been lost, they would make sense from the standpoint of his theory: "On the view of descent with modification, we may conclude that the existence of organs in a rudimentary, imperfect, and useless condition, or quite aborted, far from presenting a strange difficulty, as they assuredly do on the ordinary doctrine of creation, might even have been anticipated, and can be accounted for by the laws of inheritance."[1]

Unfortunately, Darwin confused matters when he discussed flowers. The female organs of a flower include pistils, but we also find pistils in the male flowers of some species. In a female flower the pistil guides pollen tubes to the ovary at its base. But of course a male flower lacks ovaries, so what role does the pistil play in it? Darwin said the pistil of the male flower "is in a rudimentary state." So, did he mean it's "useless?" No, the male pistil "remains well developed... for the purpose of brushing the pollen out of the surrounding anthers." Apparently assuming that all pistils performed two functions in primitive flowers, Darwin wrote, "An organ serving for two purposes, may become rudimentary or utterly aborted for one, even the more important purpose; and remain perfectly efficient for the other."[2]

So Darwin used "rudimentary" in two senses in *The Origin of Species*. In one sense it meant having become completely useless, while in another sense it meant having lost one function but retained another.

In *The Descent of Man*, Darwin tried to clear up the confusion. He wrote that rudimentary organs "are either absolutely useless... or they are of such slight service to their present possessors, that we cannot suppose that they were developed under the conditions which now exist. Organs in this latter state are not strictly rudimentary, but they are tending in this direction."[3] So in *The Descent of Man*, Darwin settled on his first definition of rudimentary, that is, useless.

In modern literature the term *vestigial* is most often used to mean what Darwin meant by rudimentary in *The Descent of Man*—that is, wholly useless. So the argument for evolution goes something like this: A vestigial structure has no purpose, so it cannot be explained by a theory of creation; instead, it is evidence of descent with modification from an ancestral structure that was once useful.

The Human Appendix

ONE OF the vestigial structures Darwin listed was the human appendix: "Not only is it useless, but it is sometimes the cause of death."[4]

The human appendix is a blind-ended tube several inches long that extends from a pouch where the small intestine joins the large intestine. It is also called the "vermiform" appendix, meaning worm-like (See Figure 6-1).

But we now know that the human appendix is not useless. Instead, it has at least two functions: One is to help fight infections; the other is to provide a safe haven for beneficial bacteria.

Fighting infections: The appendix, as it turns out, is part of the human immune system. This system fights infections by recognizing molecules called antigens on the surfaces of harmful viruses and bacteria, then producing antibodies that lock onto those antigens to target the harmful cells for destruction. These functions are performed primarily by blood cells called "lymphocytes," which interact with other cells in "lymphoid tissues." There are many lymphoid tissues in the human body; tonsils are among them.

British anatomist Richard Berry reported that the human appendix "is characterized by its large amount of lymphoid tissue." In fact, the appendix "well deserves the name which has been applied to it of 'abdominal tonsil.'" Berry concluded that the appendix "is not, therefore, a vestigial structure."[5]

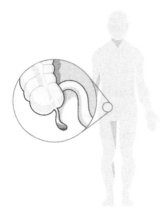

FIGURE 6-1. THE HUMAN APPENDIX: The appendix is a worm-like structure extending from a pouch near the spot where the small intestine joins the large intestine in the lower right abdomen.

Berry provided this insight not recently, but all the way back in 1900. Other scientists have since confirmed this view. In 1978, Chilean biologist Pedro Gorgollón used an electron microscope to show that the appendix, at least in children up to twelve years old, is "a well-developed lymphoid organ, suggesting that it has important immunological functions."[6] American anatomist Dale Bockman wrote in 1983 that the human appendix is a "prominent example" of lymphoid tissue "whose function is to react to the wide variety of antigens present in the gastrointestinal tract."[7] In 1991, an international team of biologists reported that lymphocytes from the appendix express higher levels of an immunologically important molecule than lymphocytes from elsewhere in the body,[8] and in 1998 Italian anatomist Giacomo Azzali documented the "intense" activity of lymphocytes in the appendix.[9] In 2004, Pakistani biologist Aliya Zahid wrote that instead of being "an evolutionary remnant of little significance to normal physiology," the appendix is "one of the guardians of the internal environment of the body from the hostile external environment."[10]

Sheltering beneficial bacteria: In addition to defending the body against harmful bacteria, the human appendix provides shelter for beneficial bacteria. Certain kinds of bacteria in our intestines help us to digest food and supply us with needed vitamins. In cases of severe diarrhea, when beneficial bacteria are flushed out along with harmful bacteria, the former need to be replenished in order to restore good health. In 2007, American biologists Randal Bollinger and William Parker and their colleagues suggested that the human appendix might serve as a "safe house" for beneficial bacteria so they can re-colonize the intestine after diarrhea.[11]

Subsequent research supported their suggestion. In 2011, medical researcher Gene Im and his colleagues reported that patients who had had their appendices removed were at increased risk for a serious form of recurrent diarrhea.[12] According to French scientist Michel Laurin and his colleagues, the idea that the appendix is a "safe-house for beneficial bacteria is supported by a host of observations in immunology and microbiology, and is consistent with observations made by medical science." Laurin and his colleagues therefore concluded that the human appendix "cannot be considered a vestige."[13,14]

Yet Darwin's followers continue to call the appendix vestigial. In a 2006 book titled *Why Darwin Matters*, Michael Shermer wrote that "humans are replete with useless vestigial structures, a distinctive sign of our evolutionary ancestry." One of those "useless vestigial structures," according to Shermer, is the human appendix.[15] A website updated in 2016 titled "Understanding Evolution," which is maintained by the University of California at Berkeley, explains that "all life bears the scars of its history — including humans. Our awkward wisdom teeth and appendix are simply historical holdovers that evolution has not managed to rid us of."[16]

There is a holdover here, but it's not the appendix. It's Darwin's now hopelessly outdated view that the appendix is useless and therefore vestigial.

Even some recent biology textbooks perpetuate the myth. The 2014 edition of Raven and Johnson's *Biology* tells students that the human appendix "is apparently vestigial…. Although some functions have been suggested, it is difficult to assign any current function to the human vermiform appendix." The textbook concludes, "It is difficult to understand vestigial structures such as these as anything other than evolutionary relics, holdovers from the past." Thus "they are readily understandable as a result of descent with modification."[17]

Useless Organ, or Useless Argument?

IN 1981, Canadian biologist Steven Scadding wrote, "The entire argument that vestigial organs provide evidence for evolution is invalid." Scadding pointed out that anatomical and experimental evidence indicated that the human appendix, once thought to be vestigial, actually functions as a lymphoid organ. Scadding concluded, "Vestigial organs represent simply a special case of homologous organs, i.e. structures similar in fundamental structure, position, and embryonic development, but not necessarily in function." Thus vestigial organs "provide no special evidence for the theory of evolution."[18]

Another Canadian biologist, Bruce Naylor, called Scadding's argument "erroneous" and demanded "an immediate and forceful response" lest it "provide ammunition" for creationists. According to Naylor, "vestigial" does not mean useless, but "surviving in small or degenerate form," so an organ with some function can still be considered vestigial. He also argued that, according to the design argument, "perfectly designed organisms necessitated the existence of a creator," but "Darwin was able to show that organisms are often something less than perfectly created machines" and thus better explained by evolution. Naylor concluded that vestigial organs "provide one of the more powerful evidences for the theory of evolution" and that "the theory of special creation (and the argument from 'design'), whatever its theological attributes, has been convincingly falsified scientifically."[19]

Scadding replied, "The entire argument of Darwin and others regarding vestigial organs hinges on their uselessness and inutility." Otherwise, he explained, the argument from vestigiality is nothing more than an argument from homology, and "Darwin treated these arguments separately recognizing that they were in fact independent." In other words, if an organ in Species A accomplishes one purpose, and a similar organ in Species B accomplishes some other useful purpose, the organs could be homologous, but a homology inference should not be conflated with an argument for evolution from "bad design."

Scadding also objected that Naylor's "less than perfectly designed" argument was "based on a theological assumption about the nature of God," namely, that God would not create "less than perfectly created machines." Scadding concluded, "Whatever the validity of this theological claim, it certainly cannot be defended as a scientific statement, and thus should be given no place in a scientific discussion of evolution."[20]

Zombie Science vs. Scadding

IN 2003, some defenders of evolution blasted people who cite Scadding's argument against using vestigial organs as evidence for evolution. According to Reed Cartwright and Douglas Theobald, such people ignore Naylor's criticisms, and "the failure to note that a subsequent paper raised objections demonstrates the poverty of their position. If they were not aware of Naylor's response, they are guilty of poor scholarship. On the other hand, if they were aware of it, then they are guilty of misrepresentation."[21]

But Cartwright and Theobald ignored the contents of Scadding's reply to Naylor, and simply repeated Naylor's re-definition of vestigiality and his claim that vestigial structures need to be functionless only with respect to their original purposes. By their own logic, then, these writers are guilty either of poor scholarship or willful misrepresentation.

In 2009, Jerry Coyne wrote that the appendix is one of "many vestigial features proving that we evolved." According to Coyne, "our appendix is simply the remnant of an organ that was critically important to our leaf-eating ancestors, but of no real value to us." Coyne acknowledged that the human appendix "may be of some small use," since it "may function as part of the immune system," and it may provide "a refuge for useful gut bacteria." Nevertheless, Coyne argued, "the appendix is still vestigial, for it no longer performs the function for which it evolved."[22]

Coyne doesn't establish his remnant claim independently. And in any case, if "vestigial" is redefined to mean change of function rather than lack of function, then the word would describe many structures never before considered vestigial. For example, if the human arm evolved from the foreleg of a four-footed mammal, then the human arm would be vestigial because its original function has changed. This is not what most people mean by vestigial.[23]

Some defenders of evolution have argued that the pelvic bones of whales are vestigial. In 2014, however, a team of scientists published evidence that a cetacean's pelvis plays an essential role in reproduction. According to one news report, "common wisdom has long held that those bones are simply vestigial," but the new research "flies directly in the face of that assumption." The news report quoted one of the scientists: "Our research really changes the way we think about the evolution of whale pelvic bones in particular, but more generally about structures we call 'vestigial.'"[24]

Biologist Paul Z. Myers, a vocal defender not only of evolution but also of materialism, was furious. He criticized the scientist quoted in the 2014 news report for "parroting common misconceptions about vestigial organs." According to Myers, "an organ is vestigial if it is reduced in size or utility compared to homologous organs in other animals."[25] To support his point, Myers quoted Darwin's confused comment about male pistils, but Myers ignored Scadding's argument that "vestigiality" then reduces to homology. Myers also ignored the fact that whale hips fulfill their role in reproduction just fine.

Human Tails?

MIDWAY THROUGH embryo development, the spinal column of a human fetus (and the fetuses of some other vertebrates) projects beyond the rest of the body (See Figure 3-2). Darwin considered this evidence that humans are descended from animals with tails. After development is complete, the spinal column in humans and some apes ends in a small triangular bone called the "coccyx." The coccyx consists of three to five vertebrae that are fused together in most adult humans.[26]

Darwin regarded the human coccyx as a rudimentary tail. "Though functionless as a tail," he wrote, it "plainly represents this part in other vertebrate animals." He argued that rudimentary organs, being useless, "are no longer subjected to natural selection. They often become wholly suppressed. When this occurs, they are nevertheless liable to occasional reappearance through reversion," and "in certain rare and anomalous cases" the coccyx has been known "to form a small external rudiment of a tail."[27]

We now know that the human coccyx is not useless. It is actually an important attachment point for various muscles, tendons and ligaments. Nevertheless, it is true that in very rare cases a human baby is born with an external projection in its lower back.

Actual cases: Such a projection usually consists of skin-covered fat and contains some blood vessels, nerves, and muscle. In 1984, pathologists Anh Dao and Martin Netsky classified projections at or near the base of the spine into two groups: "true tails," which are fleshy protuberances consisting of skin-covered fat and some blood vessels, nerves and muscle, but no bones; and "pseudotails," which are pathological deformities of the spine and spinal cord.[28] The labels are misleading, because the true tails of animals such as cats and monkeys contain vertebrae. So the "true tails" of Dao and Netsky are nothing like the functional tails of other animals.

According to Dao and Netsky, "the true, or persistent, vestigial tail of humans arises from the most distal [outer] remnant of the embryonic tail."[29] In 1989, however, pediatric neurosurgeons Sarah Gaskill and Arthur Marlin reported that Dao and Netsky's so-called "true tails" are sometimes associated with spinal cord defects that if left uncorrected "may ultimately cause permanent neurological damage." Furthermore, such projections can occur in locations other than the tail end of the embryonic spine. This fact, they argued, "would tend to discount the hypothesis that these tails are remnants from early development."[30]

In 2004, embryologists Fabiola Müller and Ronan O'Rahilly wrote that the projection at the lower end of a human embryo "does not produce even a temporary 'tail' in the human." They argued that the term tail-bud "should be used for tailed species only, and thus is not appropriate for the human."[31]

In 2005, neurosurgeon Daniel J. Donovan and neurologist Robert C. Pedersen wrote, "Conclusions regarding the evolutionary significance of the tail and distinctions between true tail and pseudotail are clinically unimportant and should be abandoned."[32] In 2014, pediatric neurosurgeon Michael Egnor wrote that he found the distinction between true tails and pseudotails meaningless. He had operated on quite a few children who had what some people would call a "tail," but "none of them—and none of the reports in the literature that I know of—are actual tails." Egnor concluded that a human "tail" is just a birth defect, and "there is no reason whatsoever to associate it with any sort of 'evolutionary regression' or any such nonsense."[33]

A phony case: In 2014, physicist Karl Giberson engaged in a public discussion with philosopher of science Stephen Meyer on the question "Should Christians Embrace Darwin?"[34] During the discussion Giberson defended evolution and Meyer criticized it. Giberson argued that nature is full of examples of bad design, and (according to his account of the exchange) to make his point he "showed pictures of otherwise healthy humans" who had been born with tails. He asked rhetorically why the human genome contains instructions for such features, and he answered: "The scientific explanation is that we inherited these instructions from our tailed ancestors but the instructions for producing them have been shut off in our genomes.... Sometimes the 'ignore these genes' message gets lost in fetal development, however, and babies are born with perfectly formed, even functional tails."[35]

Giberson showed the picture reproduced in Figure 6-2. It turns out that it was a photoshopped fake, though Giberson apparently didn't know it at the time.[36]

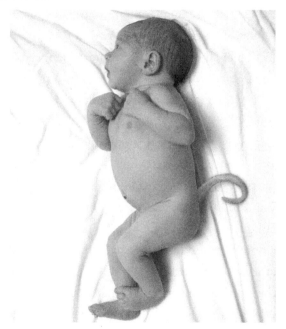

FIGURE 6-2. THE PHOTOSHOPPED HUMAN TAIL GIBERSON USED AS EVIDENCE FOR EVOLUTION: Human baby with tail. Copyright by Larry Dunstan/Science Photo Library.

He subsequently apologized for using the faked photograph, though he insisted that what he did was no worse than accidentally showing a picture of Plato when talking about Aristotle.[37] Actually, it was more like using a photoshopped picture of Plato as evidence that Plato *was* Aristotle. Despite his embarrassing gaffe, Giberson continued to maintain that human tails *do* provide evidence for evolution.

Junk DNA

As we saw in Chapter 4, Francis Crick argued in 1958 that the function of DNA is to specify the amino acid sequences of proteins.[38] The assumption that proteins build the body led to the idea of a "genetic program" that specifies the principal features of an organism.[39]

By 1970, however, biologists knew that most of our DNA does not encode proteins. In 1972, biologist Susumu Ohno published an article wondering why there is "so much 'junk' DNA in our genome."[40] In 1976, Richard Dawkins offered an explanation based on evolutionary thinking:

> It appears that the amount of DNA in organisms is more than is strictly necessary for building them: A large fraction of the DNA is never translated into protein. From the point of view of the individual organism this seems paradoxical. If the 'purpose' of DNA is to supervise the building of bodies, it is surprising to find a large quantity of DNA which does no such thing. Biologists are racking their brains trying to think what useful task this apparently surplus DNA is doing. But from the point of view of the selfish genes themselves, there is no paradox. The true 'purpose' of DNA is to survive, no more and no less. The simplest way to explain the surplus DNA is to suppose that it is a parasite, or at best a harmless but useless passenger, hitching a ride in the survival machines created by the other DNA.[41]

Then in 1980, two papers appeared back to back in the journal *Nature*: "Selfish genes, the phenotype paradigm and genome evolution," by W. Ford Doolittle and Carmen Sapienza, and "Selfish DNA: the ultimate parasite," by Leslie Orgel and Francis Crick. The first paper argued that many organisms contain "DNAs whose only 'function' is survival within genomes," and that "the search for other explanations may prove, if not intellectually sterile, ultimately futile."[42] The second argued similarly that "much DNA in higher organisms is little better than junk," and its accumulation in the course of evolution "can be compared to the spread of a not-too-harmful parasite within its host." Orgel and Crick concluded that since such DNA probably has no function, "it would be folly in such cases to hunt obsessively for one."[43]

Fortunately for the advance of empirical science, some biologists disagreed with this neo-Darwinian interpretation. Thomas Cavalier-Smith considered it "premature" to dismiss non-protein-coding DNA as junk,[44] and Gabriel Dover wrote that "we should not abandon all hope of arriving at an understanding of the manner in which some sequences might affect the biology of organisms in completely novel and somewhat unconventional ways."[45] So some biologists were skeptical of the notion of junk DNA from the very beginning, though most accepted it.

Using Junk DNA to Bash Design

DEFENDERS OF evolution have cited junk DNA to argue for neo-Darwinism, and as is so often the case, they also have used the notion to argue against intelligent design. In 1994, biologist and textbook-writer Kenneth Miller wrote, "The human genome is littered with pseudogenes [DNA sequences thought to have lost a function they once had], gene fragments, 'orphaned' genes, 'junk' DNA, and so many repeated copies of pointless DNA sequences that it cannot be attributed to anything that resembles intelligent design." Miller continued:

> If the DNA of a human being or any other organism resembled a carefully constructed computer program, with neatly arranged and logically structured modules each written to fulfill a specific function, the evidence of intelligent design would be overwhelming. In fact, the genome resembles nothing so much as a hodgepodge of borrowed, copied, mutated, and discarded sequences and commands that has been cobbled together by millions of years of trial and error against the relentless test of survival."[46]

In 2005, biologist and textbook-writer Douglas Futuyma wrote that we can "identify several patterns that confirm the historical reality of evolution." One of those patterns is that "every eukaryote's genome contains numerous nonfunctional DNA sequences." Such patterns are "inconsistent with the notion that an omnipotent Creator, who should be able to adhere to an optimal design, provided them."[47]

The next year Michael Shermer asked "why the Intelligent Designer added to our genome junk DNA." According to Shermer, "rather than being intelligently designed, the human genome looks more and more like a mosaic of mutations, fragment copies, borrowed sequences, and discarded strings of DNA that were jerry-built over millions of years of evolution."[48] The same year Francis Collins argued in his book *The Language of God* that "junk DNA" provides evidence for evolution, though he later stopped using the term in light of new evidence that such DNA is functional.[49]

In 2007 philosopher Philip Kitcher published a book in which he argued that "if you were designing the genomes of organisms, you would certainly not fill them up with junk." Yet "the most striking feature of the genome analyses we now have is how much apparently nonfunctional DNA there is." According to Kitcher, "From the Darwinian perspective all this is explicable."[50]

The same year Kitcher's book was published, however, biologists published preliminary evidence that so-called "junk DNA" is not junk after all.

The ENCODE Project

THE FIRST draft of the human genome was published in 2003, but it merely provided a catalog of DNA sequences and did not shed any light on how they functioned. So a second project, called ENCODE (for ENCyclopedia Of DNA Elements), was undertaken to investigate the functions of DNA sequences. ENCODE published its first results in 2007.

After sampling one percent of the DNA in a human cell, the ENCODE team reported that they had found "convincing evidence that the genome is pervasively transcribed," with a majority of its nucleotide subunits being represented in RNA transcripts.[51] Furthermore, although it was previously thought that only one strand (the "sense" strand) of DNA is transcribed into RNA, the evidence showed that both strands are transcribed. A 2008 report concluded that "antisense transcripts thus appear to be a pervasive feature of human cells."[52]

Not only were RNAs being transcribed from much of our so-called "junk DNA," but more and more of those RNAs were also turning out to serve important functions.[53] Two classes of non-protein-coding DNA that many biologists believed were junk are Long Interspersed Nuclear Elements (LINEs) and Short Interspersed Nuclear Elements (SINEs). In 2007, British biologists reported that RNAs transcribed from LINEs are responsible for silencing a gene expressed in human fetuses but not adults.[54]

Then in 2009, American biologists showed that RNAs transcribed from SINEs help to control gene expression and concluded that this "has refuted the historical notion that SINEs are merely 'junk DNA'."[55] The same year other regions of so-called "junk" DNA were discovered to play an essential role in placental development. As a British biologist noted in 2009, it "used to be an open question" whether these regions "simply represented junk or selfish DNA" but they are now known to make "a specific contribution to normal physiology."[56]

In September 2012, over four hundred ENCODE researchers reported much more comprehensive evidence in thirty articles published in *Nature, Genome Research*, and *Genome Biology*.[57] They concluded that the data enabled them to "assign biochemical functions for 80% of the genome."[58] Since the project had not sampled all cell types, the final figure was expected to be even higher.

Since 2012 there has been a virtual flood of new reports of functions in RNAs transcribed from non-protein-coding DNA. Such RNAs help to specify the three-dimensional structure of chromosomes,[59,60] and their three-dimensional positioning inside the nucleus,[61,62] both of which have profound effects on gene expression. Non-protein-coding RNAs are involved in fat metabolism,[63,64] maintenance of the immune system,[65,66] and proper functioning of stem cells.[67,68] Non-protein-coding RNAs also are necessary for the development of nerve cells and the nervous system,[69,70] for bone cells and the skeleton,[71,72] and for muscles.[73,74] More functions of such RNAs are discovered every month.

So the evidence demonstrates that most of our DNA is transcribed into RNA and that many of those RNAs have biological functions. The idea that most of our DNA is junk, it would seem, is dead.

But Wait—Evolution Requires Junk DNA!

ACCORDING TO some evolutionary biologists, however, "junk DNA" is very much alive because evolutionary theory demands it. Canadian biologists Alexander Palazzo and T. Ryan Gregory point out that less than ten percent of sequences are conserved (that is, similar) between humans and other mammals. Evolutionary theory attributes sequence conservation to function, and Palazzo and Gregory argue that unconserved sequences are not functional, so the number of human sequences that are functional must be much less than the eighty percent reported by ENCODE.[75]

Yet function has been identified in many non-protein-coding RNAs whose sequences have *not* been conserved.[76] As the subtitle of a report in the journal *Trends in Genetics* put it, a "lack of conservation does not mean lack of function."[77] So any estimate of functionality based on sequence conservation is an underestimate.

Nevertheless, defenders of evolution continue to argue that functionality in human DNA is closer to ten percent than eighty percent. In 2013, W. Ford Doolittle (who argued for junk DNA in 1980) distinguished between two definitions of function: "causal role" (whatever does not occur after deleting or blocking the expression of a region of DNA) and "selected effect" (whatever has been or is subject to natural selection). According to Doolittle, only the latter is really significant.[78] Several dozen members of the ENCODE team replied that there are three ways to approach biological function: The genetic approach observes the consequences of perturbing DNA, the evolutionary approach measures selection, and the biochemical approach measures molecular activity. Each approach has its strengths and limitations, and the results from ENCODE "reinforce the principle that each approach provides complementary information and that we need to use combinations of all three to elucidate genome function in human biology and disease."[79] Nevertheless, Doolittle insisted that "only 'in the light of evolution' does biology make sense," so the evolutionary approach takes priority.[80] If this means labeling functional DNA *junk*, so be it.

In 2013, biologist Dan Graur criticized the "evolution-free gospel of ENCODE" and accused its researchers of "playing fast and loose with the term 'function,' by divorcing genomic analysis from its evolutionary context."[81] In a lecture at the University of Houston, Graur argued that "if the human genome is indeed devoid of junk DNA as implied by the ENCODE project, then a long, undirected evolutionary process cannot explain the human genome." In other words: "If ENCODE is right, then evolution is wrong." But for Graur, evolution *can't* be wrong. His solution to the problem? "Kill ENCODE."[82]

So zombie science insists paradoxically *both* that DNA is the secret of life *and* that most of it is junk. On both counts, zombie science is wrong.

Evolution as a Science-Stopper

IN SPITE of the evidence, defenders of evolution continue to insist that the human appendix, the human tail, and most non-protein-coding DNA sequences are useless leftovers from a long process of unguided evolution.

One of the surest ways to discourage empirical research into the possible functions of a feature is to decide at the outset that it has none. British anatomist Arthur Keith wrote in 1912 that "for many years the appendix vermiformis has been regarded as one of the vestigial structures of man's body, an opinion which has prejudiced us against any real endeavor to discover its nature and function."[83]

Maybe there are biological features that really have no significant function, but any theory that claims non-function at the outset obstructs scientific progress.

Evolution is not just zombie science. From the perspective of empirical science, it may also be the biggest science-stopper in history.

7. The Human Eye

THE HUMAN EYE, ONCE THOUGHT TO BE A MAJOR STUMBLING BLOCK for Darwin's theory, has now become an icon of evolution. But it serves as an icon in two very different ways: First, defenders of evolution argue that eyes can evolve very easily. Second, alleged flaws in the human eye are used as evidence for unguided evolution and against intelligent design.

In *The Origin of Species* Darwin included a chapter titled "Difficulties On Theory," and in one of its sections he discussed "organs of extreme perfection and complication." Chief among these is the eye: "To suppose that the eye, with all its inimitable contrivances for adjusting the focus to different distances, for admitting different amounts of light, and for the correction of spherical and chromatic aberration, could have been formed by natural selection, seems, I freely confess, absurd in the highest possible degree." Yet Darwin immediately suggested a way to overcome the difficulty:

> If numerous gradations from a perfect and complex eye to one very imperfect and simple, each grade being useful to its possessor, can be shown to exist; if further, the eye does vary ever so slightly, and the variations be inherited, which is certainly the case; and if any variation or modification in the organ be ever useful to an animal under changing conditions of life, then the difficulty of believing that a perfect and complex eye could be formed by natural selection, though insuperable by our imagination, can hardly be considered real.[1]

Numerous Gradations?

MODERN ANIMALS do, indeed, have eyes that range from relatively simple to very complex. Flatworms have eyespots that consist of a single layer of photosensitive cells. Jellyfish also have simple eyespots, though box jellyfish have additional eyes that are more complex.[2] The giant clam and the chambered nautilus have pinhole eyes, with light-sensing cells inside a deep pit with a small opening.[3] Insects have compound eyes that generally consist of thousands of individual photoreceptor units called "ommatidia." Shrimp also have compound eyes. Cephalopods and vertebrates have camera eyes, each with a single lens that focuses incoming rays on light-sensing cells at the back of the eyeball. (Cephalopods, from the Greek words meaning "head" and "foot," are mollusks with tentacles growing from their heads. An octopus and a squid are cephalopods.)

In 1977, zoologist Luitfried von Salvini-Plawen and evolutionary biologist Ernst Mayr published a comprehensive review of the distribution of various kinds of eyes in modern animals. The presence of similar eyes in unrelated species (cephalopods and vertebrates are just one example) convinced the authors that eyes must have originated independently some forty to sixty-five times in the history of life. Indeed, they argued, eyes are so oddly distributed in the various phyla that they cannot be placed into a single phylogenetic tree. In other words, the distribution of eyes would seem to be a problem for Darwin's theory that all animals have descended from a common ancestor. Nevertheless, Salvini-Plawen and Mayr managed to conclude, "The original purpose of our investigation had been to test the validity of Darwin's assertion that the evolution of eyes is no stumbling block for his theory of natural selection. As we have seen, Darwin passed this test with flying colors."[4]

But do the many kinds of eyes in modern animals actually provide the "numerous gradations" needed by Darwin's theory? Not really.

The Fossil Record

WHAT DARWIN's theory needs is not a range of eyes that exists in the present, but a range over the history of life: Not a horizontal slice of time, but a vertical one. If the eyes of early animals started out "very imperfect and simple," and eyes in some phyla gradually became more perfect and complex in the course of geological time, *that* might constitute evidence for Darwin's theory.

But complex eyes were already present in some of the earliest animals. Trilobites are extinct members of the arthropod phylum, which includes modern insects and crustaceans (such as shrimp). When trilobites first appeared in the Cambrian explosion, many of them possessed compound eyes that were "already of a highly developed type."[5] According to trilobite expert Riccardo Levi-Setti "some of the recently discovered properties of [a] trilobite's eye lenses represent an all-time feat of function optimization." What does this signify? Levi-Setti continues:

> We are confronted here with a very successful scheme of eye structure: the composite or compound eye, made of arrays of separate optical elements, the ommatidia, pointing in slightly diverging directions and each performing an identical function.... Evidence of the success of such a scheme is widespread experience, since the eyes of insects and crustaceans, in fact of most arthropods, still follow a design closely related to that developed by trilobites.[6]

Other Cambrian findings only make matters worse. In 2011, a team of paleontologists reported the discovery in Australia of Early Cambrian non-trilobite arthropods with well-developed eyes. According to the report, the eyes' "finer features such as ommatidial lenses are preserved in superb detail and three-dimensional relief." The ommatidia show specializations that are "otherwise unknown in the Early Cambrian," but are comparable to those of modern dragonflies. The team concluded that "highly developed vision in the Early Cambrian was not restricted to trilobites."[7]

Highly developed vision may not have been restricted to arthropods, either. Fossil eyes have been reported in Cambrian cephalopods and vertebrates, leading an international team of paleontologists to conclude in 2013, "The available fossil record illustrates that the Cambrian explosion spawned the simultaneous birth of the principal invertebrate compound eye and the vertebrate camera-style eye."[8]

Did the complex eyes in the Cambrian explosion evolve from simpler eyes that preceded it? In 2004 a team of paleontologists reported the discovery of tiny worm-like Precambrian animals with external pits the team speculated might be "the remains of external sensory structures."[9] According to Swedish biologist Dan-Eric Nilsson, the team had described "the oldest known fossil animal with eyes."[10] After examining the remains more closely, however, another team of paleontologists concluded in 2012 that the features reported by the first team were "effects of mineralization that do not represent biological tissues." Not only were the eyes not eyes; the fossils were not even animals![11]

So fossil animals provide no more help for Darwin's theory than modern animals. Yet defenders of evolution still believe that eyes evolved gradually before the Cambrian. In other words, they invoke ghost lineages.

No evidence? No problem, at least for zombie science

A Master Control Gene?

SWISS BIOLOGIST Walter Gehring and his colleagues reported in 1994 that fruit flies, mice, and humans have a very similar gene involved in eye development. Mutations in the gene, called *Pax-6*, result in reduced or missing eyes. Noting that *Pax-6* is also found in worms, squids, birds, and fish, Gehring and his colleagues suggested that *Pax-6* is a "master control gene" that initiates eye development throughout the animal kingdom. They also suggested that Salvini-Plawen and Mayr's conclusion that mouse and fly eyes evolved independently "has to be re-examined" because of the similarity of their *Pax-6* genes.[12]

In 1995, Gehring and some other colleagues reported experiments in which they artificially caused a fruit fly's *Pax-6* gene to be expressed in places outside the eyes. They were thereby able to induce eyes on the wings, legs, and antennae. These ectopic (out-of-place) eyes "appeared morphologically normal and consisted of groups of fully differentiated ommatidia with a complete set of photoreceptor cells," though there was no evidence they could transmit images to the brain. Gehring and his colleagues also inserted mouse *Pax-6* into a fruit fly embryo, activated it outside the normal eye, and thereby induced the formation of ectopic eyes. The eye structures, however, were fruit fly-type compound eyes and not mouse-type camera eyes.[13]

Gehring and his colleagues subsequently reported that squid *Pax-6*, like mouse *Pax-6*, can also induce ectopic eyes in fruit fly embryos, though again the eyes were fruit fly eyes, not squid eyes.[14] Reciprocally, fruit fly *Pax-6* can induce ectopic eyes in frog embryos, though the eyes are frog eyes rather than fruit fly eyes.[15]

Gehring's claim that *Pax-6* is a master control gene for the formation of eyes has at least two problems. The first is that a fruit fly has five eyes: its two compound eyes and three simple eyes (called "ocelli") in the center of its forehead. *Pax-6* affects the development of the two compound eyes but does not affect the ocelli.[16] If *Pax-6* is a master control gene for eye formation, why isn't it involved in the formation of the fly's simple eyes?

The second (and more serious) problem is that the very experiments used to support the claim that *Pax-6* is a master control gene actually contradict it. If *Pax-6* were in control, the fruit fly gene would presumably generate a fruit fly eye, the mouse gene a mouse eye, the squid gene a squid eye, and so on. In fact, *Pax-6* is not a master control gene at all; it is just a switch. The ignition switch from a car can be installed into a boat or an airplane and serve the same function. But the car's ignition switch doesn't turn a boat or an airplane into a car. Calling an ignition switch a "master control device" doesn't tell us anything about the nature or origin of the vehicle in which it is found.

Pax-6 is just one example of a remarkable and widespread phenomenon in embryos: An identical or very similar gene can switch on a developmental pathway in many different kinds of animals—though the resulting structures are determined by the species, not the gene. Other examples include the *Hox* genes mentioned in Chapter 3. In every case, the final structure is not determined by *Pax-6* or *Hox* genes, but by the organism as a whole.

Obviously, there is much more to eye development than a "master control gene."

Gehring and Kazuho Ikeo subsequently wrote that the occurrence of *Pax-6* in so many phyla is one reason to believe in their common ancestry, but another reason is that a separate origin of eyes "in over forty different phyla is not compatible with Darwin's theory."[17] This would have come as news to Salvini-Plawen and Mayr, who had concluded in 1977 that Darwin's theory passed "with flying colors."

So whether eyes originated over forty times or once, evolution must not be doubted.

Can Eyes Evolve Easily?

IN 1994, Dan-Eric Nilsson and his colleague Susanne Pelger published some calculations allegedly showing that eyes can evolve quickly and easily. According to Nilsson and Pelger, a camera eye could evolve from a patch of light-sensing cells in less than 400,000 years.[18]

Two years before Nilsson and Pelger submitted their article for publication, Richard Dawkins gave a lecture in London arguing that natural selection can produce complex and seemingly improbable features (such as eyes) by an accumulation of small, incremental steps. He devoted about five minutes of his lecture to Nilsson's as-yet-unpublished work. According to Dawkins, Nilsson had demonstrated how eyes could evolve "in very small steps, on his computer."[19]

Dawkins continued: Nilsson "assumed that each step, which means each mutation, caused only a one percent change in the size of something, like, say, the steepness of a cup. He also devised a way of measuring the efficiency of an eye. He did this by telling the computer to measure various things about the eye that it had just drawn itself. And then the computer worked out, using the rules of physics, how good an image that eye would be capable of producing. And the question was, with those rules built into it, would there be a smooth gradient of improvement, starting out with a flat retina and ending with a proper eye like ours? And you've guessed it, the answer is yes."[20] On a screen behind Dawkins flashed a series of ten drawings, starting with a flat retina and ending with a camera eye.

We saw in Chapter 4 that attributing beneficial anatomical changes to mutations is biologically unjustified, but let's overlook that here.

In 1995, after Nilsson and Pelger's work had appeared in print, Dawkins published a book doubling down on his earlier claim. "Is there a smooth gradient of change, from flat skin to full camera eye, such that every intermediate is an improvement?" he asked. And he answered:

> Nilsson and Pelger began with a flat retina atop a flat pigment layer and surmounted by a flat, protective transparent layer. The transparent layer was allowed to undergo localized random mutations of its refractive index. They then let their model deform itself at random, constrained only by the requirement that any change must be small and must be an improvement on what went before. The results were swift and decisive. A trajectory of steadily mounting acuity [sharpness of vision] led unhesitatingly from the flat beginning through a shallow indentation to a steadily deepening cup, as the shape of the model eye deformed itself on the computer screen.[21]

But Nilsson and Pelger had done nothing of the sort. They started out with a series of eight drawings to represent what they believed had been the course of eye evolution. (Their eight published drawings were different from the ten drawings used by Dawkins in his 1991 lecture.) The first drawing was of a flat circular patch of light-sensing cells sandwiched between a transparent protective layer and a layer of dark pigment. The last was of a camera eye, and the other six drawings were hypothetical intermediates between those two.

Biologically, the drawings were quite unrealistic. First, they were two-dimensional, not three-dimensional like real eyes. Second, they ignored all the other changes that would have to accompany the deformation of a flat patch, such as modifications in head anatomy and nerve connections. Third (and most significantly), they assumed the steady, unidirectional evolution of a light-sensing patch into a camera eye without any random variations, delays, or deviations from the predetermined path. There was no selection against harmful mutations, because no harmful mutations were permitted. So the drawings did not really illustrate evolution, which is *not* unidirectional and has no endpoint in mind. Contrary to Dawkins's claim, Nilsson and Pelger did not "let their model deform itself at random," nor did they watch as "the shape of the model eye deformed itself on the computer screen." They just drew some figures that they decided beforehand represented evolutionary intermediates between simple and complex eyes. If anything, the drawings represented intelligent design,[22] though of course design much less sophisticated than actual eyes, primitive or otherwise.

According to Nilsson and Pelger, they measured four parameters in their drawings: the length of straight structures, the arc length of curved structures, and the height and width of the two-dimensional cup formed by the rounding up of the layers. Assuming a series of one percent changes in each of these four parameters (each change moving unerringly in the direction of forming a camera eye), they estimated the number of steps it would take for the first of their drawings to become the second, the second to become the third, and so on. Then they added up the numbers they had gotten and concluded that "1829 steps of 1% are needed for the entire model sequence."[23] Combining this with some assumptions about variability, heritability, selection, and generation time, Nilsson and Pelger calculated that a camera eye could easily evolve in about 364,000 years. They concluded, "It is obvious that the eye was never a real threat to Darwin's theory of evolution."[24]

Nilsson and Pelger's calculations gave the illusion that they had quantified a natural evolutionary process. But all they had really done was produce some imaginative drawings and make some measurements of them. Their "model" consisted solely of their drawings, which were not based on any calculations at all.

So in what sense did Nilsson and Pelger create a "computer model"? None at all. A computer model is a program that simulates as realistically as possible something that has happened, might have happened, or might happen in the future. In the case of the eye, such a program would have started with measurements of the three straight lines in the flat patch, applied a formula calculating how those lines would transform under random variation and selection, and projected the results of the calculations on a computer screen. But Nilsson and Pelger had done exactly the opposite. Their result came first, and their calculations came later.

In 2003, mathematician David Berlinski exposed just how meaningless Nilsson and Pelger's calculations were. Berlinski also blasted Richard Dawkins for falsely describing their work as a "computer model." And he blasted Nilsson and Pelger for failing to correct Dawkins's false description. Berlinski rightly described the whole affair as "a scientific scandal."[25]

Nevertheless, Nilsson and Pelger are still cited in biology textbooks and scientific articles as having demonstrated mathematically how eyes evolved. Mark Ridley's 2004 textbook *Evolution* states that Nilsson and Pelger made a computer simulation that "allowed the shape of the model eye to change at random." According to Ridley the model eye "then evolved in the computer, with each new generation formed from the optically superior eyes in the previous generation; changes that made the optics worse were rejected, as selection would reject them in nature."[26] A 2008 article in the *Proceedings of the National Academy of Sciences USA* referred to their work as "computer-based modeling."[27] And according to a *Scientific Reports* paper published in 2013, "as mathematically predicted by Nilsson and Pelger, a patch of light-sensitive epithelial tissue could evolve by natural selection into a camera eye within only about 364,000 generations."[28]

So some imaginative drawings magically evolved into "computer-based modeling" that "mathematically predicted" how supposedly easy it is for eyes to evolve. Isn't zombie science amazing!

A Patch of Light-Sensing Cells?

THE SCIENTISTS mentioned above who argued that eyes evolve easily assumed the prior existence of light-sensing cells. But this assumption actually requires either monumental faith or monumental ignorance about the nature and complexity of a "light-sensitive patch."

In animal eyes, light detection involves a series of chemical reactions called a "phototransduction cascade." The first chemical in the cascade is "retinal," a form of vitamin A, which changes its shape when light strikes it. The retinal is bound to a complex protein called an "opsin" (there are over a thousand different varieties of opsin),[29] which changes shape when the retinal does. The opsin's change of shape then triggers a chain of chemical reactions that culminates in the generation of a nerve impulse. It's true that some single-celled organisms detect light using a single molecule unlike retinal or opsin, but the molecule cannot generate a nerve impulse that would enable true vision.[30]

In his book *Darwin's Black Box*, biochemist Michael Behe argued that the human phototransduction cascade is "irreducibly complex," which he defined as "a single system composed of several well-matched, interacting parts that contribute to the basic function, wherein the removal of any one of the parts causes the system to effectively cease functioning."[31] According to Behe, an irreducibly complex system cannot be the result of natural selection, which kicks in only after the basic function is in place. Natural selection might conceivably help to improve an irreducibly complex system, but it cannot make one. Walter Gehring and Kazuho Ikeo acknowledged this in 1999, writing that the prototypical eye "as pointed out by Darwin, cannot be explained by selection, because selection can drive evolution only when the eye can function at least to a small extent. Once the prototype has evolved, presumably by stochastic [random] events, selection can optimize it."[32]

But do we have good reasons to believe that random events could start the ball rolling? Behe went on to argue that we have good reasons to conclude that they can't, and that an irreducibly complex system such as the phototransduction cascade is evidence for intelligent design rather than unguided evolution.

Of course, defenders of evolution rejected Behe's argument. Among other things, they accused him of lacking the imagination to think of a way natural selection might have produced irreducibly complex systems. But Behe had anticipated that criticism and addressed it in his book, noting that despite decades of work and thousands of published articles, the defenders of evolution had failed to provide the very explanation they demanded from Behe. "No one had ever explained in detailed, scientific fashion how mutation and natural selection could build the complex, intricate structures discussed in this book,"[33] he wrote.

Some recent scientific articles may sound as though they have risen to Behe's challenge, with titles such as "Opening the 'black box': The genetic and biochemical basis of eye evolution" (2008);[34] "Evolution of opsins and phototransduction" (2009);[35] "The evolution of phototransduction from an ancestral cyclic nucleotide gated pathway" (2010);[36] and "Metazoan opsin evolution reveals a simple route to animal vision" (2012).[37] Impressive titles, but the articles don't actually respond to Behe's challenge.

According to the first, which was obviously targeting Behe, opsin "did not originate from nothing, nor was it newly breathed into an ancient animal genome by a designer. Instead, opsins arose by mutation of an existing receptor to render it light-sensitive."[38] But this was no more than sheer assertion, unsupported by evidence.

The second article offered more imaginative storytelling. It listed some amino acid differences between various opsins, and "speculated that an ancestral gene that performed a particular function has diversified over the course of evolution and has brought new functionality to that organism."[39]

In a similar vein, the third proposed a phylogenetic tree and inferred from it that "the origin of phototransduction in animals may have involved the alteration of only a single component—the receptor—allowing gain of light sensitivity" in an ancient pathway.[40] The fourth also proposed a phylogenetic tree and inferred from it "a simple scenario of opsin evolution. The first opsin originated from the duplication of the common ancestor of the [hormone] melatonin and opsin genes," followed by mutations in the duplicates.[41]

All of these were simply speculations, based on hypothetical evolutionary trees, imaginary ancestors, and blind faith in the power of mutations. All of them presupposed the prior existence of a protein that evolved into retinal-plus-opsin with just a few accidental changes. None of the articles even attempted to explain in "detailed, scientific fashion" how the ancestral protein might have evolved—much less explain the coordinated origin of other parts of the impressively sophisticated phototransduction cascade.

Clearly, the claim that eyes can evolve easily is not based on empirical science.

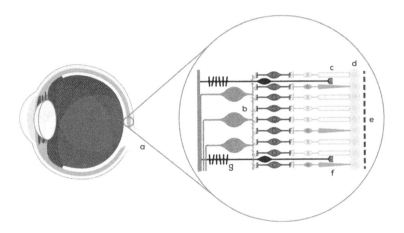

FIGURE 7-1. A SIMPLIFIED VIEW OF THE HUMAN EYE AND RETINA: (a) optic nerve; (b) nerve cells; (c) rod cell; (d) retinal pigment epithelium (RPE); (e) choriocapillaris; (f) cone cell; (g) Müller cell.

Bad Design?

WHILE SOME defenders of evolution argue that eyes can evolve easily, others claim that the human eye is badly designed, supposedly proving that it evolved by an unguided process.

In the human eye, as in all vertebrate eyes, the light-sensing cells point towards the back of the retina. The nerve cells that transmit signals to the brain are between the light-sensing cells and the incoming light (See Figure 7-1). By contrast, in the camera eye of a cephalopod the light-sensing cells point toward the incoming light.

In 1986, Richard Dawkins offered this withering assessment of vertebrate eyes:

> Any engineer would naturally assume that the photocells would point towards the light, with their wires leading backwards towards the brain. He would laugh at any suggestion that the photocells might point away from the light, with their wires departing on the side nearest the light. Yet this is exactly what happens in all vertebrate retinas. Each photocell is, in effect, wired in backwards, with its wire sticking out on the side nearest the light. The wire has to travel over the surface of the retina, to a point where it dives through a hole in the retina (the so-called "blind spot") to join the optic nerve.

Vertebrate eyes work pretty well, Dawkins conceded, but "it is the principle of the thing that would offend any tidy-minded engineer!"[42]

Six years later, evolutionary biologist George Williams was even harsher. "There would be no blind spot if the vertebrate eye were really intelligently designed," he wrote. "In fact it is stupidly designed," while "the retina of a squid is right side up." Williams, like Dawkins, attributed the difference to different evolutionary histories.[43]

Similarly, in 1994, biologist (and textbook-writer) Kenneth Miller wrote that the human eye—"that supposed paragon of intelligent design"—is badly designed. "Quite naturally," he wrote, "you (and any other designer) would choose the orientation that produces the highest degree of visual quality. No one, for example, would suggest that the neural wiring connections should be placed on the side that faces the light, rather than on the side away from it. Incredibly, this is exactly how the human retina is constructed." By contrast, a cephalopod retina is "wired right-side-out." According to Miller, evolution "can explain the inside-out nature of the vertebrate eye quite simply." Miller continued:

The vertebrate retina evolved as a modification of the outer layer of the brain. Over time, evolution progressively modified this part of the brain for light-sensitivity. Although the layer of light-sensitive cells gradually assumed a retina-like shape, it retained its original orientation, including a series of nerve connections on its surface. Evolution, unlike an intelligent designer, cannot start over from scratch to achieve the optimal design.[44]

In 2005, biologist Douglas Futuyma published a textbook claiming that "no intelligent engineer would be expected to design" the "functionally nonsensical arrangement" of nerve cells in the human retina.[45] The same year, biologist Jerry Coyne wrote that the human eye is "certainly not the sort of eye an engineer would create from scratch." Instead, "the whole system is like a car in which all the wires to the dashboard hang inside the driver's compartment instead of being tucked safely out of sight." Like Dawkins, Williams, Miller, and Futuyma, Coyne attributed this to evolution, which "is constrained to operate by modifying whatever features have evolved previously. Thus evolution yields fitter types that often have flaws. These flaws violate reasonable principles of intelligent design."[46]

So from the perspective of evolutionary theory, the human eye looks badly designed, and the theory provides no incentive to investigate further. But what if we look at the human eye from the perspective of function? What if its supposedly bad design actually enables it to function better?

Advantages of the Inverted Retina

THE TWO main types of light-sensing cells in a vertebrate retina are rods and cones (See Figure 7-1, c and f). The former are exquisitely sensitive to light, and they function very well in dim light or at night. Indeed, they can detect a single photon.[47] But they "see" only in black and white. The cone cells are far less numerous than rod cells, and they are not as sensitive to light, but they "see" in color.

Both rods and cones require lots of nutrients and vast amounts of energy. A classic textbook on the eye called them "greedy."[48] In mammals, they have the highest metabolic rate of any tissue in the body.[49] About three-quarters of the blood supply to the eye flows through a dense network of capillaries called the "choriocapillaris," which is situated behind the retina[50,51] (See Figure 7-1, e). Oxygen and nutrients—including modified Vitamin A—are transported from the blood in the choriocapillaris to the rods and cones by an intermediate layer of specialized cells called the "retinal pigment epithelium" (RPE)[52,53] (See Figure 7-1, d).

In addition to transporting oxygen and nutrients to the hungry rods and cones, the RPE performs another essential function. Rods and cones contain stacks of discs that are densely packed with light-sensing molecules. In the process of detecting light, toxic chemicals are generated that must be removed if the light-sensing cells are to continue operating. In 1967, Richard Young showed experimentally that a photoreceptor cell continually renews itself by shedding discs at the end closest to the RPE and replacing them with newly synthesized discs at the other end.[54] The RPE then engulfs and digests the shed discs, neutralizing the toxins.[55] RPE cells can even detach themselves and "rove the neural retina cleaning up debris."[56]

If the rods and cones were to face the incoming light, as evolutionists claim they should, the blood-filled choriocapillaris and the RPE would have to be in front of the retina, where they would block almost all of the light. By contrast, nerve cells are comparatively transparent, and they block very little of the incoming light. Because of the high metabolic requirements of rods and cones and their need to regenerate themselves, the inverted retina is actually much more efficient than the "tidy-minded" design imagined by evolutionary biologists.

The blind spot is not a serious problem, first of all because it is so small and second of all because the blind spot produced by the left eye is not in the same place as the blind spot produced by the right eye. This means that in humans with two good eyes, the field of vision of one eye covers for the blind spot of the other eye, and vice versa.

Most of the research cited above documenting the essential functions of the choriocapillaris and RPE was published before 1986. But

Dawkins, Williams, Miller, Futuyma, and Coyne didn't bother to check the scientific literature. They simply assumed that evolution is true and that they knew how an eye *should* be designed. Then they concluded that the human eye is badly designed, claimed it as evidence for evolution, and ignored the contrary evidence. This is zombie science at work.

Müller Cells

THERE IS even more evidence that the human eye is well designed. Among the specialized cells in the vertebrate retina are Müller cells, first described in the nineteenth century. Müller cells extend all the way through the retina, from the inner surface to the rods and cones (See Figure 7-1, g).

In 2007, a team of scientists presented evidence that Müller cells "assume the role of optical fibers and reliably transfer light with low scattering from the retinal surface to the photoreceptor cell layer."[57] In 2010, two Israeli physicists published calculations showing that the fiber-optic function of Müller cells "is an effective and biologically convenient way to improve the resolution of the eye." Indeed, they concluded that the vertebrate retina is "an optimal structure designed for improving the sharpness of images."[58]

When asked about this, Kenneth Miller still insisted that the retina is badly designed. "The shape, orientation and structure of the Müller cells help the retina to overcome one of the principal shortcomings of its inside-out wiring," he said.[59] Müller cells are merely "a retrofit: A successful and highly functional adaptation made necessary by the original architecture of the retina, but a retrofit."[60]

So we are supposed to believe that evolution left us with a flawed retina, then provided us with a retrofit to correct the flaw. And we are supposed to ignore powerful evidence that the inverted retina provides crucial advantages. There is a vision problem here, but it isn't the one evolutionists are talking about.

A Textbook Case of Myopia

THE 2014 Raven and Johnson biology textbook ignores the evidence described above and informs its readers that "because natural selection can only work on the variation present in a population, it should not be surprising that some organisms do not appear perfectly adapted to their environments." It then regurgitates the usual claim that "an excellent example of imperfect design is the eye of vertebrate animals, in which the photoreceptors face backward, toward the wall of the eye." By contrast, the authors conclude, "the eyes of cephalopods "are more optimally designed."[61]

But are they? The textbook (like George Williams and Kenneth Miller) provides no evidence that cephalopod eyes are more optimally designed. As long ago as 1984, however, a team of Italian biologists had pointed out that cephalopod eyes are physiologically inferior to vertebrate eyes. In vertebrate eyes, the initial processing of visual images occurs in the retina, by nerve cells adjacent to the photoreceptor cells (See Figure 7-1, b). In cephalopod eyes, nerve impulses from the photoreceptor cells must travel all the way to the brain to be processed. According to the Italian biologists, cephalopods must therefore transfer visual information through fibers "with the drawback of being 'long and noisy' channels." The result is slower processing and fuzzier signals. Moreover, a cephalopod eye "is just a 'passive' retina which is able to transmit only information, dot by dot, coded in a far less sophisticated fashion than in vertebrates."[62]

What if the nerve cells that process images were directly behind the photoreceptors in a cephalopod eye? Because the photoreceptors cannot be moved closer to the lens without producing out-of-focus images, the eye would then have to be considerably larger. As two European biologists pointed out in 2009, the inverted retina provides a "space-saving advantage." The vertebrate retina "has thus to be considered superior instead of inferior" to a cephalopod retina.[63]

Yet the evolutionary story continues to be told. "One of the all-time most famous examples of quirky designs in nature is the vertebrate retina," wrote American biologist Nathan Lents in 2015. "The photoreceptor cells of the retina appear to be placed backward, with the wiring facing the light and the photoreceptor facing inward.... This is not an optimal design for obvious reasons. The photons of light must travel around the bulk of the photoreceptor cell in order to hit the receiver tucked in the back. It's as if you were speaking into the wrong end of a microphone."

According to Lents, "there are no working hypotheses about why the vertebrate retina is wired in backwards. It seems to have been a random development that then 'stuck' because a correction of that magnitude would be very difficult to pull off with random mutations.... During the evolution of the cephalopod eye, the retina took shape in a more logical way, with the photoreceptors facing outward toward the light. Vertebrates were not so lucky."[64]

This story is completely and demonstrably false, but apparently it's just too good to give up. Like many other stories we have encountered in this book, it is a product of zombie science.

8. Antibiotic Resistance and Cancer

CHARLES DARWIN DID NOT KNOW ABOUT ANTIBIOTICS (THE WORD was not used in its medical sense until the twentieth century), and although people had known about cancer for centuries, Darwin did not mention it in *The Origin of Species*. Darwin's modern followers, however, use antibiotic resistance and cancer as evidence that his theory is true. Indeed, they go further and claim that modern medicine needs evolutionary theory to deal with these problems. Thanks partly to a new a field called "Darwinian medicine," antibiotic resistance and cancer have become icons of evolution.

Darwinian Medicine

IN 1991, evolutionary biologist George Williams and psychiatrist Randolph Nesse announced the "dawn of Darwinian medicine." They argued that medicine would advance more rapidly "if medical professionals were as attuned to Darwin as they have been to Pasteur." Williams and Nesse listed four areas in which they believed that evolutionary theory could provide "new insights into the causes of medical disorders."

The four areas were infectious diseases, injuries and toxins, genetic diseases, and diseases caused by abnormal environments.[1]

The first area (infectious diseases) is discussed below. In the second area, Williams and Nesse pointed out that some bodily reactions to injuries and toxins (such as swelling and fever) can be beneficial, and they attributed such reactions to adaptive evolution. In the third area the authors acknowledged that "Darwinian theory has little to contribute" to our understanding of rare single-gene diseases, but they argued that common diseases of old age (and aging itself) may be due to genes that "can be favorably selected if they also have beneficial effects early in life." In the fourth area, Williams and Nesse maintained that many "diseases of civilization" (such as obesity and diabetes) occur because we evolved to live in Stone Age conditions, not in the environments of the modern world.[2]

But we don't need "Darwinian medicine" to interpret reactions such as swelling and fever. The benefits of fever, for example, were discussed and even experimentally documented before Williams and Nesse wrote their 1991 article, with no help from evolutionary theory.[3,4] The idea that aging is due to genes that are beneficial early in life is mere speculation. And we don't need evolution to recognize that an environment is harmful and devise ways to correct it. In these three areas, Darwinian medicine is nothing more than materialistic storytelling.

Infectious Diseases

IN THE area of infectious diseases, evolutionary biologist Paul Ewald has claimed that we can harness evolution to make disease-causing bacteria less harmful. Ewald argues that diseases transmitted from person to person tend to be less harmful than diseases spread through food or water, because the former require basically healthy people for their transmission while the latter can spread even after killing the victim.[5] According to Ewald, in a waterborne cholera epidemic the disease-causing bacteria "evolve to become more exploitative, using us more extensively as their food sources, and thereby become more harmful to us." If we clean up the water supply, however, "then we force the disease organisms to be transmitted only by routes that require healthy people. So what we should be finding if we clean up water supplies is that we drive the organisms to evolve toward mildness."[6]

But we don't need evolutionary theory to know that we should clean up our water supplies. Ever since British physician John Snow discovered in the 1840s that cholera is spread by contaminated drinking water, public health officials have been preventing the disease by ensuring that our drinking water is safe.[7] Evolution had nothing to do with it.

In fact, mortality from *all* infectious diseases in the West began declining before Darwin, due to better nutrition and public health improvements such as clean water and better sewage disposal.[8] The decline was also due to improved personal hygiene, as the story of Hungarian obstetrician Ignác Semmelweis illustrates. While working in an Austrian hospital in 1847, Semmelweis noticed that the death rate of mothers from childbed fever was much higher in wards run by medical students than in wards run by midwives. He also noticed that the medical students would go directly from the morgue to the obstetric ward without adequately washing their hands. By simply requiring the medical students to wash their hands in a chlorine solution after leaving the morgue, Semmelweis dramatically reduced the incidence of childbed fever.[9]

Also without any help from evolutionary theory, modern immunization techniques have triumphed over two major infectious diseases: smallpox and polio. In the 1790s, English physician Edward Jenner started vaccinating people against smallpox, and by 1980 a global immunization campaign had eradicated smallpox throughout the world.[10] In 1955, American virologist Jonas Salk developed a vaccine against polio, and in 1961 Albert Sabin developed a version that could be given orally. As a result, polio cases worldwide have been reduced by ninety-nine percent.[11] Evolution had nothing to do with these victories.

Antibiotic Resistance

ACCORDING TO advocates of Darwinian medicine, however, there is one aspect of infectious diseases that absolutely requires the application of evolutionary theory: antibiotic resistance.

Microbiologists grow bacteria in shallow dishes (named "Petri dishes" after German scientist Julius Petri) that contain agar, a jelly-like substance obtained from algae. In 1928, English microbiologist Alexander Fleming was growing staphylococcus ("staph") bacteria in his laboratory when he noticed a Petri dish contaminated by mold. Remarkably, there were no staph colonies around the mold, suggesting that the latter was producing a substance that killed or inhibited the bacteria. The mold was a species of *Penicillium* (another species of which is used to make blue cheese), so Fleming called the substance "penicillin."[12]

Fleming was not a chemist, and he was unable to purify and concentrate penicillin enough to make it clinically useful. It wasn't until the 1940s that Australian pharmacologist Howard Florey and German biochemist Ernst Chain, working in England, succeeded in purifying and producing penicillin in large quantities.[13] In 1945 Fleming, Florey and Chain shared the Nobel Prize for their achievements.

Penicillin is effective against many diseases, but not against tuberculosis. In 1944, Russian-born American microbiologist Selman Waksman and his research assistant, Albert Schatz, announced the discovery of a substance they obtained from soil bacteria that was effective against tuberculosis bacteria. Because the soil bacteria were named *Streptomyces griseus*, Waksman and Schatz called the substance "streptomycin."[14] Waksman was also the first person to use the word "antibiotic" to refer to a substance produced by one microorganism that kills or inhibits the growth of another.

Soon after the discovery of streptomycin, American plant physiologist Benjamin Duggar collected thousands of soil samples and began a systematic search for other antibiotic-producing microorganisms.[15] In 1948, Duggar announced the discovery of aureomycin, derived from *Streptomyces aureofaciens*.[16] Auroemycin was the first of a long line of antibiotics called "tetracyclines" because of their chemical structure.

What role did Darwinism play? Evolutionary theory contributed nothing to the discovery of antibiotics. Alexander Fleming said in 1945 that while discovering penicillin he felt like a pawn "being moved about on the board of life by some superior power."[17] Years later, penicillin pioneer Ernst Chain described Darwinian evolution as "a hypothesis based on no evidence and irreconcilable with the facts." He went even further:

> This hypothesis willfully neglects the principle of teleological purpose which stares the biologist in the face wherever he looks....

These classical evolutionary theories are a gross oversimplification of an immensely complex and intricate mass of facts, and it amazes me that they were swallowed so uncritically and readily, and for such a long time, by so many scientists without a murmur of protest.[18]

Selman Waksman, the co-discoverer of streptomycin, was more succinct, insisting simply that he saw no role for evolution in the discovery of streptomycin. In 1956, he wrote that applying Darwinian assumptions in his work was "totally unjustified."[19]

In 2005, American chemist Philip Skell wrote that "my own research with antibiotics during World War II received no guidance from insights provided by Darwinian evolution." Skell was curious whether his experience was the rule or the exception, so he "asked more than seventy eminent researchers if they would have done their work differently if they had thought Darwin's theory was wrong. The responses were all the same: No." After reviewing the major biological discoveries of the twentieth century, Skell concluded that "Darwin's theory had provided no discernible guidance" in any of them but had been brought in afterwards as a "narrative gloss."[20]

Even before Florey and Chain had developed methods for purifying and concentrating penicillin, bacteria had been discovered that were resistant to it.[21]

Indeed, we now know that antibiotic resistance predates the modern use of antibiotics and occurs naturally in the wild.[22,23]

Among bacteria that are normally susceptible to penicillin, a few naturally carry a complex enzyme called beta-lactamase, which inactivates the antibiotic. If a population of bacteria has a few cells containing beta-lactamase, and the population is treated with penicillin, those cells can survive and multiply. The result is a population of penicillin-resistant bacteria.

Beta-lactamase is much too complex to evolve from scratch by mutation and selection. Its origin is unknown. So although the proliferation of penicillin-resistant bacteria can be described as microevolution, evolutionary theory has contributed nothing to our understanding of how such beta-lactamase originated in the first place.

But some cases of antibiotic resistance *are* due to mutation. Streptomycin acts by binding to and inactivating the bacterial ribosome, a complex assembly of proteins and RNAs that translates messenger RNAs into proteins. A mutation can alter the structure of a bacterial ribosome so that streptomycin no longer binds to it.

Such mutations come at a price. The bacterial cell now has defective ribosomes. But if the mutation is not *too* damaging, the cell can still survive. When a population of bacteria containing one or more cells with the appropriate mutation is exposed to streptomycin, the mutant cells can grow and reproduce. The result is a population of streptomycin-resistant bacteria.

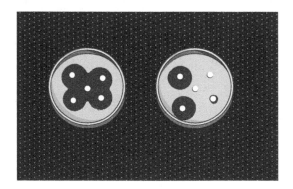

FIGURE 8-1 ANTIBIOTIC RESISTANCE: The agar in these Petri dishes was completely smeared with bacteria (one species on the left, another on the right); then sterile paper disks soaked in various antibiotics were placed on the mats of bacteria and the two dishes were incubated overnight at body temperature so the bacteria could grow. Clear zones around the disks indicate that the bacteria were susceptible to the antibiotic and did not grow. The absence of clear areas around two of the disks on the right indicates that this second species is resistant to the antibiotics in those two disks. The smaller clear zone around one disc indicates partial resistance.

Antibiotic-resistant bacteria can be detected in the laboratory by spreading bacteria over the agar in a Petri dish, then carefully placing small, sterile paper disks soaked in various antibiotics on the culture and incubating it at body temperature. If the bacteria are susceptible to the antibiotics, they will not grow near the disks; if they are resistant they will grow unhindered (See Figure 8-1).

Do We Need Evolutionary Theory to Overcome Antibiotic Resistance?

SINCE THE modern introduction of antibiotics, the number and kinds of antibiotic-resistant bacteria have increased enormously. Will Darwinian medicine save the day?

The proliferation of antibiotic resistance is clearly an example of microevolution, but it is just as clearly not an example of macroevolution. Bacteria that become resistant to antibiotics do not thereby become new species. Yet many people in the scientific establishment routinely equivocate on the word "evolution," switching back and forth between microevolution and macroevolution as though they were the same thing.

In some cases the equivocation might be due to misunderstanding, but in other cases it is a deliberate attempt to mislead. When anthropologist Eugenie Scott was serving as executive director of the aggressively pro-evolution National Center for Science Education, she wrote about how to deal with "anti-evolutionism." Scott would introduce college students to evolution "as an issue of the history of the planet: as the way we try to understand change through time. The present is different from the past. Evolution happened, there is no debate within science as to whether it happened, and so on." Only afterwards would she bring in Darwin's "Big Idea," which is what "we want students to know about organic evolution."[24]

This is called "bait-and-switch." Start with an idea everyone accepts, then slip in something more controversial and hope no one notices.

In 2001, journalist Carl Zimmer published a book titled *Evolution: The Triumph of an Idea.* In it, Zimmer claimed that antibiotic resistance "didn't just happen: It unfolded according to the principles of natural selection, as the bacteria with the best genes for fighting the drugs prospered. Without understanding evolution, a researcher has little hope of figuring out how to create new drugs and determine how they should be administered."[25]

Is this true? Do physicians dealing with antibiotic resistance need Darwin's "Big Idea?" As we saw, they didn't need it in the early days of penicillin and streptomycin. And they don't need it now. Instead, they need to focus on prevention and cure.

Preventing Antibiotic Resistance

So WHAT works in the fight against antibiotic resistance? One is identifying key mistakes in the fight, and correcting them as much as possible. The two factors that contribute most to the emergence of antibiotic resistance are the improper use of antibiotics and the failure to isolate affected patients.

The indiscriminate use of antibiotics tends to increase the proportion of resistant bacteria in a population. Since antibiotics are not effective against viral infections such as a cold or flu, they should not be used in those cases. According to a 2016 report commissioned by the British government, this calls for "new, rapid diagnostics to cut unnecessary use of antibiotics."[26]

Widespread use of antibiotics to prevent diseases in livestock also increases the proportion of resistant bacteria in a population. The 2016 report recommends a "global public awareness campaign" to reduce the use of antibiotics in healthy animals.[27] So the first line of defense against resistance to antibiotics is to use them only when necessary.

When antibiotics are necessary, they should be used properly. Physicians instruct patients to complete a course of treatment by taking all the prescribed medication, thereby killing all the disease-causing bacteria. If antibiotic treatment is stopped prematurely, bacteria that are slightly resistant might remain and spread to other people. Perhaps the fight against antibiotic resistance would benefit if physicians emphasized this more to their patients.

Patients infected with antibiotic-resistant bacteria should be isolated from others to prevent the spread of resistant strains. This is already common practice in hospitals in the developed world, though some hospitals are more stringent than others. In parts of the developing world there is a need not only for better isolation practices but also for more basic hygiene, such as thorough handwashing.

These preventive measures have no need for evolutionary theory.

Overcoming Antibiotic-Resistant Infections

So, HOW about curing patients already infected with antibiotic-resistant bacteria? Does that require evolutionary theory? No, it does not.

Some scientists have been studying metabolic pathways in bacteria to discover new targets for antibiotics or ways to increase the effectiveness of existing antibiotics. A team of American biomedical engineers led by James Collins reported in 2013 that they had successfully identified "novel enzyme targets for compounds which may have no antimicrobial properties alone, but which enhance the killing efficacy of current antibacterial agents."[28]

Drugs such as penicillin that inhibit cell wall synthesis are among the most effective in combating bacterial infection, and for a long time microbiologists knew of only one metabolic pathway for cell wall synthesis. In 2016, however, a team of American microbiologists reported the discovery of another pathway, and they concluded that it "provides an attractive new avenue to target this pathway for antibiotic development."[29]

Another approach relies on live microbes. Bacteriophages ("phages," for short) are viruses that infect only bacteria. There are two types of bacteriophage: those that kill the bacterial cell and those that enter a bacterial cell and modify its DNA. The second type can aggravate the problem of antibiotic resistance by facilitating the transfer of resistance genes from one bacterial population to another, but in recent years this type has been used successfully in molecular biology and genetic engineering. The first type cannot spread resistance and has been used effectively to treat infections that are due to antibiotic-resistant bacteria.[30]

Indeed, soon after the discovery of phages a century ago, they were used to combat bacterial infections in human patients. The therapeu-

tic use of phages was largely abandoned in the West after the advent
of antibiotics, but it was continued in Eastern European countries such
as Georgia.[31] In Poland, a clinic specializing in phage therapy has been
operating since 2005.[32]

Because of the modern rise in antibiotic resistance, there is now re-
newed interest in phage therapy in the West. In 2009, a British team reported a "controlled clinical trial of a therapeutic bacteriophage preparation [that] showed efficacy and safety" in treating chronic ear infections
caused by antibiotic-resistant bacteria.[33]

Taking another approach, microbiologist Daniel Kadouri has been
studying two species of predatory bacteria that attack and feed on disease-causing bacteria that are resistant to multiple antibiotics.[34] The
predatory bacteria are non-toxic in mice, they provoke no sustained response from a mouse's immune system, and they do not grow on or in
mammalian cells; they feed only on other bacteria.

In 2016, Kadouri and his colleagues reported that the predatory bacteria are also non-toxic and non-inflammatory in cultured human cells.[35]
Pending clinical trials, predatory bacteria may be useful in combating
some antibiotic-resistant infections in humans.

Despite these public health and technical advances, there is still a
need for new antibiotics. As microbiologists Julian Davies and Dorothy
Davies wrote in 2010, "It is vital that there should be absolutely no letup
in the search for new antimicrobial agents."[36] And as biologists Gautam
Dantas and Morten Sommer wrote in 2014, "What is most desperately
needed are new antibiotics, and as many of them as possible."[37]

Happily there is reason for optimism on this front. New antibiotics
can be natural (from microbes) or synthetic (from laboratories). Finding new natural antibiotics has been difficult because most soil microorganisms cannot be grown in a laboratory. But the invention of a new
technology called the "iChip" (for isolation chip), composed of several
hundred miniature diffusion chambers, has made it possible to recover
many such microorganisms.[38] In 2015 a team of scientists using iChips

reported the discovery of a new antibiotic effective against staph and tuberculosis bacteria.[39]

Many antibiotics have been produced through "semisynthesis," the chemical modification of naturally occurring antibiotics. In 2005, however, a team of scientists led by chemical biologist Andrew Myers reported a completely synthetic route to a diverse range of tetracycline antibiotics.[40] By 2016, Myers and his colleagues had synthesized two new antibiotics that are now candidates for clinical use.[41,42]

None of these approaches relied on evolutionary theory—not even microevolutionary theory.

In one attempt to apply evolutionary theory to antibiotic resistance, physician Robert Woods teamed up with evolutionary biologist Andrew Read in 2014 to treat a patient with an infection that was resistant to multiple antibiotics. Woods and Read hoped that by applying evolutionary principles they would be able to help the patient. After a year of trying, however, they reported that "it was impossible to make evidence-based decisions about the evolutionary risks associated with the various treatment options." Sadly, the patient died. "It remains to be seen," Woods and Read concluded, "whether evolutionary science can help" with chronic bacterial infections.[43]

Another Icon Too Good to Give Up

So ANTIBIOTIC resistance is not evidence for (macro)evolution, and evolutionary theory is not needed for its prevention or treatment. Yet antibiotic resistance is still being used to persuade people of Darwin's "Big Idea."

In 2016, microbiologist Michael Baym and his colleagues constructed a huge rectangular Petri dish about two feet wide and four feet long. They called it a "microbial evolution and growth arena (MEGA) plate," and they filled it with agar that contained different concentrations of antibiotics. The agar at the ends contained no antibiotics, while successive regions in between contained increasing concentrations, with the highest in the middle. Then they inoculated the ends with bacteria and warmed

the MEGA plate so the bacteria could grow. As the bacteria spread toward the middle they encountered higher and higher concentrations of
antibiotics, which temporarily halted their growth until resistant strains
appeared and continued spreading.[44] After ten days the bacteria had
reached the middle of the plate, and time-lapse photography condensed
their spread into a two-minute video.[45]

After viewing the movie, science writer Ed Yong wrote in *The Atlantic*, "You're seeing evolution in action. You're watching living things
facing down new challenges, dying, competing, thriving, invading, and
adapting—all in a two-minute movie." Yong reported that for evolutionary biologist Pamela Yeh the video also "shows the importance of ran-
domness in evolution," since the bacteria causing the spreading were not
always the most antibiotic-resistant; they were just lucky enough to be
near the leading edge where they had room to grow.[46]

But the MEGA plate is only a teaching aid. Depending on how it is
used, it can either inform or misinform. In their report Baym and his
colleagues emphasized that "the MEGA-plate is not intended to directly
simulate natural or clinical settings, but… its relative simplicity and ability to visually demonstrate evolution makes the MEGA-plate a useful
tool for science education and outreach."[47] Perhaps, but unfortunately
neither the report nor the video pointed out that only microevolution
was involved. The goal was not to enlighten students about the distinction between microevolution and macroevolution, but apparently to use
the former to indoctrinate them in the latter.

Invading Education

DESPITE THE ineffectiveness of Darwinian medicine, its advocates are
ratcheting up their campaign to increase the emphasis on evolution in
universities and medical schools. The push has been on for more than
a decade. In 2003, Randolph Nesse and Joshua Shiffman attempted to
convince national medical education leaders to institute "new undergraduate prerequisites… and appropriate board examination questions
to ensure that medical graduates have a basic understanding of evolution-

ary biology." In other words, Nesse and Shiffman recommended forcing students to study evolution before they could become physicians.[48]

In 2006 Nesse, along with evolutionary biologist Stephen Stearns and geneticist Gilbert Omenn, recommended including "questions about evolution in medical licensing examinations; this will motivate curriculum committees to incorporate relevant basic science education." They also recommended ensuring "evolutionary expertise in agencies that fund biomedical research."[49] In other words, they recommended increasing the evolution content of medical education and research, not by persuading physicians and medical researchers of the practical value of Darwinian medicine, but by applying pressure from the top down through licensing and funding agencies.

In 2012, biologist Ajit Varki wrote that "nothing in medicine makes sense, except in the light of evolution."[50] The same year, Nesse, Stearns, and Omenn joined with nine other biologists in arguing that medical students should learn not only the proximate causes of diseases (such as harmful microorganisms or metabolic imbalances) but also the "ultimate causes"—that is, evolution. According to Nesse and his colleagues, "testing competency in evolution" should become "part of gaining admission to medical school." The authors also encouraged evolutionary biologists "to reach out to premedical students."[51]

Funny, the call to "reach out" seems more at home in religion or politics than in science.

The Importance of Asking Why

IN 2005, biologists Eugene Harris and Avelin Malyango wrote that "the questions our students ask are like the endless series of 'why' questions that children ask." According to Harris and Malyango, learning the proximate causes of diseases doesn't satisfy medical students' curiosity. Instead, the authors argued, "we can help answer our students' questions by providing them with evolutionary answers."[52] And a decade later, Nesse and eight other biologists similarly argued that evolution "encourages asking, investigating, and answering why? questions about vulnerability to disease." Specifically, "evolutionary biology gives students the tools to understand why our bodies seem so exquisitely designed, yet susceptible to innumerable maladies."[53]

The next year, in 2016, medical school professors Paola Palanza and Stefano Parmigiani wrote that since "evolution is the foundation for biology and biology the foundation for medicine, it follows that evolution ought to be a foundation for medicine." Instead of demonstrating these claims, they hurried on to their recommendations. Among other things, physicians should understand "when and how the species of *Homo sapiens* developed from other species," and that the human eye "has a sub-optimal design." After all, "a humanistic culture is important for scientists."[54]

So the push to teach more evolution to medical students is justified by the desire to promote a "humanistic culture" and convince future physicians that the human body is not well designed. This is not empirical science. This is a propaganda campaign on behalf of zombie science.

FIGURE 8-2. CANCER: Left: A malignant tumor (misshapen cells irregularly arranged) has started to grow in a layer of normal cells (uniformly shaped cells in regular rows). Center: the tumor has grown larger and has begun to invade tissues above and below the layer of normal cells. Right: the tumor has grown even larger and more invasive, and malignant cells are beginning to break off to start new tumors elsewhere in the body.

Cancer

DARWINIAN MEDICINE claims that evolution is necessary for understanding and treating not only antibiotic resistance, but also cancer. In cancer, some of a body's cells divide without stopping and then invade surrounding tissues. The result (except in blood cancers such as leukemia) is a tumor (See Figure 8-2). In some cases, cancer cells can break off and travel to other places in the body and form new tumors. The disease can be fatal: In the United States, over half a million people die each year from cancer.[55] Yet according to some people, cancer is an icon of evolution.

Cancer as Speciation?

CANCER CELLS reproduce autonomously. That is, they may divide and grow outside the body, if provided with appropriate conditions and nutrients. Some biologists have argued that because autonomous reproduction is characteristic of biological species, the development of cancer is an example of speciation and the various types of cancer are separate species.

In 1958, Julian Huxley wrote that once cancer "has crossed the threshold of autonomy, the resultant tumor can be logically regarded as a new biologic species."[56] In 1991, evolutionary biologists Leigh Van Valen and Virginia Maiorana argued that HeLa cells, a widely used tissue-culture cell line derived from a cancerous tumor, should be regarded as a separate species of single-celled organisms.[57] Physician Mark Vincent wrote in 2010 that "cancer really is a form of speciation" and called it "the animal within."[58]

Molecular biologist Peter Duesberg and his colleagues sounded a similar note in 2011, stating that the origin of cancer from healthy cells "is a form of speciation." The most common characteristic of cancer cells is that they have too few or too many chromosomes, or their chromosomes have been broken and rearranged. The number and appearance of a cell's chromosomes constitute its "karyotype," and according to Duesberg and his colleagues the karyotypes of cancer cells may appear to be abnormal when compared to non-cancerous cells, but they are no more abnormal than "the karyotype of a cat would be abnormal compared to that of a dog."[59]

Changes in karyotype actually can produce speciation in plants. Normally, when two species hybridize their different chromosomes do not match up during cell division, and the resulting hybrid is sterile. Sometimes, however, chromosomes in plant hybrids undergo spontaneous doubling, so each chromosome has a matching counterpart and the offspring is a fertile new species. In the first decades of the twentieth century, Swedish scientist Arne Müntzing used two plant species to make an artificial hybrid that underwent chromosome doubling to produce hempnettle, a member of the mint family already found in nature.[60] And chromosome doubling enabled Russian scientist Georgii Karpechenko to produce a new species not found in nature by hybridizing a radish and a cabbage. (Unfortunately, the result, called a radocabbage, consisted of the root of a cabbage and the top of a radish.)[61]

So chromosome doubling can lead to speciation in plants, but it does not lead to the open-ended evolution of new forms required by evolutionary theory. For those who consider cancer an example of evolution in action, the larger question is not whether cancer cells can be considered new species, but whether cancer provides support for the grand materialistic narrative of common descent by mindless evolutionary processes. Some evolutionists say yes. Let's look at their arguments more closely.

Cancer as Evolution by Mutation and Selection

COMPUTATIONAL BIOLOGIST Joshua Swamidass does not consider cancer an example of speciation, but he regards it as a good example of evolution by mutation and natural selection. Indeed, Swamidass argues that in cancer "we can see the evolution of new functions (new information!)," because "cancer regularly innovates with proteins of novel function."[62]

This idea that cancer is an example of evolution by mutation and selection is not new. In 1976, pathologist Peter Nowell attributed "tumor evolution" to the "stepwise selection of variant sublines."[63] In 1996, cancer researchers Mohammad Ilyas and Ian P. M. Tomlinson described cancer as "Darwinian evolution through selection of advantageous somatic mutations."[64] In 2003, Robert Gatenby and Thomas Vincent published an evolutionary model of cancer.[65] And in 2012 Mel Greaves and Carlo Maley wrote, "The basic principle of a Darwinian evolutionary system is the purposeless genetic variation of reproductive individuals who are united by common descent, together with natural selection of the fittest variants. Cancer is a clear example of such a system."[66]

What about Swamidass's claim that "cancer regularly innovates with proteins of novel function"? Many cancers have mutations in genes of the *Ras* family or in the *TP53* gene, and some of these are called "gain-of-function" mutations. But how novel are the functions that are gained? *Ras* genes produce signaling proteins that induce cells to divide. In normal cells Ras proteins are turned off much of the time, but when mutated they get stuck in the "on" position and induce cancer cells to divide without stopping.[67] Yet the Ras protein hasn't gained a new function; it has simply lost the ability to turn off its old one.

The *TP53* gene encodes a protein called p53 that has many functions. Not only does it bind to specific DNA sequences, but it also interacts with many other molecules involved in cell metabolism.[68] In normal cells, p53's functions prevent the cell from becoming cancerous, so the protein is called a "tumor suppressor." When *TP53* mutates in cancer cells its tumor suppressor function is abolished, and the mutant protein (designated mutp53) accumulates at a much higher concentration than normal p53 (designated "wild-type" p53, or wtp53). The mutant protein still binds to DNA, but it has lost its sequence specificity, so it interacts with regions of DNA that are unaffected by normal p53. Like wtp53, mutp53 also continues to interact with many other molecules in the cell, but those interactions are altered to the point where the cell divides without stopping and invades other tissues.[69]

This does not necessarily mean, however, that mutp53 acts through mechanisms different from those of wtp53. The mutant protein binds to more regions of DNA than wtp53, not because it has gained anything, but only because it has lost its sequence specificity. And the other effects of mutp53 are probably not as novel as they seem. Thus, Israeli cancer researchers Moshe Oren and Varda Rotter argue that "given the high concentration of mutp53 protein in tumor cells, relatively weak molecular interactions, which are marginal within the wtp53 protein, may now be amplified by mass action and reach a threshold that allows them to exert a measurable impact on biochemical processes within the cell."[70]

In 2012, philosopher of biology Pierre-Luc Germain pointed out that the adaptations in cancer cells "are not complex adaptations, in other words they are not the result of cumulative evolution.... Instead, it is the pre-existing wiring of the cell which best accounts for these features." That is, "healthy cells—their structure, possible states, pathways, and weak spots—already contain the resources to be drawn upon and developed by cancer cells."[71] So cancer is not a good example of the evolution of new functions.

Do We Need Evolutionary Theory to Overcome Cancer?

THE FIRST line of defense against cancer (like the first line of defense against antibiotic resistance) is prevention. In most cases the causes of cancer are not yet understood, and there is no guaranteed way to prevent it, but statistics show that cancer is less likely to occur among people who have a healthy diet and lifestyle and who avoid smoking. The second line of defense is early detection, which is aided by modern diagnostic techniques and technologies. The latter include X-rays and computerized tomography (CAT scans), ultrasound, and magnetic resonance imaging. The third line of defense is treatment. If a tumor is detected early enough, it may be eliminated by surgery or localized radiation treatment.

If those don't work, there is chemotherapy. Most of us know someone who has contracted cancer and endured this unpleasant treatment option. Since cancer cells grow more quickly than most cells in the body, standard chemotherapy drugs block the process of cell division. Unfortunately, such drugs also affect rapidly dividing healthy cells, producing side effects such as anemia and hair loss. Like bacteria, some cancer cells may be (or can become) resistant to the chemicals being used to kill them. As with antibiotic resistance, chemotherapy resistance can sometimes be overcome by targeting metabolic pathways in cancer cells to make chemotherapy drugs more effective. The discovery and synthesis of new drugs is also important. As in the case of antibiotic resistance, evolutionary theory plays no role in any of this.

There may be an exception, though not one that provides any real aid and comfort to the grand materialistic story. American physician Robert Gatenby and his colleagues argue that an "evolution-guided treatment strategy" can be effective in treating some cancers.[72] What do they mean? Gatenby and his colleagues note that chemotherapy-resistant cancer cells (like antibiotic-resistant bacteria) tend to be less fit than non-resistant cells. When both non-resistant and resistant cancer cells are present, the former grow at the expense of the latter when chemotherapy is withdrawn. So Gatenby and his colleagues argue that the standard practice of trying to kill all the cancer cells is mistaken, and that it is better to use lower and less frequent doses that leave some chemotherapy-susceptible cells alive. Although the tumor would still be still present, it would not grow as quickly or might not grow at all.

The treatment would, in essence, spare robust cancer cells so they can outgrow weakling cancer cells whose only advantage is resistance to the chemotherapy. The patient's life might be prolonged, and because chemotherapy would be administered at lower doses, the quality of life would be better. In 2009, Gatenby and his colleagues published experimental evidence that their "adaptive therapy" might work.[73]

Perhaps adaptive therapy can help some cancer patients; let's hope so. But is it really based on evolutionary thinking? Microevolutionary thinking, but not macroevolutionary thinking. Darwin's "Big Idea" was all about the latter.

Cancer as an Icon of Evolution

So THE value of evolutionary theory in treating cancer is questionable, at best. But some people argue that cancer is at least of value in providing evidence for evolutionary theory. Something doesn't seem right here. According to evolutionary theory, the human body originated by mutation and selection, though the evidence shows that those processes cannot produce anything like a human body. Now we have evidence that mutation and selection can produce cancer, which destroys the human body. How does that support evolutionary theory?

Darwinian evolution needs examples of biological processes that build new forms and functions. Cancer destroys those things. Saying cancer is evidence for biological evolution is like saying I have a theory that explains the rise of modern civilization, and the evidence for my theory is the night of the living dead.

9. Zombie Apocalypse

THE ICONS OF EVOLUTION ARE NOT TEXTBOOK MISTAKES. They are used to promote a grand materialistic story even after scientists have shown that the icons misrepresent the evidence. They are tools of zombie science.

When it comes to evolution, it seems, establishment science is less interested in evidence and critical thinking than it is in promoting the doctrine that all life can be explained materialistically. Here is how Harvard geneticist and evolutionary biologist Richard Lewontin put it (emphasis in the original):

> Our willingness to accept scientific claims that are against common sense is the key to an understanding of the real struggle between science and the supernatural. We take the side of science in spite of the patent absurdity of some of its constructs, in spite of its failure to fulfill many of its extravagant promises of health and life, in spite of the tolerance of the scientific community for unsubstantiated just-so stories, because we have a prior commitment to materialism. It is not that the methods and institutions of science somehow compel us to accept a material explanation of the phenomenal world, but, on the contrary, that we are forced by our a priori adherence to material causes to create an apparatus of investigation and a set of concepts that produce material explanations, no matter how counter-intuitive, no matter how mystifying to the uninitiated. Moreover, that materialism is absolute, for we cannot allow a Divine Foot in the door.[1]

Darwin's "Big Idea" is that unguided natural processes produced the first living cells, and that unguided natural processes transformed those cells into the vast array of living things we now have. It's a big claim, and it's contrary to the evidence. Some of the Big Idea's constructs are patently absurd, and it relies heavily on unsubstantiated just-so stories. Yet materialism compels us to accept it. Zombie science rules. And its rule is corrupting our culture.

In 2001, the American Public Broadcasting Service (PBS) released an eight hour-long series titled *Evolution*, which is still being shown to public school students. One of the most popular episodes—titled "Why sex?"—featured evolutionary psychologist Geoffrey Miller. According to the narrator, Miller "believes the human brain, like the peacock's magnificent tail, is an extravagance that evolved—at least in part—to help us attract a mate, and pass on genes." Miller himself says that in the course of evolution "there was a sort of decision-making process that was selecting our brains. But it wasn't God, it was our ancestors. They were choosing their sexual partners for their brains, for their behavior, during courtship."

With a performance of Handel's *Messiah* in the background, the narrator then says, "Miller is just getting started when he argues that the size of our brains can be attributed to our ancestors' sexual choices. He's also convinced that artistic expression, no matter how sublime, has its roots in our desire to impress the opposite sex."[2]

So Handel wrote his *Messiah* to get some sex. Evolutionary thinking is like reverse alchemy: It turns gold into lead. And this process is evident in religion, education, and science itself.

Corrupting Religion

AMERICAN PHILOSOPHER Daniel Dennett wrote in 1995 that "Darwin's dangerous idea" is like a "universal acid: It eats through just about every traditional concept." Indeed, it "cuts much deeper into the fabric of our most fundamental beliefs than many of its sophisticated apologists have yet admitted, even to themselves."[3]

Among our most fundamental beliefs, of course, is religion.

Before Darwin, Christianity and science got along quite well, despite what many people may think. Indeed, the founders of most modern disciplines in biology and other scientific fields such as chemistry and physics were Christians. The false idea that religion and science have always been at war with each other was promoted by two books written in the late nineteenth century by followers of Darwin who were hostile to Christianity. In 1874, chemist John Draper published his *History of the Conflict Between Religion and Science*, and in 1896 educator Andrew Dickson White published *A History of the Warfare of Science with Theology in Christendom*. Modern scholars have repeatedly shown that their "warfare metaphor" profoundly misrepresents the true history of the relationship between Christianity and science.[4,5]

There never was a war between religion and empirical science, but there *is* a war between religion and materialistic science, and the battleground is evolution.

Polls show that religion in America is on the decline. In the past two decades there has been a threefold increase in the number of people who say "none" when asked what their religion is.[6] About half of those raised in a religion say that they left because they stopped believing, and many of these say they stopped believing because of science in general and evolution in particular.[7]

Most people learn about evolution outside of church, but over the past decade believers in evolution have been increasingly successful in persuading clergy to bring evolution into their sanctuaries. In 2004, biologist Michael Zimmerman started the "Clergy Letter Project" to "let the public know that numerous clergy from most denominations have tremendous respect for evolutionary theory and have embraced it as a core component of human knowledge, fully harmonious with religious faith."[8] Zimmerman solicited signatures on a letter that included the following:

> We the undersigned, Christian clergy from many different traditions, believe that the timeless truths of the Bible and the discoveries of modern science may comfortably coexist. We believe that the the-

ory of evolution is a foundational scientific truth, one that has stood up to rigorous scrutiny and upon which much of human knowledge and achievement rests…. We ask that science remain science and that religion remain religion, two very different, but complementary, forms of truth.[9]

This view that science and religion occupy completely separate realms was championed by Stephen Jay Gould, who called the realms "nonoverlapping magisteria." According to Gould, "the net of science covers the empirical universe: what is it made of (fact) and why does it work this way (theory). The net of religion extends over questions of moral meaning and value."[10] In other words, Gould argues that the world of objective reality belongs to science (which for him is materialistic), while religion is confined to the realm of subjective feelings and imagination. In effect, this is just a restatement of materialistic philosophy. It's a bully tactic to convince religious believers that they are not entitled to say anything about objective reality.

Attempts to recruit Christian clergy to the cause of promoting evolution are motivated in part by the influence the clergy have over others. Eugenie Scott said in 2002, "I have found that the most effective allies for evolution are people of the faith community. One clergyman with a backward collar is worth two biologists at a school board meeting any day!"[11]

In addition to the Clergy Letter Project, Zimmerman initiated "Evolution Sunday," to be celebrated every year on the Sunday closest to Darwin's birthday (February 12). Evolution Sunday encourages clergy and congregations to learn about and promote evolution. In 2006, *The New York Times* reported that "ministers at several hundred churches around the country preached yesterday against recent efforts to undermine the theory of evolution."[12] In 2008, Zimmerman expanded Evolution Sunday to Evolution Weekend, thereby including Jewish congregations.[13]

In 2008, the United Methodist Church endorsed the Clergy Letter Project and urged "United Methodist clergy participation."[14] In 2009, the Southwestern Washington Synod Assembly of the Evangelical Lutheran Church of America passed a resolution endorsing the Clergy Letter Project and "affirming the teaching of the theory of evolution as a core component of human knowledge."[15] In June 2016, the General Assembly of the Presbyterian Church (U.S.A.) also voted to endorse the Clergy Letter.[16]

With so many clergy drinking Darwin's universal acid, it's no wonder that religion in America is declining.

Corrupting Education

IN SEPTEMBER 2014, psychology professor David Barash wrote in *The New York Times* that "every year around this time, with the college year starting, I give my students The Talk." In The Talk, Barash tells students that evolution is "the underpinning of all biological science," and that Gould's magisteria are "not nearly as nonoverlapping" as Gould claimed. Indeed, "as evolutionary science has progressed, the available space for religious faith has narrowed." So materialistic science can invade the space Gould claimed was reserved for religion. Barash concludes that "the more we know of evolution, the more unavoidable is the conclusion that living things, including human beings, are produced by a natural, totally amoral process, with no indication of a benevolent, controlling creator."[17] So Barash begins his "science" course each year with a lecture bashing religion.

Indoctrination into materialistic science begins well before college. In 2004, child psychologist Deborah Kelemen wrote that young children are "intuitive theists" who are "disposed to view natural phenomena as resulting from nonhuman design."[18] Since Kelemen regards this view as incompatible with science, she and her colleagues proposed in 2014 to indoctrinate young children with "theory-driven interventions using picture storybooks." They wrote:

> Repeated, spaced instruction on gradually scaled-up versions of the logic of natural selection could ultimately place students in a better position to suppress competing intuitive theoretical explanations such that they could elaborate a richer, more abstract, and broadly applicable knowledge of this process. Storybook interventions such

as the ones reported here seem a promising start from which to promote scientific literacy in the longer term.[19]

Intervention usually refers to an effort to help someone overcome an abnormal addiction. For Kelemen and her colleagues, however, it means convincing children to overcome a normal intuition and adopt the counterintuitive belief that natural selection can produce the illusion of design. According to the authors, this belief constitutes "scientific literacy."

Indoctrination into zombie science continues into high school, with help from the icons of evolution. Even so, political science professors Michael Berkman and Eric Plutzer lament the success of "evolution deniers" and lay the blame largely at the feet of high school teachers, whom they call "enablers of doubt" because of their own uncertainty about evolution.[20]

In 2011, the two professors argued that the situation would be improved by "requiring an evolution course for all preservice biology teachers" (prospective teachers still undergoing training).[21] In 2015, Berkman said: "Evolution is fundamental to biology, but more importantly we think that when you are communicating a skepticism about evolution you're communicating a skepticism about science generally."[22]

Public school teachers who encourage students to think critically about the evidence for evolutionary theory may find themselves targeted by the National Center for Science Education (NCSE, first mentioned in Chapter 3), which insists that any criticism of evolution is tantamount to religion. Eugenie Scott and her NCSE associate Glenn Branch also wrote in 2003 that teaching students there is a scientific controversy over evolution is equivalent to teaching that there is a legitimate historical controversy over whether the Holocaust occurred. According to Scott and Branch, "It is unfair to students to miseducate and confuse them about the nature of the scientific process, by teaching them that there are empirical problems with evolution."[23] Partly because of efforts by the NCSE, some teachers who profess skepticism about evolution have been fired.[24] Thus, empirical science and critical thinking suffer, while zombie science flourishes.

Corrupting Science

DENNETT'S "UNIVERSAL acid" doesn't just eat through religion and education; it also eats through science—the very discipline on which it claims to depend. We have seen throughout this book how a belief in evolution leads to misrepresentations of the evidence. But belief in evolution corrupts science even more deeply than that.

Chemist Linus Pauling, winner of two Nobel prizes, wrote in 1958 that "science is the search for the truth."[25] In 2000 Bruce Alberts, then President of the U. S. National Academy of Sciences, said (quoting Israeli statesman Shimon Peres): "Science and lies cannot coexist. You don't have a scientific lie, and you cannot lie scientifically. Science is basically the search of truth." Thus "a system that does not permit the search for truth cannot be a scientific system."[26]

In 2014, however, cognitive scientist Donald Hoffman and mathematician Chetan Prakash argued that evolution produces perceptions that are not true. According to them, human perception "evolved by natural selection," and evolutionary theory predicts that natural selection "drives true perceptions to extinction when they compete with perceptions tuned to fitness."[27] So according to Darwinian theory, human perceptions are more about survival than truth.

They're not alone in making this argument. According to biologists Ajit Varki and Danny Brower, the modern human mind evolved when early humans overcame their awareness of mortality by acquiring "a massive capacity for denial."[28] Varki and Brower argue that all non-humans are aware of their own mortality and thus are inhibited from embarking on enterprises—such as scientific discoveries and technological innovations—that transcend the life of a single individual. By evolving a capacity for denying mortality, subhuman creatures became humans and modern culture emerged. But "reality denial" quickly extended to other aspects of reality and produced religion, which unfortunately leads many people to reject what Varki and Brower regard as the ultimate reality of "biological evolution by natural selection [which] is now established as an incontrovertible fact."[29]

But if evolution maximizes fitness by eliminating true perceptions, how do Hoffman and Prakash know their perception of evolution is true? And if modern humans evolved to deny reality, how do Varki and Brower know they're not denying reality when they claim evolution cannot be doubted?

Oxford professor C. S. Lewis pointed out in 1947 that a theory "which made it impossible to believe that our thinking was valid, would be utterly out of court." The theory of evolution "would itself have been reached by thinking, and if thinking is not valid that theory would, of course, be itself demolished. It would have destroyed its own credentials."[30]

Lewis was a Christian, but New York University professor Thomas Nagel is not. Nevertheless, Nagel made a similar argument in 2012. He pointed out that mind is "a basic aspect of nature." But the materialistic doctrine of evolution denies the reality of mind, so it "provides an account of our capacities that undermines their reliability, and in so doing undermines itself."[31] Although Nagel prefers not to believe in God, and he is not an advocate of intelligent design, he argues that a "satisfactory explanation" of mind would require "natural teleological laws" that make intelligible the existence of conscious organisms.[32] Since "the materialist neo-Darwinian conception of nature" does not make conscious organisms intelligible, Nagel concludes that it "is almost certainly false." In fact, he says he is "willing to bet that the present right-thinking consensus will come to seem laughable in a generation or two."[33]

For now, however, materialistic science rules.

Valuing Survival over Truth

FOR EMPIRICAL science the highest value is truthfulness, but for materialistic science the highest value is survival of the fittest. Of course there have been scientists in the past who put self-interest above the search for truth, and there are many scientist in the present who still consider truthfulness the highest value. But the pursuit of self-interest—in the form of professional survival—is on the rise.

It has long been the case that many people in the academic world need to publish their thoughts or findings in order to keep their jobs and advance in their careers. The phrase "publish or perish" has been common for almost a century. And what is true for academics in general is even truer for scientists. Unfortunately, "publish or perish" in the scientific establishment has led to a growing tendency to sacrifice truth for professional survival.

When published scientific articles are found to be untrue, they are sometimes retracted. The data on retractions can serve as a rough indicator of the growing problem. In 2011, *Nature* assistant editor Richard Van Noorden reported that "in the past decade, the number of retraction notices has shot up 10-fold, even as the literature has expanded by only 44%."[34]

Science journalist Paul Voosen wrote in 2015 that "science today is riven with perverse incentives," most of them financial. Universities and financing agencies reward scientists based on their publication records, encouraging the submission of results that have not been carefully checked and often cannot be replicated afterwards. Voosen quoted biologist Arturo Casadevall as saying that "scientists themselves are playing this game because once they succeed, the rewards are so great they basically force everyone to do it." Voosen also quoted biologist Ferric Fang as saying that as a result science is "increasingly populated by predators." According to Voosen, solving the problem will require changing "an entire scientific culture."[35]

In 2016, scientists Paul Smaldino and Richard McElreath called the phenomenon "the natural selection of bad science," noting that "selection for high output leads to poorer methods and increasingly high false discovery rates."[36]

Some papers have to be retracted because of hasty or careless work, but a growing percentage of retracted papers result from deliberate fraud. In 2012 Fang, Casadevall, and Grant Steen reported that "the percentage of scientific articles retracted because of fraud has increased [about] 10-fold since 1975." The authors listed some articles that were known to be based on fraud but were not retracted, and they concluded that "the current number of articles retracted because of fraud represents an underestimation of the actual number of fraudulent articles in the literature."[37]

So materialistic science (in the practical sense as well as the theoretical sense) is corrupting empirical science. But the effect of materialism on science is most obvious in the current controversy over intelligent design.

Zombie Science vs. Intelligent Design

FOR MOST of the twentieth century, opposition to evolution came mainly from a biblically inspired young Earth creationism that rejected not only the claim that unguided evolution could produce all features of living things but also the claim that the Earth is billions of years old. Even though establishment science lacked evidence for the first claim, it had enough evidence for the second to prevail over young Earth creationism in most (though not all) academic and scientific institutions.

In the 1990s, however, a form of opposition to evolution with no position on the age of the Earth rose to prominence in America: intelligent design (ID). According to ID, it is possible to infer from evidence that some features of the natural world, including some features of living things, are better explained by an intelligent cause than by unguided natural processes.[38-41] So unlike young Earth creationism, ID is based strictly on scientific evidence rather than a combination of scientific evidence *and* Bible-based arguments.

The validity of ID's inference to design is controversial. What follows is not a defense of ID, but a brief account of the scientific establishment's reaction to it—a reaction that is quite revealing.

In 1999, the Kansas State Board of Education voted to include microevolution but not macroevolution in its science teaching standards. Establishment science accused the Board of eliminating evolution entirely and trying to sneak creationism into the curriculum.[42] Although the new standards did not mention ID, the Board was accused of promoting it. A month later, Kansas State University biologist Scott Todd wrote, "Even if all the data point to an intelligent designer, such an hypothesis is excluded from science because it is not naturalistic."[43]

The distinction between empirical science and materialistic science could not be more obvious.

But ruling intelligent design out of court as unscientific is not enough for some evolutionists. In 2002, evolutionary biologist Massimo Pigliucci equated ID with creationism, and wrote that "creationism is more properly called *evolution denial*," a form of denial "analogous to the denial of the Holocaust." According to Pigliucci, "in the case of creationism, the sinister characters are associated principally with the so-called intelligent design movement," which is "bent on literally destroying science as we know it."[44]

In 2005, anthropologist Pat Shipman published an article titled "Being stalked by intelligent design," in which she wrote that "I and my colleagues in science are being stalked with careful and deadly deliberation" because "the intelligent design movement is a deliberate campaign to undermine the teaching of science in America."[45] Biologist and journal editor Gerald Weissmann wrote that "zealots of many stripes," including those of ID, "are chipping away at evolutionary science." Weissmann warned that "our heritage of reason, formed in the Enlightenment, is becoming eclipsed" by "the Endarkenment," against which "experimental science is our defense."[46]

In the same vein, physicist Marshall Berman wrote that ID "poses a threat to all of science and perhaps to secular democracy itself." He predicted that if ID wasn't stopped "the curtain of Dark Ages II" would begin to fall.[47] And in 2006 science journalist Robyn Williams called ID a form of terrorism.[48]

According to philosopher Niall Shanks, "A culture war is currently being waged in the United States by religious extremists who hope to turn the clock of science back to medieval times.... The chief weapon in this war is a version of creation science known as intelligent design theory."[49] Shanks warned, "When reason rooted in evidence about the world is abandoned, we will all have much to fear."[50]

In 2008, biologist and textbook-writer Kenneth Miller (first mentioned in Chapter 2) claimed that "to the ID movement the rationalism of the Age of Enlightenment, which gave rise to science as we know it, is the true enemy." If ID prevails, he wrote, "the modern age will be brought to an end."[51] For Miller, what is at stake "is nothing less than America's scientific soul."[52]

Clearly, these writers confuse empirical and technological science on the one hand with zombie science on the other. Modern civilization depends on the first two, but it is threatened by the third. Pigliucci's "science as we know it" is zombie science. Shipman's "teaching of science" is indoctrination into zombie science. If Weissmann really wants to use experimental science to fend off an "Endarkenment," then he should direct his warning at zombie science, not ID. It is zombie science rather than ID that abandons Shanks's "reason rooted in evidence." And whatever Miller may think, zombie science is not "America's scientific soul."

Why this hysteria over ID? Because if the evidence shows that *even one feature* of living things is due to intelligent design instead of unguided natural processes, the whole edifice of zombie science comes crashing down.

In popular zombie lore, a zombie apocalypse is the breakdown of society as a result of an initial zombie outbreak that spreads to become a general assault on civilization. And popular lore says that the only way to kill a zombie is to destroy its brain or cut off its head. But of course zombie science is not a material being; it's a spirit, a habit of mind. How does one overcome a spirit?

I have used the zombie metaphor throughout this book, but maybe the popular lore on battling vampires contains the best metaphor for fighting the dogmatic materialism masquerading as empirical science. One way to kill a vampire, according to popular lore, is to expose it to direct sunlight. And one thing ID proponents have is lots of light, in the form of a growing body of evidence against evolution and for intelligent design. Just reflecting on all of the evidence, and how much new evidence in favor of ID has emerged in the past twenty years, is enough to get me humming one of my favorite tunes.

Here comes the sun...

Little darling, I feel that ice is slowly melting.

Little darling, it seems like years since it's been clear.

Here comes the sun, here comes the sun,

And I say it's alright.[53]

Too optimistic? I don't think so. A growing number of biologists acknowledge that there are problems with modern evolutionary theory. In 1997, molecular biologist James Shapiro wrote that there are "far more unresolved questions than answers about evolutionary processes," and he argued that what is needed is a "third way" between creationism and Darwinism to investigate "possible intelligent cellular action in evolution." Shapiro was not advocating ID. Instead, he argued that all cells possess something akin to intelligence and a capacity for "natural genetic engineering."[54]

In 2007, Massimo Pigliucci published a paper asking whether we need "an extended evolutionary synthesis" that goes beyond neo-Darwinism.[55] The following year, Pigliucci and fifteen other biologists gathered at the Konrad Lorenz Institute for Evolution and Cognition Research just north of Vienna to discuss the question. Science journalist Suzan Mazur called this group "the Altenberg 16."[56] When Mazur saw the hostility directed at the Altenberg 16 by mainstream evolutionary biologists, she wrote that "the evolution industry" was "as much about the posturing, salesmanship, stonewalling and bullying that goes on as it is about actual scientific theory."[57]

Undaunted, the Altenberg 16 published a collection of their essays in 2010. The authors were not creationists or ID supporters, and they did not challenge materialistic descent with modification. But they did challenge the Darwinian idea that organisms could evolve solely by the gradual accumulation of small variations preserved by natural selection, and the neo-Darwinian idea that DNA is "the sole agent of variation and unit of inheritance."[58]

The same year, cognitive scientists Jerry Fodor and Massimo Piattelli-Palmarini (who were not among the Altenberg 16) observed that "much of the vast neo-Darwinian literature is distressingly uncritical. The possibility that anything is seriously amiss with Darwin's account of evolution is hardly considered." Fodor and Piattelli-Palmarini did not propose abandoning materialism or embracing ID, but they argued that the role of natural selection has been greatly exaggerated and that "internal factors" in the organism are more important than environmental factors.[59]

In 2011 James Shapiro (also not one of Altenberg 16) published a book titled *Evolution: A View from the 21st Century*. In it, he expounded on his concept of natural genetic engineering and provided evidence that cells can reorganize their genomes in purposeful ways. Many scientists react to the phrase natural genetic engineering the same way they react to intelligent design, because it seems "to violate the principles of naturalism that exclude any role for a guiding intelligence outside of nature." But Shapiro argued that "the concept of cell-guided natural genetic engineering fits well within the boundaries of twenty-first century biological science. Despite widespread philosophical prejudices, cells are now reasonably seen to operate teleologically [i.e., purposefully]: Their goals are survival, growth, and reproduction."[60]

In 2014 Shapiro, along with British physiologist Denis Noble and website developer Raju Pookottil, started an online forum for scientists and other scholars who "see the need for a deeper and more complete exploration of all aspects of the evolutionary process." They called their enterprise The Third Way of Evolution, and many scholars are now affiliated with it. The website makes it clear that it and the scientists listed on it "do not support or subscribe to" creationism or intelligent design.[61] Nevertheless, it demonstrates a growing dissatisfaction with modern evolutionary theory. According to Mazur, the group has been dubbed "the Oxford 50."[62]

In 2015, *Nature* published an exchange of views among scientists who believe that evolutionary theory needs rethinking and scientists who believe it is fine as it is.

Those who believe that the theory needs rethinking suggested that those defending it might be "haunted by the specter of intelligent design" and thus want "to show a united front to those hostile to science." Nevertheless, the former concluded that recent findings in several fields require a "conceptual change in evolutionary biology."[63] These same scientists also published an article in which they proposed "an alternative conceptual framework" that they called the "extended evolutionary synthesis," which retains the fundamentals of evolutionary theory "but differs in its emphasis on the role of constructive processes in development and evolution."[64]

Also in 2015, Noble published an article arguing for "a new conceptual framework" in evolutionary biology. Noble criticized the idea that DNA contains a "blueprint" for the organism and argued that the neo-Darwinian conception was wrong. Instead, an organism is best understood as a network in which "there is no privileged level of causation" and which behaves as a whole.[65] American biologist Clarence Williams criticized Noble and insisted that "neo-Darwinism is just fine." Noble replied that an "honest response" to new evidence in biology "is to say that the central tenets of neo-Darwinism are no longer valid."[66,67]

Noble and several others—most notably Austrian biologist Gerd Müller—organized a public meeting to discuss an extended evolutionary synthesis at the Royal Society in London in November, 2016. Invited speakers included Noble, Shapiro, and Müller, among others.[68,69]

Müller opened the meeting by pointing out that current evolutionary theory fails to explain (among other things) the origin of new anatomical structures (that is, macroevolution). Most of the other speakers agreed that the current theory is inadequate, though two speakers defended it. Although some proponents of intelligent design were in the audience, none of the speakers considered ID an option. One speaker even caricatured ID as "God did it," and at one point another participant blurted out, "*Not* God—we're excluding God."[70]

The advocates of an extended evolutionary synthesis proposed various mechanisms that they argued were ignored or downplayed in current theory, but none of their proposed mechanisms moved beyond microevolution. By the end of the meeting it was clear that none of the speakers had met the challenge posed by Müller on the first day.[71]

Despite its failure to solve the problem of macroevolution, the meeting showed that current evolutionary theory is broken, and a growing number of scientists know it.

When I was a boy growing up in northern New Jersey, a lake near our house would freeze hard in the winter, and I would skate on it with my friends. As the weather grew warmer in the early spring, the ice would become honeycombed with pockets of meltwater. Although the spring ice still looked thick and solid, my friends and I knew that it was no longer strong enough to hold our weight, and we stopped skating on it.

Today, evolutionary theory is like spring ice. It still covers the lake, and to many people it still looks solid. But it's honeycombed with meltwater. It can no longer carry the weight it once did. Summer is on the way.

A Scientific Revolution?

IN 1962, historian of science Thomas Kuhn published his now-famous work titled *The Structure of Scientific Revolutions*. According to Kuhn, most scientific work is "normal science," focused on solving problems within a "paradigm." Kuhn's concept of paradigm had several meanings, including worldview and research program. A paradigm typically dominates funding, faculty appointments, and scientific journals, and its practitioners resist all attempts to replace it with a new paradigm. They have mastered the old paradigm and devoted their careers to it. They have little incentive to help it crumble and strong incentives to keep it intact. So replacement doesn't happen easily. When replacement does occur, it is a "scientific revolution."

People involved in a scientific revolution often debate the very definition of science. Kuhn wrote, "The reception of a new paradigm often necessitates a redefinition of the corresponding science," the "standard that distinguishes a real scientific solution from a mere metaphysical speculation." For example, Newton's theory of gravity was resisted on the grounds that "gravity, interpreted as an innate attraction between every pair of particles of matter, was an occult quality." Critics of Newtonianism claimed that it was not science and "its reliance upon innate forces would return science to the Dark Ages."[72]

The current conflict between evolution and ID has the characteristics of a scientific revolution. Defenders of evolution control research funding, scientific journals, and faculty appointments. They resist all challenges to their paradigm, and they view even minor amendments such as the "extended evolutionary synthesis" with suspicion. Most fundamentally, defenders of evolution insist on retaining the materialistic definition of science that became dominant after Darwin.

Kuhn wrote that at first a new paradigm "may have few supporters, and on occasions the supporters' motives may be suspect. Nevertheless, if they are competent, they will improve it, explore its possibilities, and show what it would be like to belong to the community guided by it."[73] This has been happening with ID.

ID advocates have been improving and exploring their approach theoretically for several decades. In a 1998 book titled *The Design Inference*, mathematician William Dembski developed the concept of "specified complexity" and argued that something that is both complex and specified (that is, corresponds to an independently given pattern) can only be produced by intelligence.[74] Dembski further developed the concept in his 2002 book *No Free Lunch: Why Specified Complexity Cannot Be Purchased without Intelligence*.[75] Not surprisingly, Dembski's books sustained withering criticisms from defenders of evolution. In 2007, Dembski and computer engineer Robert Marks started the Evolutionary Informatics Lab in Waco, Texas, to explore specified complexity mathematically.[76]

They and their colleagues have since published dozens of articles and book chapters elaborating on the concept.[77]

In 2011, Dembski and Marks joined many other scientists at a conference at Cornell University that discussed new perspectives on biological information. A contract was signed with a major European scientific publisher for a volume containing the papers from the conference, but when defenders of evolution got word of it they pressured the publisher to breach the contract. The volume was subsequently published in 2013 by a different scientific publisher.[78] Clearly, there is a growing scientific community guided by intelligent design.

According to Kuhn, an important issue in a scientific revolution "is which paradigm should in the future guide research." A "decision between alternative ways of practicing science is called for, and in the circumstances the decision must be based less on past achievement than on future promise."[79] In 2014, physicist David Snoke wrote, "Many have demanded that the intelligent design paradigm must come up with a successful, predictive, quantitative program for biology, but it seems that such a program already exists right under our noses." Snoke pointed to systems biology, which "analyzes living systems in terms of systems engineering concepts such as design, information processing, optimization, and other explicitly teleological concepts." Although most systems biologists believe in evolution, "they cannot avoid using design language and design concepts in their research, and a straightforward look at the field indicates it is really a design approach."[80]

Scientists who explicitly accept intelligent design are also developing the new paradigm with empirical research. In 2005, molecular biologist Douglas Axe started the Biologic Institute in Redmond, Washington to support both theoretical and experimental work guided by the assumption that "life appears to have been designed because it really *was* designed."[81] In 2014, Axe and his colleagues Ann Gauger and Mariclair Reeves published laboratory evidence that "structural similarities among enzymes with distinct functions are better interpreted as supporting shared design principles than shared evolutionary histories."[82]

Also in 2014, a large conference was held in Brazil to discuss ID. Organized by the Sociedade Brasileira do Design Inteligente (Brazilian Society for Intelligent Design), the conference attracted hundreds of people, including many interested scientists. According to one of the participants, the crowd represented a major change from previous years. In 1998, he said, "all the people in Brazil willing to be publicly identified as ID theorists" would have fit into a VW van.[83]

So despite fierce opposition from establishment science, scientific interest in intelligent design is growing. In fact, its growth took an upward turn in 2016. Because evolution's defenders currently control public funding for science (which amounts to billions of dollars annually in the United States), ID must rely on private funding. In 2016, the Discovery Institute in Seattle received a grant to fund more than a dozen research projects directed by ID-friendly scientists at universities around the world.

Here comes the sun, and the reign of zombie science is coming to an end.

Supplement

How to Make a Plain Paper Cover for Your Book

1. Cut a piece of paper (a brown paper bag will do) 3-4 inches higher than the height of the book and 3-4 inches wider than twice the width of the book. (Top figure.)
2. Fold the top and bottom of the paper so it is just a little larger than the height of the book. (Second figure from the top.)
3. Open the book, fold the left side of the paper over the front cover, then slide the cover into the fold. (Third figure from the top.)
4. Do the same for the back cover. The paper cover is now finished. (Bottom figure.) If necessary, use tape to secure the flaps to the outer paper cover.

For more help go to http://www.wikihow.com/Create-a-Paper-Bag-Book-Cover.

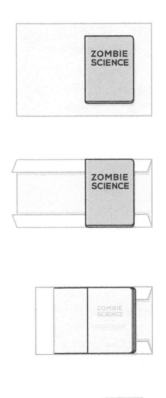

ENDNOTES

ILLUSTRATIONS

All illustrations by Anca Sandu and Brian Gage unless otherwise specified.

CHAPTER 1 (PAGES 15–23)

1. John W. Gofman and Frank Lindgren, "The role of lipids and lipoproteins in atherosclerosis," *Science* 111 (1950): 166–171. doi:10.1126/science.111.2877.166. PMID:15403115.

2. Ancel Keys, "Atherosclerosis: A problem in newer public health," *Journal of Mount Sinai Hospital, New York* 20 (1953): 118–139. PMID:13085148.

3. Jacob Yerushalmy and Herman E. Hilleboe, "Fat in the diet and mortality from heart disease; a methodologic note," *New York State Journal of Medicine* 57 (1957): 2343–2354. PMID:13441073.

4. David Kritchevsky, "History of recommendations to the public about dietary fat." *Journal of Nutrition* 128 Supplement (1998): 449S–452S. PMID:9478046.

5. Irvine H. Page, Edgar V. Allen, Francis L. Chamberlain, Ancel Keys, Jeremiah Stamler, and Fredrick J. Stare, "Dietary fat and its relation to heart attacks and strokes," *Circulation* 23 (1961): 133–136. doi:10.1161/01.CIR.23.1.133.

6. U. S. Senate Select Committee on Nutrition and Human Needs, *Dietary Goals for the United States* (2nd edition; Washington, DC: U.S. Government Printing Office, 1977). http://zerodisease.com/archive/Dietary_Goals_For_The_United_States.pdf.

7. U.S. Department of Agriculture, *The Food Guide Pyramid* (Washington, DC: Human Nutrition Information Service, Home and Garden Bulletin No. 252, 1992). http://www.cnpp.usda.gov/sites/default/files/archived_projects/FGPPamphlet.pdf.

8. U.S. Department of Agriculture, *USDA's Food Guide: Background and Development* (Washington, DC: Human Nutrition Information Service, 1993). http://www.cnpp.usda.gov/sites/default/files/archived_projects/FGPBackgroundAndDevelopment.pdf.

9. U.S. Department of Agriculture, *Scientific Report of the 2015 Dietary Guidelines Advisory Committee* (February, 2015): 17. http://www.health.gov/dietaryguidelines/2015-scientific-report/PDFs/Scientific-Report-of-the-2015-Dietary-Guidelines-Advisory-Committee.pdf.

10. Anahad O'Connor, "Nutrition panel calls for less sugar and eases cholesterol and fat restrictions," *The New York Times* (February 19, 2015). http://well.blogs.nytimes.com/2015/02/19/nutrition-panel-calls-for-less-sugar-and-eases-cholesterol-and-fat-restrictions/.

11. Alvin Plantinga, "Methodological Naturalism?" *Origins & Design* 18:1 (1997). http://www.leaderu.com/orgs/arn/odesign/od181/methnat181.htm.

12. Alvin Plantinga, "Methodological Naturalism? Part 2," *Origins & Design* 18:2 (1997). http://www.arn.org/docs/odesign/od182/methnat182.htm.

13. Francis Darwin, ed., *The Life and Letters of Charles Darwin, Including an Autobiographical Chapter* (London: John Murray, 1887), I:309. http://darwin-online.org.uk/content/frame set?itemID=F1452.1&viewtype=text&pageseq=327.

14. Charles R. Darwin, *On the Origin of Species by Means of Natural Selection*, 1st ed. (London: John Murray, 1859), 459.

15. Ibid., 372.

16. Charles R. Darwin, *On the Origin of Species by Means of Natural Selection*, 4th ed. (London: John Murray, 1866), 513.

17. Darwin, *Origin of Species* (1859), 90.

18. Neal C. Gillespie, *Charles Darwin and the Problem of Creation* (Chicago: University of Chicago Press, 1979), 147.

19. Alfred Russel Wallace, "Sir Charles Lyell on geological climates and the origin of species," *Quarterly Review* 126 (April 1869): 359–394, 391 and 394. http://people.wku.edu/ charles.smith/wallace/S146.htm.

20. Michael A. Flannery, *Alfred Russel Wallace: A Rediscovered Life* (Seattle, WA: Discovery Institute Press, 2011), 67.

21. Jonathan Wells, "Darwin's straw god argument," Discovery Institute (2008). http://www. discovery.org/a/8101.

22. Theodosius Dobzhansky, *Genetics and the Origin of Species* (New York: Columbia University Press, 1937), 12.

23. Theodosius Dobzhansky, "Nothing in biology makes sense except in the light of evolution," *American Biology Teacher* 35 (1973): 125–129. doi:10.2307/4444260.

24. Stephen Dilley, "Nothing in biology makes sense except in light of theology?" *Studies in History and Philosophy of Biological and Biomedical Sciences* 44 (2013): 774–786. doi:10.1016/j.shpsc.2013.06.006.

25. Jonathan Wells, *Icons of Evolution: Science or Myth?* (Washington, DC: Regnery Publishing, 2000).

CHAPTER 2 (PAGES 25–48)

1. Charles R. Darwin, *On the Origin of Species by Means of Natural Selection*, 1st ed. (London: John Murray, 1859), 413.

2. Ibid., 488.

3. Ibid., 484.

4. Ibid., 129–130.

5. Ibid., between 116 and 117.

6. Charles R. Darwin, Letter to Charles Lyell, October 11, 1859, in *The Life and Letters of Charles Darwin*, ed. Francis Darwin (London: John Murray, 1887), II:211. http://darwin-online.org.uk/content/frameset?pageseq=227&itemID=F1452.2&viewtype=side.

7. Darwin, *Origin of Species* (1859), 281–282.

8. Ibid., 308.

9. James W. Valentine, Stanley M. Awramik, Philip W. Signor and Peter M. Sadler, "The biological explosion at the Precambrian-Cambrian boundary," *Evolutionary Biology* 25 (1991): 279–356.

10. James W. Valentine, *On the Origin of Phyla* (Chicago: The University of Chicago Press, 2004), xxiii.

11. Ibid., 37.

12. Douglas H. Erwin and James W. Valentine, *The Cambrian Explosion* (Greenwood Village, CO: Roberts and Company, 2013), especially Chapter 9.

13. Stephen C. Meyer, *Darwin's Doubt* (New York: HarperCollins, 2013).

14. Niles Eldredge and Stephen Jay Gould, "Punctuated equilibria: An alternative to phyletic gradualism," in *Models in Paleobiology*, ed. Thomas J. M. Schopf (San Francisco: Freeman Cooper, 1972), 82–115.

15. Stephen Jay Gould, *The Structure of Evolutionary Theory* (Cambridge, MA: Harvard University Press, 2002), 759.

16. Brian Charlesworth, Russell Lande, and Montgomery Slatkin, "A Neo-Darwinian commentary on macroevolution," *Evolution* 36 (1982): 474–498. doi:10.2307/2408095.

17. Ronald A. Jenner, "Macroevolution of animal body plans: Is there science after the tree?" *BioScience* 64 (2014): 653–664. doi:10.1093/biosci/biu099.

18. Gareth Nelson, "Presentation to the American Museum of Natural History" (1969), in David M. Williams and Malte C. Ebach, "The reform of palaeontology and the rise of biogeography," *Journal of Biogeography* 31 (2004): 685–712. doi:10.1111/j.1365-2699.2004.01063.x.

19. Henry Gee, *In Search of Deep Time: Beyond the Fossil Record to a New History of Life* (New York: The Free Press, 1999), 32, 113–117.

20. John Barker and Judith Philip, "Phylogenetics of man-made objects: Simulating evolution in the classroom," *Science in School* 27 (2013): 26–31. http://www.scienceinschool.org/2013/issue27/phylogenetics.

21. Ibid.

22. Willi Hennig, *Phylogenetic Systematics*, trans. D. Dwight Davis and Rainier Zangerl (Urbana, IL: University of Illinois Press, 1966).

23. Kevin Padian, "Trickle-down evolution: An approach to getting major evolutionary adaptive changes into textbooks and curricula," *Integrative and Comparative Biology* 48 (2008): 175–188. doi:10.1093/icb/icn023. PMID:21669782.

24. Kenneth R. Miller and Joseph S. Levine, *Biology* (Saddle River, NJ: Pearson Education, 2014), 517.

25. James A. Lake, "The order of sequence alignment can bias the selection of tree topology," *Molecular Biology and Evolution* 8 (1991): 378–385. PMID:2072863.

26. David A. Morrison, "Why would phylogeneticists ignore computerized sequence alignment?" *Systematic Biology* 58 (2009): 150–158. doi:10.1093/sysbio/syp009. PMID:20525575.

27. David A. Morrison, "Is sequence alignment an art or a science?" *Systematic Botany* 40 (2015): 14–26. doi:10.1600/036364415X686305.

28. Antonis Rokas, Dirk Krüger, and Sean B. Carroll, "Animal evolution and the molecular signature of radiations compressed in time," *Science* 310 (2005): 1933–1938. doi:10.1126/science.1116759. PMID:16373569.

29. Casey W. Dunn, Andreas Hejnol, David Q. Matus, Kevin Pang, William E. Browne, Stephen A. Smith, Elaine Seaver, Greg W. Rouse, Matthias Obst, Gregory D. Edgecombe, Martin V. Sørensen, Steven H. D. Haddock, Andreas Schmidt-Rhaesa, Akiko Okusu, Reinhardt Møbjerg Kristensen, Ward C. Wheeler, Mark Q. Martindale, and Gonzalo Giribet, "Broad phylogenomic sampling improves resolution of the animal tree of life," *Nature* 452 (2008): 745–749. doi:10.1038/nature06614. PMID:18322464.

30. Hervé Philippe, Romain Derelle, Philippe Lopez, Kerstin Pick, Carole Borchiellini, Nicole Boury-Esnault, Jean Vacelet, Emmanuelle Renard, Evelyn Houliston, Eric Quéinnec, Corinne Da Silva, Patrick Wincker, Hervé Le Guyader, Sally Leys, Daniel J. Jackson, Fabian Schreiber, Dirk Erpenbeck, Burkhard Morgenstern, Gert Wörheide, and Michaël Manuel, "Phylogenomics revives traditional views on deep animal relationships," *Current Biology* 19 (2009): 706–712. doi:10.1016/j.cub.2009.02.052. PMID:19345102.

31. Liliana Dávalos, Andrea Cirranello, Jonathan Geisler, and Nancy Simmons, "Understanding phylogenetic incongruence: Lessons from phyllostomid bats," *Biological Reviews of the Cambridge Philosophical Society* 87 (2012): 991–1024. doi:10.1111/j.1469-185X.2012.00240.x. PMID:22891620.

32. Leonidas Salichos and Antonis Rokas, "Inferring ancient divergences requires genes with strong phylogenetic signals," *Nature* 497 (2013): 327–331. doi:10.1038/nature12130. PMID:23657258.

33. Karl J. Schmid and Diethard Tautz, "A screen for fast evolving genes from *Drosophila*," *Proceedings of the National Academy of Sciences USA* 94 (1997): 9746–9750. doi:10.1073/pnas.94.18.9746. PMID:9275195.

34. Hervé Philippe, Yan Zhou, Henner Brinkmann, Nicolas Rodrigue and Frédéric Delsuc, "Heterotachy and long-branch attraction in phylogenetics," *BMC Evolutionary Biology* 5 (2005): 50. doi:10.1186/1471-2148-5-50. PMID:16209710.

35. François Jacob, "Evolution and tinkering," *Science* 196 (1977): 1161–1166. doi.org/10.1126/science.860134. PMID:860134.

36. Daniel Fischer and David Eisenberg, "Finding families for genomic ORFans," *Bioinformatics* 15 (1999): 759–762. doi:10.1093/bioinformatics/15.9.759. PMID:10498776.

37. Jing Cai, Ruoping Zhao, Huifeng Jiang, and Wen Wang, "*De novo* origination of a new protein-coding gene in *Saccharomyces cerevisiae*," *Genetics* 179 (2008): 487–496. doi:10.1534/genetics.107.084491. PMID:18493065.

38. Diana Ekman and Arne Elofsson, "Identifying and quantifying orphan protein sequences in fungi," *Journal of Molecular Biology* 396 (2010): 396–405. doi:10.1016/j.jmb.2009.11.053. PMID:19944701.

39. Qi Zhou, Guojie Zhang, Yue Zhang, Shiyu Xu, Ruoping Zhao, Zubing Zhan, Xin Li, Yun Ding, Shuang Yang, and Wen Wang, "On the origin of new genes in *Drosophila*," *Genome Research* 18 (2008): 1446–1455. doi:10.1101/gr.076588.108. PMID:18550802.

40. Sidi Chen, Yong E. Zhang, and Manyuan Long, "New genes in *Drosophila* quickly become essential," *Science* 330 (2010): 1682–1685. doi:10.1126/science.1196380. PMID:21164016.

41. Tobias J. A. J. Heinen, Fabian Staubach, Daniela Häming, and Diethard Tautz, "Emergence of a new gene from an intergenic region," *Current Biology* 19 (2009): 1527–1531. doi:10.1016/j.cub.2009.07.049. PMID:19733073.

42. Daniel N. Murphy and Aoife McLysaght, "De novo origin of protein-coding genes in murine rodents," *PLoS One* 7 (2012): e48650. doi:10.1371/journal.pone.0048650. PMID:23185269.

43. David G. Knowles and Aoife McLysaght, "Recent de novo origin of human protein-coding genes," *Genome Research* 19 (2009): 1752–1759. doi:10.1101/gr.095026.109. PMID:19726446.

44. Dong-Dong Wu, David M. Irwin, and Ya-Ping Zhang, "De novo origin of human protein-coding genes," *PLoS Genetics* 7 (2011): e1002379. doi:10.1371/journal.pgen.1002379. PMID:22102831.

45. Caroline B. Albertin, Oleg Simakov, Therese Mitros, Z. Yan Wang, Judit R. Pungor, Eric Edsinger-Gonzales, Sydney Brenner, Clifton W. Ragsdale, and Daniel S. Rokhsar, "The octopus genome and the evolution of cephalopod neural and morphological novelties," *Nature* 524 (2015): 220–224. doi:10.1038/nature14668. PMID:26268193.

46. Henrik Kaessmann, "Origins, evolution, and phenotypic impact of new genes," *Genome Research* 20 (2010): 1313–1326. doi:10.1101/gr.101386.109. PMID: 20651121.

47. Diethard Tautz and Tomislav Domazet-Lošo, "The evolutionary origin of orphan genes," *Nature Reviews Genetics* 12 (2011): 692–702. doi:10.1038/nrg3053. PMID:21878963.

48. Anne-Ruxandra Carvunis, Thomas Rolland, Ilan Wapinski, Michael A. Calderwood, Muhammed A. Yildirim, Nicolas Simonis, Benoit Charloteaux, César A. Hidalgo, Justin Barbette, Balaji Santhanam, Gloria A. Brar, Jonathan S. Weissman, Aviv Regev, Nicolas Thierry-Mieg, Michael E. Cusick, and Marc Vidal, "Proto-genes and *de novo* gene birth," *Nature* 487 (2012): 370–374. doi:10.1038/nature11184. PMID:22722833.

49. Jeffrey Rosenfeld, Jonathan Foox, and Rob DeSalle, "Insect genome content phylogeny and functional annotation of core insect genomes," *Molecular Phylogenetics and Evolution* 97 (2016): 224–232. doi:10.1016/j.ympev.2015.10.014. PMID:26549428.

50. Carl R. Woese and George E. Fox, "Phylogenetic structure of the prokaryotic domain: The primary kingdoms," *Proceedings of the National Academy of Sciences USA* 74 (1977): 5088–5090. doi:10.1073/pnas.74.11.5088. PMID:270744.

51. Detlef D. Leipe, L. Aravind, and Eugene V. Koonin, "Did DNA replication evolve twice independently?" *Nucleic Acids Research* 27 (1999): 3389–3401. doi:10.1093/nar/27.17.3389. PMID:10446225.

52. Carl Woese, "The universal ancestor," *Proceedings of the National Academy of Sciences USA* 95 (1998): 6854–6859. doi:10.1073/pnas.95.12.6854. PMID:9618502.

53. W. Ford Doolittle, "The practice of classification and the theory of evolution, and what the demise of Charles Darwin's tree of life hypothesis means for both of them," *Philosophical Transactions of the Royal Society of London B* 364 (2009): 2221–2228. doi:10.1098/rstb.2009.0032. PMID:19571242.

54. Darwin, *Origin of Species* (1859), 457–458.

55. Gavin de Beer, *Homology: An Unsolved Problem* (London: Oxford University Press, 1971), 15–16.

56. Gavin de Beer, *Embryos and Ancestors*, 3rd ed. (Oxford: Clarendon Press, 1958), 152.

57. Ernst Mayr, *The Growth of Biological Thought* (Cambridge, MA: Harvard University Press, 1982), 232, 465.

58. David B. Wake, "Homoplasy, homology and the problem of 'sameness' in biology" in Novartis Symposium 222—*Homology*, eds. G.K. Bock and G. Cardew (Chinchester, UK: John Wiley & Sons, 1999), 24–46. See page 45.

59. Miller and Levine, *Biology* (2014), 468, 470.

60. Sylvia Mader and Michael Windelspecht, *Biology*, 12 ed. (New York: McGraw-Hill Education, 2016), 273.

61. Günter P. Wagner, *Homology, Genes, and Evolutionary Innovation* (Princeton: Princeton University Press, 2014), xii.

62. Ibid., 1–2.

63. Ibid., 90.

64. Ibid., 2.

65. Ibid., 53.

66. Ronald H. Brady, "On the independence of systematics," *Cladistics* 1 (1985): 113–126. doi:10.1111/j.1096-0031.1985.tb00416.x.

67. Edwin Ray Lankester, "On the use of the term homology in modern zoology, and the distinction between homogenetic and homoplastic agreements," *The Annals and Magazine of Natural History* 6 (1870): 34–43.

68. Simon Conway Morris, *Life's Solution* (Cambridge: Cambridge University Press, 2003), 283.

69. Thomas J. Givnish, "New evidence on the origin of carnivorous plants," *Proceedings of the National Academy of Sciences USA* 112 (2015): 10–11. doi:10.1073/pnas.1422278112. PMID:25538295.

70. Leonardo O. Alvarado-Cárdenas, Enrique Martínez-Meyer, Teresa P. Feria, Luis E. Eguiarte, Héctor M. Hernández, Guy Midgley, and Mark E. Olson, "To converge or not to converge in environmental space: Testing for similar environments between analogous succulent plants of North America and Africa," *Annals of Botany* 111 (2013): 1125–1138. doi:10.1093/aob/mct078.

71. George R. McGhee, Jr., *Convergent Evolution: Limited Forms Most Beautiful* (Cambridge, MA: MIT Press, 2011), 271, 276.

72. Conway Morris, *Life's Solution*, 283–284.

73. Ibid., 327.

74. Stephen Jay Gould, *Wonderful Life* (New York: W. W. Norton, 1989), 28.

Chapter 3 (Pages 49–79)

1. Jonathan Wells, "Survival of the fakest," *The American Spectator* (December 2000 / January 2001): 19–27. http://www.discovery.org/a/1209. The title of this article was suggested by *The American Spectator's* editor at the time, Josh Gilder.

2. Jonathan Wells, "Critics rave over *Icons of Evolution*: A response to published reviews," Discovery Institute XI:2 (2002). http://www.discovery.org/a/1180.

3. Jerry A. Coyne, "Creationism by stealth," *Nature* 410 (2001): 745–746. doi:10.1038/35071144.

4. Massimo Pigliucci, "Intelligent design theory," *BioScience* 51 (2001): 411–414. doi:10.1641/0006-3568(2001)051[0411:IDT]2.0.CO;2.

5. Kevin Padian and Alan Gishlick, "The talented Mr. Wells," *Quarterly Review of Biology* 77 (2002): 33–37. doi:10.1086/339201.

6. The misidentified Ronstadt photo was in the second edition of Prentice Hall's *Exploring Physical Science* (1997). See John L. Hubisz, *Review of Middle School Physical Science Texts* (Physical Sciences Resource Center, 2002), 55. http://www.compadre.org/psrc/document/ServeFile.cfm?ID=1289&DocID=142#Doc142.

7. Charles R. Darwin, Letter to J. D. Hooker, March 29, 1863, in *The Life and Letters of Charles Darwin*, ed. Francis Darwin (London: John Murray, 1887), III:18. http://darwin-online.org.uk/content/frameset?pageseq=30&itemID=F1452.3&viewtype=side.

8. Charles R. Darwin, Letter to J. D. Hooker, February 1, 1871. http://evolutionatbyu.com/20130104Darwin-and-spontaneous-generationV03.pdf.

9. Alexander I. Oparin, *The Origin of Life* (Moscow: Moscow Worker, 1924).

10. J. B. S. Haldane, "The origin of life," *Rationalist Annual* 148 (1928): 3–10.

11. Stanley L. Miller, "A production of amino acids under possible primitive Earth conditions," *Science* 117 (1953): 528–529. doi:10.1126/science.117.3046.528. PMID:13056598.

12. Gordon Schlesinger and Stanley L. Miller, "Prebiotic synthesis in atmospheres containing CH4, CO, and CO2. I. Amino acids," *Journal of Molecular Evolution* 19 (1983): 376–382. doi:10.1007/BF02101642. PMID:6417344.

13. Heinrich D. Holland, *The Chemical Evolution of the Atmosphere and Oceans* (Princeton: Princeton University Press, 1984), 99–100.

14. Xueshu Xie, Daniel Backman, Albert T. Lebedev, Viatcheslav B. Artaev, Liying Jiang, Leopold L. Ilag, and Roman A. Zubarev, "Primordial soup was edible: Abiotically produced Miller-Urey mixture supports bacterial growth," *Scientific Reports* 5 (2015): 14338. doi:10.1038/srep14338. PMID:26412575.

15. Kenneth A. Mason, Jonathan B. Losos, and Susan R. Singer, Raven and Johnson's *Biology*, 10th ed. (New York: McGraw-Hill, 2014), 511–512.

16. Kenneth R. Miller and Joseph S. Levine, *Biology* (Upper Saddle River, NJ: Pearson Education, 2014), 554.

17. Jane B. Reece, Lisa A. Urry, Michael L. Cain, Steven A. Wasserman, Peter V. Minorsky, and Robert B. Jackson, *Campbell Biology*, 10th ed. (San Francisco: Pearson Benjamin Cummings, 2014), 57.

18. Scott Freeman, Lizabeth Allison, Michael Black, Greg Podgorski, Kim Quillin, Jon Monroe, and Emily Taylor, *Biological Science*, 5th ed. (San Francisco: Pearson Benjamin Cummings, 2014), 33–34.

19. Sylvia Mader and Michael Windelspecht, *Biology*, 12th ed. (New York: McGraw-Hill, 2016), 319.

20. Reece, Urry, Cain, Wasserman, Minorsky, and Jackson *Campbell Biology* (2014), 520.

21. Stephen R. McNutt and C. M. Davis, "Lightning associated with the 1992 eruptions of Crater Peak Mount Spurr Volcano, Alaska," *Journal of Volcanology and Geothermal Research* 102 (2000): 45. doi:10.1016/S0377-0273(00)00181-5.

22. Adam P. Johnson, H. James Cleaves, Jason P. Dworkin, Daniel P. Glavin, Antonio Lazcano, and Jeffrey L. Bada, "The Miller volcanic spark discharge experiment," *Science* 322 (2008): 404. doi:10.1126/science.1161527. PMID:18927386.

23. Stanley L. Miller, "Production of some organic compounds under possible primitive Earth conditions," *Journal of the American Chemical Society* 77 (1955): 2351–2361. doi:10.1021/ja01614a001.

24. Eric T. Parker, Manshui Zhou, Aaron S. Burton, Daniel P. Glavin, Jason P. Dworkin, Ramanarayanan Krishnamurthy, Facundo M. Fernández, and Jeffrey L. Bada, "A plausible simultaneous synthesis of amino acids and simple peptides on the primordial Earth," *Angewandte Chemie* 53 (2014): 8132-8136. doi:10.1002/anie.201403683. PMID:24966137.

25. Eric T. Parker, H. James Cleaves, Aaron S. Burton, Daniel P. Glavin, Jason P. Dworkin, M. Zhou, Jeffrey L. Bada, and Facundo M. Fernández, "Conducting Miller-Urey experiments," *Journal of Visualized Experiments* 83 (2014): e51039. doi:10.3791/51039. PMID:24473135.

26. Stephen C. Meyer, *Signature in the Cell* (New York: HarperCollins, 2009).

27. Jack W. Szostak, "Attempts to define life do not help to understand the origin of life," *Journal of Biomolecular Structure and Dynamics* 29 (2012): 599–600. doi:10.1080/073911012010524998. PMID:22208251.

28. James Tour, "Animadversions of a synthetic chemist," *Inference* 2:2 (May 19, 2016). http://inference-review.com/article/animadversions-of-a-synthetic-chemist.

29. Ibid.

30. Charles R. Darwin, Letter to Asa Gray, September 10, 1860, in *The Life and Letters of Charles Darwin*, ed. Francis Darwin (London: John Murray, 1887), II:338. http://darwin-online.org.uk/content/frameset?pageseq=354&itemID=F1452.2&viewtype=side.

31. Charles R. Darwin, *On the Origin of Species by Means of Natural Selection*, 1st ed. (London: John Murray, 1859), 442, 449.

32. Charles R. Darwin, *On the Origin of Species by Means of Natural Selection*, 5th ed. (London: John Murray, 1869), 533.

33. Ibid., 515.

34. This widely used version of Haeckel's embryo drawings is from Figures 57 and 58 in George J. Romanes, *Darwinism Illustrated* (Chicago: Open Court, 1892), 42–43.

35. Michael K. Richardson, James Hanken, Mayoni L. Gooneratne, Claude Pieau, Albert Raynaud, Lynne Selwood, and Glenda M. Wright, "There is no highly conserved embryonic stage in the vertebrates: Implications for current theories of evolution and development," *Anatomy and Embryology* 196 (1997): 91–106. doi:10.1007/s004290050082. PMID:9278154.

36. Quoted in Elizabeth Pennisi, "Haeckel's embryos: Fraud rediscovered," *Science* 277 (1997): 1435. doi:10.1126/science.277.5331.1435a.

37. Robert J. Richards, *The Tragic Sense of Life: Ernst Haeckel and the Struggle over Evolutionary Thought* (Chicago: University of Chicago Press, 2008).

38. Nick Hopwood, *Haeckel's Embryos: Images, Evolution, and Fraud* (Chicago: University of Chicago Press, 2015).

39. Jonathan Wells, *Icons of Evolution* (Washington, DC: Regnery Publishing, 2000), 94–101.

40. Rudolf A. Raff, *The Shape of Life: Genes, Development, and the Evolution of Animal Form* (Chicago: The University of Chicago Press, 1996), 197.

41. Coyne, "Creationism by stealth," 745.

42. Jerry A. Coyne, *Why Evolution Is True* (New York: Viking Penguin, 2009), 77–79.

43. Stephen Jay Gould, "Abscheulich! (Atrocious!)," *Natural History* (March, 2000): 42–49.

44. Donald R. Prothero, *Bringing Fossils to Life*, 3rd ed. (New York: Columbia University Press, 2013), 29.

45. Mader and Windelspecht, *Biology*, 274.

46. Mason, Losos and Singer, Raven and Johnson's *Biology*, 428.

47. Miller and Levine, *Biology*, 469.

48. Casey Luskin, "Haeckel's embryo drawings make cameos in proposed Texas instructional materials," *Evolution News & Views* (June 17, 2011). http://www.evolutionnews. org/2011/06/haeckels_embryos_make_multiple047321.html.

49. Randy Olson, *Flock of Dodos: The Evolution-Intelligent Design Circus* (New York: New Video Group, 2007).

50. Jonathan Wells, "Flock of dodos, or pack of lies?" *Evolution News & Views* (February 9, 2007). http://www.evolutionnews.org/2007/02/flock_of_dodos_or_pack_of_ fals_4003165.html.

51. John G. West and Casey Luskin, "Hoax of dodos, part 1," *Evolution News & Views* (February 7, 2007). http://www.evolutionnews.org/2007/02/hoax_of_dodos_pt_1_ flock_of_do003132.html.

52. Debate at Villanova University (April 12, 2012), starting at 4:10. https://www.youtube. com/watch?v=8vDzcJNt1MM.

53. Casey Luskin, "Dodos keep on hoaxing," *Evolution News & Views* (April 13, 2012). http://www.evolutionnews.org/2012/04/thursday_night058531.html.

54. Randy Olson, *Houston, We Have a Narrative* (Chicago: University of Chicago Press, 2015), vii.

55. Pat Shipman, *Taking Wing* (New York: Simon and Schuster, 1998), 14.

56. Larry Martin (1985) "The relationship of *Archaeopteryx* to other birds," in *The Beginnings of Birds*, ed. M. K. Hecht, J. H. Ostrom, G. Viohl, and P. Wellnhofer (Eichstätt: Freunde des Jura-Museums, 1985), 182.

57. Qiang Ji and Shu'an Ji, "On the discovery of the earliest fossil bird in China (*Sinosauropteryx* gen. nov.) and the origin of birds," trans. Will Downs, *Chinese Geology* 233 (1996): 30–33. http://paleoglot.org/files/Ji%26Ji_96.pdf.

58. "Scientists: Fossil is of feathered dinosaur," *Los Angeles Times* (October 18, 1996). http:// articles.latimes.com/1996-10-18/news/mn-55101_1_feathered-dinosaur.

59. Theagarten Lingham-Soliar, Alan Feduccia, and Xiaolin Wang, "A new Chinese specimen indicates that 'protofeathers' in the Early Cretaceous theropod dinosaur

Sinosauropteryx are degraded collagen fibres," *Proceedings of the Royal Society of London B* 274 (2007): 1823–1829. doi:10.1098/rspb.2007.0352. PMID:17521978.

60. Alan Feduccia, *Riddle of the Feathered Dragons* (New Haven, CT: Yale University Press, 2012), 127.

61. Lida Xing, Ryan C. McKellar, Xing Xu, Gang Li, Ming Bai, W. Scott Persons IV, Tetsuto Miyashita, Michael J. Benton, Jianping Zhang, Alexander P. Wolfe, Qiru Yi, Kuowei Tseng, Hao Ran, and Philip J. Currie, "A feathered dinosaur tail with primitive plumage trapped in Mid-Cretaceous amber," *Current Biology* 26 (2016): 1–9. doi:10.1016/j.cub.2016.10.008. PMID:27939315.

62. "Feathers on a bird or dinosaur tail? The media are certain; the scientific evidence less so," *Evolution News & Views* (December 9, 2016). http://www.evolutionnews.org/2016/12/feathers_on_a_b103354.html.

63. Dongyu Hu, Lianhai Hou, Lijun Zhang, and Xing Xu, "A pre-*Archaeopteryx* troodontid theropod from China with long feathers on the metatarsus," *Nature* 461 (2009): 640–643. doi:10.1038/nature08322. PMID:19794491.

64. Mason, Losos and Singer, Raven and Johnson's *Biology*, 424.

65. Prothero, *Bringing Fossils to Life*, 88.

66. Darwin, *Origin of Species* (1859), 6.

67. Ibid., 90.

68. J. W. Tutt, *British Moths* (London: George Routledge, 1896).

69. H. B. D. Kettlewell, "Darwin's missing evidence," *Scientific American* 200 (1959): 48–53. doi:10.1038/scientificamerican0359-48. PMID:13635037.

70. Judith Hooper, *Of Moths and Men* (New York: Norton, 2002), 242–244.

71. Michael E. N. Majerus, *Melanism: Evolution in Action* (Oxford: Oxford University Press, 1998), 121.

72. Jerry A. Coyne, "Not black and white," *Nature* 396 (1998): 35–36. doi:10.1038/23856.

73. Kenneth Chang, "On scientific fakery and the systems to catch it," *The New York Times* (October 15, 2002), D1.

74. Jerry A. Coyne, "Evolution under pressure," *Nature* 418 (2002): 19–20. doi:10.1038/418019a.

75. Michael E. N. Majerus, "The peppered moth: The proof of Darwinian evolution," lecture at a meeting of the European Society for Evolutionary Biology, Uppsala University (August 22, 2007). http://www.gen.cam.ac.uk/images/researchpages/majerus/peppered-moth-proof-evolution-text/view.

76. Laurence M. Cook, Bruce S. Grant, Ilik J. Saccheri, and James Mallet, "Selective bird predation on the peppered moth: The last experiment of Michael Majerus," *Biology Letters* 8 (2012): 609–612. doi:10.1098/rsbl.2011.1136. PMID:22319093.

77. Majerus, "The peppered moth" (2007), 10.

78. Frank J. Sulloway, "Darwin and his finches: The evolution of a legend," *Journal of the History of Biology* 15 (1982): 1–53. doi:10.1007/BF00132004.

79. Frank J. Sulloway, "The legend of Darwin's finches," *Nature* 303 (1983): 372. doi:10.1038/303372a0.

80. Peter T. Boag and Peter R. Grant, "Intense natural selection in a population of Darwin's finches (Geospizinae) in the Galápagos," *Science* 214 (1981): 82–85. doi:10.1126/science.214.4516.82. PMID:17802577.

81. Peter R. Grant, "Natural selection and Darwin's finches," *Scientific American* 265 (October, 1991): 82–87. doi:10.1038/scientificamerican1091-82.

82. National Academy of Sciences, *Science and Creationism: A View from the National Academy of Sciences*, 2nd ed. (Washington, DC: National Academy of Sciences Press, 1999), Chapter on "Evidence Supporting Biological Evolution," 2. http://www.nap.edu/catalog/6024/science-and-creationism-a-view-from-the-national-academy-of.

83. Peter R. Grant and B. Rosemary Grant, "Hybridization of bird species," *Science* 256 (1992): 193–197. doi:10.1126/science.256.5054.193. PMID:17744718.

84. Peter R. Grant and B. Rosemary Grant, "The secondary contact phase of allopatric speciation in Darwin's finches," *Proceedings of the National Academy of Sciences USA* 106 (2009): 20141-20148. doi:10.1073/pnas.0911761106. PMID:19918081.

85. Daniel Cressey, "Darwin's finches tracked to reveal evolution in action: A new species of finch may have arisen in the Galápagos," *Nature News* (November 16, 2009). doi:10.1038/news.2009.1089.

86. Joel Achenbach, "The people who saw evolution," *Princeton Alumni Weekly* (April 23, 2014). https://paw.princeton.edu/article/people-who-saw-evolution.

87. Sangeet Lamichhaney, Jonas Berglund, Marcus Sällman Almén, Khurram Maqbool, Manfred Grabherr, Alvaro Martinez-Barrio, Marta Promerová, Carl-Johan Rubin, Chao Wang, Neda Zamani, B. Rosemary Grant, Peter R. Grant, Matthew T. Webster, and Leif Andersson, "Evolution of Darwin's finches and their beaks revealed by genome sequencing," *Nature* 518 (2015): 371–375. doi:10.1038/nature14181. PMID:25686609.

88. Bailey D. McKay and Robert M. Zink, "Sisyphean evolution in Darwin's finches," *Biological Reviews of the Cambridge Philosophical Society* 90 (2015): 689–698. doi:10.1111/brv.12127. PMID:25040800.

89. Miller and Levine, *Biology*, 472–473.

90. Mason, Losos, and Singer, Raven and Johnson's *Biology*, 9, 418–419.

91. Miller and Levine, *Biology*, 473.

92. Edward B. Lewis, "A gene complex controlling segmentation in *Drosophila*," *Nature* 276 (1978): 565–570. doi:10.1038/276565a0. PMID:103000.

93. Nobel Assembly at the Karolinska Institute, *The Nobel Prize in Physiology or Medicine* (1995). http://www.nobelprize.org/nobel_prizes/medicine/laureates/1995/press.html.

94. H. H. El Shatoury, "Developmental interactions in the development of the imaginal muscles of *Drosophila*," *Journal of Embryology and Experimental Morphology* 4 (1956): 228–239.

95. Joyce J. Fernandes, Susan E. Celniker, Edward B. Lewis, and Krishnaswamy VijayRaghavan, "Muscle development in the four-winged *Drosophila* and the role of the *Ultrabithorax* gene," *Current Biology* 4 (1994): 957–964. doi:10.1016/S0960-9822(00)00219-0. PMID:7874495.

96. Freeman, Allison, Black, Podgorski, Quillin, Monroe, and Taylor, *Biological Science*, 413.

97. "First genetic evidence uncovered of how major changes in body shapes occurred during early animal evolution," UCSD Press Release (February 6, 2002). http://ucsdnews.ucsd.edu/archive/newsrel/science/mchox.htm.

98. Matthew Ronshaugen, Nadine McGinnis, and William McGinnis, "Hox protein mutation and macroevolution of the insect body plan," *Nature* 415 (2002): 914–917. doi:10.1038/nature716. PMID:11859370.

99. Donald R. Prothero, *Evolution: What the Fossils Say and Why It Matters* (New York: Columbia University Press, 2007), 101.

100. Ibid., 195.

101. "Has evolution adequately explained the origins of life?" debate with Richard V. Sternberg, Stephen C. Meyer, Donald R. Prothero, and Michael Shermer at Saban Theater, Beverly Hills, CA (November 30, 2009), discussion starting at 1:13:20. https://www.youtube.com/watch?v=lzwHqqMMSaU.36:50-50:20.

102. Donald R. Prothero, "No longer sleeping in Seattle," *The Panda's Thumb* (December 3, 2009). http://pandasthumb.org/archives/2009/12/no-longer-sleeping-in-seattle.html.

103. Prothero, *Evolution*, 194.

104. Prothero, *Bringing Fossils to Life*, 101.

105. Ibid., 103.

106. Darwin, *Origin of Species* (1859), 488.

107. Charles R. Darwin, *The Descent of Man, and Selection in Relation to Sex* (London: John Murray, 1871), 185.

108. Niles Eldredge and Ian Tattersall, *The Myths of Human Evolution* (New York: Columbia University Press, 1982), 126–127.

109. Misia Landau, *Narratives of Human Evolution* (New Haven, CT: Yale University Press, 1991), ix–x, 148.

110. Jens L. Franzen, Philip D. Gingerich, Jörg Habersetzer, Jørn H. Hurum, Wighart von Koenigswald, and B. Holly Smith, "Complete primate skeleton from the Middle Eocene of Messel in Germany: Morphology and paleobiology," *PLoS One* 4 (2009): e5723. doi:10.1371/journal.pone.0005723. PMID:19492084.

111. Brian Handwerk, "Missing link found," *National Geographic* (May 19, 2009). http://news.nationalgeographic.com/news/2009/05/090519-missing-link-found.html.

112. James Randerson and Ed Pilkington, "Deal in Hamburg bar led scientist to Ida fossil, the 'eighth wonder of the world'," *The Guardian* (May 19, 2009). http://www.theguardian.com/science/2009/may/19/fossil-ida-missing-link-discovery.

113. Tim Arango, "Seeking a missing link, and a mass audience," *The New York Times* (May 18, 2009). http://www.nytimes.com/2009/05/19/business/media/19fossil.html.

114. Rex Dalton, "Fossil primate challenges Ida's place," *Nature* 461 (2009): 1040. doi:10.1038/4611040a. PMID:19847234.

115. Erik R. Seiffert, Jonathan M. G. Perry, Elwyn L. Simons, and Doug M. Boyer, "Convergent evolution of anthropoid-like adaptations in Eocene adapiform primates," *Nature* 461 (2009): 1118–1121. doi:10.1038/nature08429. PMID:19847263.

116. Blythe A. Williams, Richard F. Kay, E. Christopher Kirk, and Callum F. Ross, "Darwinius masillae is a strepsirrhine—a reply to Franzen et al.," *Journal of Human Evolution* 59 (2010): 567–573. doi:10.1016/j.jhevol.2010.01.003. PMID:20188396.

117. Tim D. White, Gen Suwa, and Berhane Asfaw, "*Australopithecus ramidus*, a new species of early hominid from Aramis, Ethiopia," *Nature* 371 (1994): 306–312. doi:10.1038/371306a0. PMID:8090200.

118. Ann Gibbons, "In search of the first hominids," *Science* 295 (2002): 1214–1219. doi:10.1126/science.295.5558.1214. PMID:11847320.

119. Tim D. White, Berhane Asfaw, Yonas Beyene, Yohannes Haile-Selassie, C. Owen Lovejoy, Gen Suwa, and Giday WoldeGabriel, "*Ardipithecus ramidus* and the paleobiology of early hominids," *Science* 326 (2009): 64–86. doi:10.1126/science.1175802. PMID:19810190.

120. Lee R. Berger, Darryl J. de Ruiter, Steven E. Churchill, Peter Schmid, Kristian J. Carlson, Paul H. G. M. Dirks, and Job M. Kibii, "*Australopithecus sediba*: A new species of homo-like Australopith from South Africa," *Science* 328 (2010): 195–204. doi:10.1126/science.1184944. PMID:20378811.

121. Michael Balter, "Candidate human ancestor from South Africa sparks praise and debate," *Science* 328 (2010): 154–155. doi:10.1126/science.328.5975.154. PMID:20378782.

122. Ibid.

123. Lee R. Berger, "Introduction: The mosaic nature of *Australopithecus sediba*," *Science* 340 (2013): 163–165. doi:10.1126/science.340.6129.163. PMID:23580522.

124. Ann Gibbons, "A human smile and funny walk for *Australopithecus sediba*," *Science* 340 (2013): 132–133. doi:10.1126/science.340.6129.132. PMID:23580501.

125. Lee R. Berger, John Hawks, Darryl J. de Ruiter, Steven E. Churchill, Peter Schmid, Lucas K. Delezene, Tracy L. Kivell, Heather M. Garvin, Scott A. Williams, Jeremy M. DeSilva, Matthew M. Skinner, Charles M. Musiba, Noel Cameron, Trenton W. Holliday, William Harcourt-Smith1, Rebecca R. Ackermann, Markus Bastir, Barry Bogin, Debra Bolter, Juliet Brophy, Zachary D. Cofran, Kimberly A. Congdon, Andrew S. Deane, Mana Dembo, Michelle Drapeau, Marina C. Elliott, Elen M. Feuerriegel, Daniel Garcia-Martinez, David J. Green, Alia Gurtov, Joel D. Irish, Ashley Kruger, Myra F. Laird, Damiano Marchi, Marc R. Meyer, Shahed Nalla, Enquye W. Negash, Caley M. Orr, Davorka Radovcic, Lauren Schroeder, Jill E. Scott, Zachary Throckmorton, Matthew W. Tocheri, Caroline VanSickle, Christopher S. Walker, Pianpian Wei, and Bernhard Zipfel, "*Homo naledi*, a new species of the genus Homo from the Dinaledi Chamber, South Africa," *eLife* 4 (2015): e09560. doi:10.7554/eLife.09560. PMID:26354291.

126. Ewen Callaway, "Crowdsourcing digs up an early human species," *Nature* 525 (2015): 297–298. doi:10.1038/nature.2015.18305. PMID:26381960.

127. Jeffrey H. Schwartz and Ian Tattersall, "Defining the genus Homo," *Science* 349 (2015): 931–932. doi:10.1126/science.aac6182. PMID:26315422.

128. Ann Gauger, Douglas Axe, and Casey Luskin, *Science and Human Origins* (Seattle: Discovery Institute Press, 2012).

129. Nadia Drake, "Human evolution 101," *National Geographic* (September 11, 2015). http://news.nationalgeographic.com/2015/09/human-evolution-101.html.

130. Mary-Claire King and Allan C. Wilson, "Evolution at two levels in humans and chimpanzees," *Science* 188 (1975): 107–116. doi:10.1126/science.1090005. PMID:1090005.

131. International Human Genome Sequencing Consortium, "Finishing the euchromatic sequence of the human genome," *Nature* 431 (2004): 931–945. doi:10.1038/nature03001. PMID:15496913.

132. The Chimpanzee Sequencing and Analysis Consortium, "Initial sequence of the chimpanzee genome and comparison with the human genome," *Nature* 437 (2005): 69–87. doi:10.1038/nature04072. PMID:16136131.

133. Jon Cohen, "Relative differences: The myth of 1%," *Science* 316 (2007): 1836. doi:10.1126/science.316.5833.1836. PMID:17600195.

134. Jeffery P. Demuth, Tijl De Bie, Jason E. Stajich, Nello Cristianini, and Matthew W. Hahn, "The evolution of mammalian gene families," *PLoS One* 1 (2006): e85. doi:10.1371/journal.pone.0000085. PMID:17183716.

135. Jonathan Marks, *What It Means to Be 98% Chimpanzee* (Berkeley: University of California Press, 2002), 22.

Chapter 4 (Pages 81–97)

1. Francis Crick, quoted in Horace Freeland Judson, *The Eighth Day of Creation: The Makers of the Revolution in Biology* (New York: Simon & Schuster, 1979), 175.

2. Charles Darwin, *On the Origin of Species by Means of Natural Selection*, 1st ed. (London: John Murray, 1859), 134.

3. Charles Darwin, *The Variation of Animals and Plants Under Domestication* (London: John Murray, 1868), II:357–404.

4. August Weismann, *Essays Upon Heredity* (Oxford: Clarendon Press, 1889), I:423. http://www.esp.org/books/weismann/essays/facsimile/.

5. August Weismann, *The Germ-Plasm: A Theory of Heredity*, trans. W. Newton Parker and Harriet Rönnfeldt (New York: Charles Scribner's Sons, 1893). http://www.esp.org/books/weismann/germ-plasm/facsimile/.

6. Gregor Mendel, *Versuche über Pflanzen-Hybriden* (*Experiments in Plant Hybridization*). Read at meetings of the Natural History Society of Brünn (February 8 and March 8, 1865). http://www.mendelweb.org/Mendel.html.

7. William Bateson, Letter to Adam Sedgwick, April 18, 1905. https://www.dnalc.org/view/16195-gallery-5-william-bateson-letter-page-1.html.

8. Wilhelm Johannsen, *Elemente der Exakten Erblichkeitslehre* (Jena: Gustav Fischer, 1909), 124–127. https://ia902704.us.archive.org/4/items/elementederexakt00joha/elementederexakt00joha.pdf.

9. Wilhelm Johannsen, "The genotype conception of heredity," *American Naturalist* 45 (1911): 129–159. http://www.jstor.org/stable/2455747?seq=1#page_scan_tab_contents.

10. Nils Roll-Hansen, "Sources of Wilhelm Johannsen's genotype theory," *Journal of the History of Biology* (2009): 457–493. doi:10.1007/s10739-008-9166-8. PMID:20027784.

11. Walter S. Sutton, "On the morphology of the chromosome group in *Brachystola magna*," *Biological Bulletin* 4 (1902): 24–39. http://www.biolbull.org/content/4/1/24.full.pdf.

12. Thomas H. Morgan, Alfred H. Sturtevant, Hermann J. Muller, and Calvin B. Bridges, *The Mechanism of Mendelian Heredity* (New York: Henry Holt, 1915), viii. http://www.esp.org/books/morgan/mechanism/facsimile/index.html.

13. Frederick Griffith, "The significance of pneumococcal types," *Journal of Hygiene* (London) 27 (1928): 113–159. doi:10.1017/S0022172400031879. PMID:20474956.

14. Oswald T. Avery, Colin M. MacLeod, and Maclyn McCarty, "Studies on the chemical nature of the substance inducing transformation of pneumococcal types," *Journal of Experimental Medicine* 79 (1944): 137–158. doi:10.1084/jem.79.2.137. PMID:19871359.

15. James D. Watson and Francis H. C. Crick, "Molecular structure of nucleic acids: A structure for deoxyribose nucleic acid," *Nature* 171 (1953): 737–738. doi:10.1038/171737a0. PMID:13054692. http://annals.org/article.aspx?articleid=716280.

16. James D. Watson and Francis H. C. Crick, "Genetical implications of the structure of deoxyribonucleic acid," *Nature* 171 (1953): 964–967. doi:10.1038/171964b0. PMID:13063483. http://profiles.nlm.nih.gov/SC/B/B/Y/X/_/scbbyx.pdf.

17. Alvin M. Weinberg, "Messenger RNA: Origins of a discovery," *Nature* 414 (2001): 485.

18. Francis H. C. Crick, "On protein synthesis," *Symposia of the Society for Experimental Biology* 12 (1958): 138–163.

19. François Jacob and Jacques Monod, "Genetic regulatory mechanisms in the synthesis of proteins," *Journal of Molecular Biology* 3 (1961): 318–356. doi:10.1016/S0022-2836(61)80072-7.

20. Francois Jacob, *The Logic of Life*, trans. Betty E. Spillmann (Princeton: Princeton University Press, 1973), 3.

21. Jacques Monod, quoted in Judson, *The Eighth Day of Creation* (1979), 217.

22. Richard Dawkins, *The Selfish Gene* (New York: Oxford University Press, 1976), 2, 23, 25.

23. Helena Curtis and N. Sue Barnes, *Biology*, 5th ed. (New York: Worth Publishers, 1989), 974.

24. Ernst Mayr, *Animal Species and Evolution* (Cambridge, MA: Harvard University Press, 1963), 263.

25. Ernst Mayr, *Populations, Species, and Evolution: An Abridgement of Animal Species and Evolution* (Cambridge, MA: Harvard University Press, 1970), 162.

26. Sean B. Carroll, *Endless Forms Most Beautiful: The New Science of Evo Devo* (New York: W. W. Norton, 2005), 294.

27. Brian K. Hall, *Evolutionary Developmental Biology* (London: Chapman & Hall, 1992), 9.

28. Eric H. Davidson, "How embryos work: A comparative view of diverse modes of cell fate specification," *Development* 108 (1990): 365–389. PMID:2187672.

29. Carroll, *Endless Forms*, 295.

30. Ibid., 35.

31. Eric H. Davidson, *The Regulatory Genome: Gene Regulatory Networks in Development and Evolution* (Amsterdam: Academic Press, 2006), 27–28.

32. Hall, *Evolutionary Developmental Biology*, 150.

33. Conrad H. Waddington, "The epigenotype," *Endeavour* 1 (1942): 18–20.

34. Conrad H. Waddington, *An Introduction to Modern Genetics* (London: George Allen & Unwin, 1939), 156.

35. Julie C. Kiefer, "Epigenetics in development," *Developmental Dynamics* 236 (2007): 1144–1156. doi:10.1002/dvdy.21094. PMID:17304537.

36. Susan W. Herring, "Formation of the vertebrate face: Epigenetic and functional influences," *American Zoologist* 33 (1993): 472–483. doi:10.1093/icb/33.4.472.

37. Eva Jablonka and Marion J. Lamb, "The changing concept of epigenetics," *Annals of the New York Academy of Sciences* 981 (2002): 82–96. doi:10.1111/j.1749-6632.2002. tb04913.x. PMID:12547675.

38. Jan Sapp, *Beyond the Gene: Cytoplasmic Inheritance and the Struggle for Authority in Genetics* (Oxford: Oxford University Press, 1987).

39. Wei Sun, Xintian You, Andreas Gogol-Döring, Haihuai He, Yoshiaki Kise, Madlen Sohn, Tao Chen, Ansgar Klebes, Dietmar Schmucker, and Wei Chen, "Ultra-deep profiling of alternatively spliced *Drosophila Dscam* isoforms by circularization-assisted multi-segment sequencing," *EMBO Journal* 32 (2013): 2029–2038. doi:10.1038/ emboj.2013.144. PMID:23792425.

40. Yoseph Barash, John A. Calarco, Weijun Gao, Qun Pan, Xinchen Wang, Ofer Shai, Benjamin J. Blencowe, and Brendan J. Frey, "Deciphering the splicing code," *Nature* 465 (2010): 53–59. doi:10.1038/nature09000. PMID:20445623.

41. Sandra Garrett and Joshua J. C. Rosenthal, "RNA editing underlies temperature adaptation in K+ channels from polar octopuses," *Science* 335 (2012): 848–851. doi:10.1126/science.1212795. PMID:22223739.

42. Jae Hoon Bahn, Jaegyoon Ahn, Xianzhi Lin, Qing Zhang, Jae-Hyung Lee, Mete Civelek, and Xinshu Xiao, "Genomic analysis of ADAR1 binding and its involvement in multiple RNA processing pathways," *Nature Communications* 9 (2015): 6355. doi:10.1038/ ncomms7355. PMID:25751603.

43. Robert B. Russell and Geoffrey J. Barton, "Structural features can be unconserved in proteins with similar folds," *Journal of Molecular Biology* 244 (1994): 332–350. doi:10.1006/jmbi.1994.1733. PMID:7966343.

44. Alexey G. Murzin, "Metamorphic proteins," *Science* 320 (2008): 1725–1726. doi:10.1126/science.1158868. PMID:18583598.

45. Robert G. Spiro, "Protein glycosylation: Nature, distribution, enzymatic formation, and disease implications of glycopeptide bonds," *Glycobiology* 12 (2002): 43R-56R. doi:10.1093/glycob/12.4.43R. PMID:12042244.

46. Kelley W. Moremen, Michael Tiemeyer, and Alison V. Nairn, "Vertebrate protein glycosylation: Diversity, synthesis and function," *Nature Reviews Molecular Cell Biology* 13 (2012): 448–462. doi:10.1038/nrm3383. PMID:22722607.

47. Robert H. Singer, "RNA zipcodes for cytoplasmic addresses," *Current Biology* 3 (1993): 719–721. doi:10.1016/0960-9822(93)90079-4. PMID:15335871.

48. Donald M. Engelman, "Membranes are more mosaic than fluid," *Nature* 438 (2005): 578–580. doi:10.1038/nature04394. PMID:16319876.

49. George E. Palade, "Membrane biogenesis: An overview," *Methods in Enzymology* 96 (1983): xxix–lv. doi:10.1016/S0076-6879(83)96004-4. PMID:6656627.

50. Jonathan Wells, "Membrane patterns carry ontogenetic information that is specified independently of DNA," *Bio-Complexity* 2 (2014): 1–28. doi:10.5048/BIO-C.2014.2.

51. Thomas Cavalier-Smith, "The membranome and membrane heredity in development and evolution," in *Organelles, Genomes and Eukaryote Phylogeny*, ed. Robert P. Hirt and David S. Horner (Boca Raton, FL: CRC Press, 2004), 335–351.

52. Brian C. Goodwin, "What are the causes of morphogenesis?" *BioEssays* 3 (1985): 32–36. doi:10.1002/bies.950030109. PMID:3842578.

53. Gerry Webster and Brian Goodwin, *Form and Transformation: Generative and Relational Principles in Biology* (Cambridge: Cambridge University Press, 1996), 134.

54. Giuseppe Sermonti, *Why Is a Fly Not a Horse?* (Seattle, WA: Discovery Institute Press, 2005).

55. Lenny Moss, *What Genes Can't Do* (Cambridge, MA: MIT Press, 2003), xviii.

56. Ibid., 95–96.

57. Evelyn Fox Keller, *The Century of the Gene* (Cambridge, MA: Harvard University Press, 2000), 7–9.

58. Ibid., 100–101.

59. Denis Noble, "Genes and causation," *Philosophical Transactions of the Royal Society of London A* 366 (2008): 3001–3015. doi:10.1098/rsta.2008.0086. PMID:18559318.

60. Ibid.

61. Stuart A. Newman, "The demise of the gene," *Capitalism Nature Socialism* 24 (2013): 62–72. doi:10.1080/10455752.2012.759366.

62. Michael Lynch, *The Origins of Genome Architecture* (Sunderland, MA: Sinauer Associates, 2007), 370.

63. Jonathan Webb, "The gene's still selfish: Dawkins' famous idea turns 40," *BBC News* (May 24, 2016). http://www.bbc.com/news/science-environment-36358104.

64. Ellen Goldbaum, "Master orchestrator of the genome is discovered, stem cell scientists report," *ScienceDaily* (May 8, 2015). https://www.sciencedaily.com/releases/2015/05/150508110526.htm.

65. Christopher Terranova, Sridhar T. Narla, Yu-Wei Lee, Jonathan Bard, Abhirath Parikh, Ewa K. Stachowiak, Emmanuel S. Tzanakakis, Michael J. Buck, Barbara Birkaya, and Michal K. Stachowiak, "Global developmental gene programing involves a nuclear form of fibroblast growth factor receptor-1 (FGFR1)," *PLoS One* 10 (2015): e0123380. doi:10.1371/journal.pone.0123380. PMID:25923916.

66. Goldbaum, "Master orchestrator of the genome is discovered."

67. Liz Williams, "Scientists uncover gene architects responsible for body's blueprint," 7alter+Eliza Hall Institute of Medical Research (April 14, 2015). http://www.wehi.edu.au/news/scientists-uncover-gene-architects-responsible-body's-blueprint.

68. Bilal N. Sheikh, Natalie L. Downer, Belinda Phipson, Hannah K. Vanyai, Andrew J. Kueh, Davis J. McCarthy, Gordon K. Smyth, Tim Thomas, and Anne K. Voss, "MOZ and BMI1 play opposing roles during Hox gene activation in ES cells and in body segment identity specification in vivo," *Proceedings of the National Academy of Sciences* USA 112 (2015): 5437–5442. doi:10.1073/pnas.1422872112. PMID:25922517.

69. National Cancer Institute, "*BRCA1* and *BRCA2*: Cancer risk and genetic testing" (April 1, 2015). http://www.cancer.gov/about-cancer/causes-prevention/genetics/brca-fact-sheet#q1.

70. Dean H. Hamer, Stella Hu, Victoria L. Magnuson, Nan Hu, and Angela M. L. Pattatucci, "A linkage between DNA markers on the X chromosome and male sexual orientation," *Science* 261 (1993): 321–327. doi:10.1126/science.8332896. PMID:8332896.

71. Dean Hamer and Peter Copeland, *The Science of Desire: The Search for the Gay Gene and the Biology of Behavior* (New York: Simon & Schuster, 1994).

72. Neal Risch, Elizabeth Squires-Wheeler, and Bronya J. B. Keats, "Male sexual orientation and genetic evidence," *Science* 262 (1993): 2063–2065. doi:10.1126/science.8266107. PMID:8266107.

73. George Rice, Carol Anderson, Neil Risch, and George Ebers, "Male homosexuality: Absence of linkage to microsatellite markers at Xq28," *Science* 284 (1999): 665–667. doi:10.1126/science.284.5414.665. PMID:10213693.

74. Alan R. Sanders, Eden R. Martin, Gary W. Beecham, S. Guo, Khytam Dawood, G. Rieger, Judith A. Badner, Elliot S. Gershon, R. S. Krishnappa, A. B. Kolundzija, J. Duan, P. V. Gejman, and J. Michael Bailey, "Genome-wide scan demonstrates significant linkage for male sexual orientation," *Psychological Medicine* 45 (2015): 1379–1388. doi:10.1017/S0033291714002451. PMID:25399360.

75. Tuck C. Ngun, Weilong Guo, Negar M. Ghahramani, Kajori Purkayastha, Daniel Conn, Francisco J. Sánchez, Sven Bocklandt, Michael Q. Zhang, Christina M. Ramírez, Matteo Pellegrini, and Eric Vilain, "PgmNr 95: A novel predictive model of sexual orientation using epigenetic markers," American Society for Human Genetics Annual Meeting, Session 27 (Baltimore, MD; October 8, 2015). https://ep70.eventpilotadmin.com/web/page.php?page=IntHtml&project=ASHG15&id=150123267.

76. Nalini Padmanabhan, "Epigenetic algorithm accurately predicts male sexual orientation," American Society of Human Genetics (October 8, 2015). http://www.ashg.org/press/201510-sexual-orientation.html.

77. John Greally, "Over-interpreted epigenetics study of the week," *Blog of the Center for Epigenomics at the Albert Einstein College of Medicine* (October 9, 2015). http://epgntxeinstein.tumblr.com/post/130812695958/over-interpreted-epigenetics-study-of-the-week-2.

78. Ed Yong, "No, scientists have not found the 'gay gene,'" *The Atlantic* (October 10, 2015). http://www.theatlantic.com/science/archive/2015/10/no-scientists-have-not-found-the-gay-gene/410059/.

79. Dean H. Hamer, *The God Gene: How Faith Is Hardwired into Our Genes* (New York: Anchor Books, 2004).

80. John Horgan, "'Gene-whiz' science strikes again: Researchers discover a liberal gene," *Scientific American Blog Network* (October 29, 2010). http://blogs.scientificamerican.com/cross-check/gene-whiz-science-strikes-again-researchers-discover-a-liberal-gene/.

CHAPTER 5 (PAGES 99–114)

1. Charles Darwin, *On the Origin of Species by Means of Natural Selection*, 1st ed. (London: John Murray, 1859), 179, 184.

2. Francis Darwin and A. C. Seward, eds., *More Letters of Charles Darwin* (London: John Murray, 1903), I:162. http://darwin-online.org.uk/content/frameset?pageseq=205&itemID=F1548.1&viewtype=side.

3. Philip D. Gingerich, Neil A. Wells, Donald E. Russell, and S. M. Ibrahim Shah, "Origin of whales in epicontinental remnant seas: New evidence from the early

Eocene of Pakistan," *Science* 220 (1983): 403–406. doi:10.1126/science.220.4595.403. PMID:17831411.

4. Percival Davis, Dean H. Kenyon, and Charles B. Thaxton, *Of Pandas and People: The Central Question of Biological Origins*, 2nd ed. (Dallas, TX: Haughton Publishing, 1993), 101–102.

5. J. G. M. Thewissen, S. Taseer Hussain, and Muhammad Arif, "Fossil evidence for the origin of aquatic locomotion in archaeocete whales," *Science* 263 (1994): 210–212. doi:10.1126/science.263.5144.210. PMID:17839179.

6. Philip D. Gingerich, S. Mahmood Raza, Muhammad Arif, Mohammad Anwar, and Xiaoyuan Zhou, "New whale from the Eocene of Pakistan and the origin of cetacean swimming," *Nature* 368 (1994): 844–847. doi:10.1038/368844a0.

7. Stephen Jay Gould, "Hooking Leviathan by its past," *Natural History* 103 (May 1994): 8–14.

8. Sunil Bajpai and J. G. M. Thewissen, "A new, diminutive whale from Kachchh (Gujarat, India) and its implications for locomotor evolution of cetaceans," *Current Science* (New Delhi) 79 (2000): 1478–1482.

9. J. G. M. Thewissen, Lisa Noelle Cooper, Mark T. Clementz, Sunil Bajpai, and Brahma N. Tiwari, "Whales originated from aquatic artiodactyls in the Eocene epoch of India," *Nature* 450 (2007): 1190–1194. doi:10.1038/nature06343. PMID:18097400.

10. Philip D. Gingerich, Munir ul-Haq, Wighart von Koenigswald, William J. Sanders, B. Holly Smith, and Iyad S. Zalmout, "New protocetid whale from the middle Eocene of Pakistan: Birth on land, precocial development, and sexual dimorphism," *PLoS One* 4 (2009): e4366. doi:10.1371/journal.pone.0004366. PMID:19194487.

11. Kevin Padian, "The tale of the whale," *Reports of the National Center for Science Education* 17:6 (1997): 26–27. http://ncse.com/rncse/17/6/tale-whale.

12. Gingerich, "New protocetid whale," 14.

13. J. G. M. Thewissen, *The Walking Whales: From Land to Water in Eight Million Years* (Berkeley: University of California Press, 2014), 169.

14. J. G. M. Thewissen and Sunil Bajpai, "Whale origins as a poster child for macroevolution," *BioScience* 15 (2001): 1037–1049. doi:10.1641/0006-3568(2001)051[1037:WOAAPC]2.0.CO;2.

15. Kate Wong, "The mammals that conquered the seas," pp. 182–191 in *Evolution: A Scientific American Reader* (Chicago: University of Chicago Press, 2006), 189.

16. Thewissen, "Whales originated from aquatic artiodactyls," 1190.

17. Everhard J. Slijper, *Whales*, trans. A. J. Pomerans, 2nd ed. (Ithaca, NY: Cornell University Press, 1962), 100–101, 108.

18. Frank E. Fish, John T. Beneski, and Darlene R. Ketten, "Examination of the three-dimensional geometry of cetacean flukes using computed tomography scans: Hydrodynamic implications," *Anatomical Record* 290 (2007): 614–623. doi:10.1002/ar.20546. PMID:17516428.

19. Slijper, *Whales*, 151.

20. Gregory S. Schorr, Erin A. Falcone, David J. Moretti, and Russel D. Andrews, "First long-term behavioral records from Cuvier's beaked whales (*Ziphius cavirostris*) reveal record-breaking dives," *PLoS One* 9 (2014): e92633. doi:10.1371/journal.pone.0092633. PMID:24670984.

21. Slijper, *Whales*, 139–140.

22. Richard E. Brown and James P. Butler, "The absolute necessity of chest-wall collapse during diving in breath-hold diving mammals," *Aquatic Mammals* 26 (2000): 26–32.

23. Sam H. Ridgway, B. L. Scronce, and John Kanwisher, "Respiration and deep diving in the bottlenose porpoise," *Science* 166 (1969): 1651–1654. doi:10.1126/science.166.3913.1651. PMID:5360592.

24. Konrad J. Falke, Roger D. Hill, Jesper Qvist, Robert C. Schneider, Michael Guppy, Graham C. Liggins, Peter W. Hochachka, Richard E. Elliott, and Warren M. Zapol, "Seal lungs collapse during free diving: Evidence from arterial nitrogen tensions," *Science* 229 (1985): 556–558. doi:10.1126/science.4023700. PMID:4023700.

25. Birgitte I. McDonald and Paul J. Ponganis, "Lung collapse in the diving sea lion: Hold the nitrogen and save the oxygen," *Biology Letters* 8 (2012): 1047–1049. doi:10.1098/rsbl.2012.0743. PMID:22993241.

26. Shawn R. Noren and Terrie M. Williams, "Body size and skeletal muscle myoglobin of cetaceans: Adaptations for maximizing dive duration," *Comparative Biochemistry and Physiology* A 126 (2000): 181–191. doi:10.1016/S1095-6433(00)00182-3. PMID:10936758.

27. Slijper, *Whales*, 133.

28. Per F. Scholander, "The master switch of life," *Scientific American* (December, 1963): 92–106.

29. Roger G. Spragg, Paul J. Ponganis, James J. Marsh, Gunnar A. Rau, and Wolfgang Bernhard, "Surfactant from diving aquatic mammals," *Journal of Applied Physiology* 96 (2004): 1626–1632. doi:10.1152/japplphysiol.00898.2003. PMID:14688033.

30. Natalie J. Miller, Anthony D. Postle, Sandra Orgeig, Grielof Koster, and Christopher B. Daniels, "The composition of pulmonary surfactant from diving mammals," *Respiratory Physiology and Neurobiology* 152 (2006): 152–168. doi:10.1016/j.resp.2005.08.001. PMID:16140043.

31. Sentiel A. Rommel, D. Ann Pabst, William A. McLellan, James G. Mead, and Charles W. Potter, "Anatomical evidence for a countercurrent heat exchanger associated with dolphin testes," *Anatomical Record* 232 (1992): 150–156. doi:10.1002/ar.1092320117. PMID:1536461.

32. Sentiel A. Rommel, D. Ann Pabst, and William A. McLellan, "Reproductive thermoregulation in marine mammals," *American Scientist* 86 (1998): 440–448. doi:10.1511/1998.5.440.

33. Slijper, Whales, 381–382.

34. Genevieve Johnson, Alexandros Frantzis, Chris Johnson, Voula Alexiadou, Sam H. Ridgway, and Peter T. Madsen, "Evidence that sperm whale (*Physeter macrocephalus*) calves suckle through their mouth," *Marine Mammal Science* 26 (2010): 990–996. doi:10.1111/j.1748-7692.2010.00385.x.

35. Slijper, *Whales*, 382–383, 386.

36. Thewissen, *Walking Whales*, 186–187.

37. Heinz-Georg Belting, Cooduvalli S. Shashikant, and Frank H. Ruddle, "Modification of expression and cis-regulation of *Hoxc8* in the evolution of diverged axial morphology," *Proceedings of the National Academy of Sciences USA* 95 (1998): 2355–2360. doi:10.1073/pnas.95.5.2355. PMID:9482889.

38. Cooduvalli S. Shashikant, Chang B. Kim, Marc A. Borbély, Wayne C. H. Wang, and Frank H. Ruddle, "Comparative studies on mammalian *Hoxc8* early enhancer sequence reveal a baleen whale-specific deletion of a cis-acting element," *Proceedings of the National Academy of Sciences USA* 95 (1998): 15446–15451. doi:10.1073/pnas.95.26.15446. PMID:9860988.

39. Lars Bejder and Brian K. Hall, "Limbs in whales and limblessness in other vertebrates: Mechanisms of evolutionary and developmental transformation and loss," *Evolution and Development* 4 (2002): 445–458. doi:10.1046/j.1525-142X.2002.02033.x. PMID:12492145.

40. Robert W. Meredith, John Gatesy, Joyce Cheng and Mark S. Springer, "Pseudogenization of the tooth gene enamelysin (*MMP20*) in the common ancestor of extant baleen whales," *Proceedings of the Royal Society of London B* 278 (2011): 993–1002. doi:10.1098/rspb.2010.1280. PMID:20861053.

41. Ping Feng, Jinsong Zheng, Stephen J Rossiter, Ding Wang, and Huabin Zhao, "Massive losses of taste receptor genes in toothed and baleen whales," *Genome Biology and Evolution* 6 (2014): 1254–1265. doi:10.1093/gbe/evu095. PMID:24803572.

42. Shixia Xu, Yuan Chen, Yuefeng Cheng, Dan Yang, Xuming Zhou, Junxiao Xu, Kaiya Zhou, and Guang Yang, "Positive selection at the ASPM gene coincides with brain size enlargements in cetaceans," *Proceedings of the Royal Society of London B* 279 (2012): 4433–4440. doi:10.1098/rspb.2012.1729. PMID:22977148.

43. Stephen H. Montgomery, Nicholas I. Mundy, and Robert A. Barton, "*ASPM* and mammalian brain evolution: A case study in the difficulty in making macroevolutionary inferences about gene-phenotype associations," *Proceedings of the Royal Society of London B* 281 (2014): 20131743. doi:10.1098/rspb.2013.1743. PMID:24452019.

44. Morris Agaba, Edson Ishengoma, Webb C. Miller, Barbara C. McGrath, Chelsea N. Hudson, Oscar C. Bedoya Reina, Aakrosh Ratan, Rico Burhans, Rayan Chikhi, Paul Medvedev, Craig A. Praul, Lan Wu-Cavener, Brendan Wood, Heather Robertson, Linda Penfold, and Douglas R. Cavener, "Giraffe genome sequence reveals clues to its unique morphology and physiology," *Nature Communications* 7 (2016): 11519. doi:10.1038/NCOMMS11519. PMID:27187213.

45. Wolf-Ekkehard Lönnig, *The Evolution of the Long-Necked Giraffe (Giraffa camelopardalis L.): What do we really know? Testing the Theories of Gradualism, Macromutation, and Intelligent Design* (Münster, Germany:Verlagshaus Monsenstein und Vannerdat OHG, 2011).

46. John W. Drake, Brian Charlesworth, Deborah Charlesworth, and James F. Crow, "Rates of spontaneous mutation," *Genetics* 148 (1998): 1667–1686. PMID:9560386.

47. Rick Durrett and Deena Schmidt, "Waiting for two mutations: With applications to regulatory sequence evolution and the limits of Darwinian evolution," *Genetics* 180 (2008): 1501–1509. doi:10.1534/genetics.107.082610. PMID:18791261.

48. Richard V. Sternberg, "The problem of whale origins," debate with Stephen C. Meyer, Donald R. Prothero, and Michael Shermer at Saban Theater, Beverly Hills, CA (November 30, 2009), 36:50–50:20. https://www.youtube.com/watch?v=lzwHqqMMSaU.

49. Mónica R. Buono, Marta S. Fernández, Marcelo A. Reguero, Sergio A. Marenssi, Sergio N. Santillana, and Thomas Mörs, "Eocene Basilosaurid Whales from the La Meseta

Formation, Marambio (Seymour) Island, Antarctica," *Ameghiniana* 53 (2016): 296–315 doi:10.5710/AMGH.02.02.2016.2922.

49. "An unbearable rush: Antarctic whale fossil poses a challenge to evolution that won't go away," *Evolution News & Views* (November 16, 2016). http://www.evolutionnews. org/2016/11/an_unbearable_r_1103292.html.

Chapter 6 (Pages 115–130)

1. Charles R. Darwin, *On the Origin of Species by Means of Natural Selection*, 1st ed. (London: John Murray, 1859), 168, 455–456.

2. Ibid., 451–452.

3. Charles R. Darwin, *The Descent of Man and Selection in Relation to Sex* (London: John Murray, 1871), I:17–18, 32.

4. Ibid., 27.

5. Richard J. A. Berry, "The true caecal apex, or the vermiform appendix: Its minute and comparative anatomy," *Journal of Anatomy and Physiology* 35 (1900): 83–100. PMID:17232459.

6. Pedro Gorgollón, "The normal human appendix: A light and electron microscopic study," *Journal of Anatomy* 126 (1978): 87–101. PMID:649505.

7. Dale E. Bockman, "Functional histology of appendix," *Archivum Histologicum Japonicum* 46 (1983): 271–292. doi:10.1679/aohc.46.271. PMID:6357136.

8. Kohtaro Fujihashi, Jerry R. McGhee, Cummins Lue, Kenneth W. Beagley, Tetsuya Taga, Toshio Hirano, Tadamitsu Kishimoto, Jiri Mestecky, and Hiroshi Kiyono, "Human appendix B cells naturally express receptors for and respond to interleukin 6 with selective IgA1 and IgA2 synthesis," *Journal of Clinical Investigation* 88 (1991): 248–252. doi:10.1172/JCI115284. PMID:2056119.

9. Giacomo Azzali, "Three-dimensional and ultrastructural aspects of the lymphatic vascularization of the vermiform appendix," *Journal of Submicroscopic Cytology and Pathology* 30 (1998): 545–553. PMID:9851063.

10. Aliya Zahid, "The vermiform appendix: Not a useless organ," *Journal of the College of Physicians and Surgeons—Pakistan* 14 (2004): 256–258. PMID:15228837.

11. R. Randal Bollinger, Andrew S. Barbas, Errol L. Bush, Shu S. Lin, and William Parker, "Biofilms in the large bowel suggest an apparent function of the human vermiform appendix," *Journal of Theoretical Biology* 249 (2007): 826–831. doi:10.1016/j. jtbi.2007.08.032. PMID:17936308.

12. Gene Y. Im, Rani J. Modayil, Cheng T. Lin, Steven J. Geier, Douglas S. Katz, Martin Feuerman, and James H. Grendell, "The appendix may protect against *Clostridium difficile* recurrence," *Clinical Gastroenterology and Hepatology* 9 (2011): 1072–1077. doi:10.1016/j. cgh.2011.06.006. PMID:21699818.

13. Michel Laurin, Mary Lou Everett, and William Parker, "The cecal appendix: One more immune component with a function disturbed by post-industrial culture," *Anatomical Record* 294 (2011): 567–579. doi:10.1002/ar.21357. PMID:21370495.

14. Heather F. Smith, William Parker, Sanet H. Kotzé, and Michel Laurin, "Morphological evolution of the mammalian cecum and cecal appendix," *Comptes Rendus Palevol* 16 (2017): 39–57. doi:10.1016/j.crpv.2016.06.001.

15. Michael Shermer, *Why Darwin Matters: The Case Against Intelligent Design* (New York: Henry Holt, 2006), 18.

16. University of California Museum of Paleontology, *Understanding Evolution* (2016). http://evolution.berkeley.edu/evolibrary/article/0_0_0/mantisshrimp_10.

17. Kenneth A. Mason, Jonathan B. Losos, and Susan R. Singer, Raven and Johnson's *Biology*, 10th ed. (New York: McGraw-Hill, 2014), 429–430.

18. Steven R. Scadding, "Do 'vestigial organs' provide evidence for evolution?" *Evolutionary Theory* 5 (1981): 173–176.

19. Bruce G. Naylor, "Vestigial organs are evidence of evolution," *Evolutionary Theory* 6 (1982): 91–96.

20. Steven R. Scadding, "Vestigial organs do not provide scientific evidence for evolution," *Evolutionary Theory* 6 (1982): 171–173.

21. Reed A. Cartwright and Douglas Theobald, "Citing Scadding (1981) and misunderstanding vestigiality," *TalkOrigins Archive* (December 8, 2003). http://www.talkorigins.org/faqs/quotes/scadding.html.

22. Jerry A. Coyne, *Why Evolution Is True* (New York: Viking Penguin, 2009), 60–62.

23. Jonathan Wells, "The myth of vestigial organs and bad design," *Evolution News & Views* (May 4, 2009). http://www.evolutionnews.org/2009/05/the_myth_of_vestigial_organs_a020111.html.

24. Matthew Dean and James Dines, "Whale sex: It's all in the hips," *ScienceDaily* (September 8, 2014). http://www.sciencedaily.com/releases/2014/09/140908121536.htm.

25. Paul Z. Myers, "Vestigial: Learn what it means!" *Pharyngula*, accesssed September 23, 2014. http://scienceblogs.com/pharyngula/2014/09/23/vestigial-learn-what-it-means/.

26. Jason T. K. Woon, Vivekanandan Perumal, Jean-Yves Maigne, and Mark D. Stringer, "CT morphology and morphometry of the normal adult coccyx," *European Spine Journal* 22 (2013): 863–870. doi:10.1007/s00586-012-2595-2. PMID:23192732.

27. Darwin, *Descent of Man*, 17, 29.

28. Anh H. Dao and Martin G. Netsky, "Human tails and pseudotails," *Human Pathology* 15 (1984): 449–453. doi:10.1016/S0046-8177(84)80079-9. PMID:6373560.

29. Ibid., 449.

30. Sarah J. Gaskill and Arthur E. Marlin, "Neuroectodermal appendages: The human tail explained," *Pediatric Neuroscience* 15 (1989): 95–99. doi:10.1159/000120450. PMID:2635301.

31. Fabiola Müller and Ronan O'Rahilly, "The primitive streak, the caudal eminence and related structures in staged human embryos," *Cells, Tissues, Organs* 177 (2004): 2–20. doi:10.1159/000078423. PMID:15237191.

32. Daniel J. Donovan and Robert C. Pedersen, "Human tail with noncontiguous intraspinal lipoma and spinal cord tethering: Case report and embryologic discussion," *Pediatric Neurosurgery* 41 (2005): 35–40. doi:10.1159/000084863. PMID:15886511.

33. Michael Egnor, "The myth of human 'tails': A physician and surgeon's perspective," *Evolution News & Views* (May 23, 2014). http://www.evolutionnews.org/2014/05/the_myth_of_hum085921.html.

34. Andrew McDiarmid, "'Should Christians embrace Darwin?' An evening with Karl Giberson and Stephen Meyer," *Evolution News & Views* (April 11, 2014). http://www.evolutionnews.org/2014/04/should_christia084351.html.

35. Karl W. Giberson, "My debate with an 'intelligent design' theorist," *The Daily Beast* (April 21, 2014). http://www.thedailybeast.com/articles/2014/04/21/my-debate-with-an-intelligent-design-theorist.html.

36. David Klinghoffer, "So, here's the source of Karl Giberson's tailed-baby photo," *Evolution News & Views* (May 29, 2014). http://www.evolutionnews.org/2014/05/heres_what_seem086161.html.

37. David Klinghoffer, "Karl Giberson apologizes for photoshopped image of tailed baby," *Evolution News & Views* (June 6, 2014). http://www.evolutionnews.org/2014/06/karl_giberson_a086461.html.

38. Francis H. C. Crick, "On protein synthesis," *Symposia of the Society for Experimental Biology* 12 (1958): 138–163. PMID:13580867.

39. Alexandre E. Peluffo, "The 'genetic program': Behind the genesis of an influential metaphor," *Genetics* 200 (2015): 685–696. doi:10.1534/genetics.115.178418. PMID:26170444.

40. Susumu Ohno, "So much 'junk' DNA in our genome," *Brookhaven Symposia in Biology* 23 (1972): 366–70. PMID:5065367. http://www.junkdna.com/ohno.html.

41. Richard Dawkins, *The Selfish Gene* (New York: Oxford University Press, 1976), 47.

42. W. Ford Doolittle and Carmen Sapienza, "Selfish genes, the phenotype paradigm and genome evolution," *Nature* 284 (1980): 601–603. doi:10.1038/284601a0. PMID:6245369.

43. Leslie E. Orgel and Francis H. C. Crick, "Selfish DNA: the ultimate parasite," *Nature* 284 (1980): 604–607. doi:10.1038/284604a0. PMID:7366731.

44. Thomas Cavalier-Smith, "How selfish is DNA?" *Nature* 285 (1980): 617–618. doi:10.1038/285617a0. PMID:7393317.

45. Gabriel Dover, "Ignorant DNA?" *Nature* 285 (1980): 618–620. doi:10.1038/285618a0. PMID:7393318.

46. Kenneth R. Miller, "Life's Grand Design," *Technology Review* 97 (February–March 1994): 24–32. http://www.millerandlevine.com/km/evol/lgd/index.html.

47. Douglas J. Futuyma, *Evolution* (Sunderland, MA: Sinauer Associates, 2005), 48–49.

48. Shermer, *Why Darwin Matters*, 74–75.

49. Francis S. Collins, *The Language of God: A Scientist Presents Evidence for Belief* (New York: Free Press, 2006), 136–139.

50. Philip Kitcher, *Living With Darwin: Evolution, Design, and the Future of Faith* (New York: Oxford, 2007), 57–58.

51. ENCODE Project Consortium, "Identification and analysis of functional elements in 1% of the human genome by the ENCODE pilot project," *Nature* 447 (2007): 799–816. doi:10.1038/nature05874. PMID:17571346.

52. Yiping He, Bert Vogelstein, Victor E. Velculescu, Nickolas Papadopoulos, and Kenneth W. Kinzler, "The antisense transcriptomes of human cells," *Science* 322 (2008): 1855–1857. doi:10.1126/science.1163853. PMID:19056939.

53. Jonathan Wells, *The Myth of Junk DNA* (Seattle: Discovery Institute Press, 2011), 47–69.

54. Elizabeth A. Shepard, Pritpal Chandan, Milena Stevanovic-Walker, Mina Edwards, and Ian R. Phillips, "Alternative promoters and repetitive DNA elements define the species-dependent tissue- specific expression of the FMO1 genes of human and mouse," *Biochemical Journal* 406 (2007): 491–499. doi:10.1042/BJ20070523. PMID:17547558.

55. Ryan D. Walters, Jennifer F. Kugel, and James A. Goodrich, "InvAluable junk: the cellular impact and function of *Alu* and B2 RNAs," *IUBMB Life* 61 (2009): 831–837. doi:10.1002/iub.227. PMID:19621349.

56. Jonathan P. Stoye, "Proviral protein provides placental function," *Proceedings of the National Academy of Sciences USA* 106 (2009): 11827–11828. doi:10.1073/pnas.0906295106. PMID:19617545.

57. Nature ENCODE Explorer (2016). http://www.nature.com/encode/#/threads.

58. ENCODE Project Consortium, "An integrated encyclopedia of DNA elements in the human genome," *Nature* 489 (2012): 57–74. doi:10.1038/nature11247. PMID:22955616.

59. Fan Lai, Ulf A. Orom, Matteo Cesaroni, Malte Beringer, Dylan J. Taatjes, Gerd A. Blobel, and Ramin Shiekhattar, "Activating RNAs associate with Mediator to enhance chromatin architecture and transcription," *Nature* 494 (2013): 497–501. doi:10.1038/nature11884. PMID:23417068.

60. Pei Han and Ching-Pin Chang, "Long non-coding RNA and chromatin remodeling," *RNA Biology* 12 (2015): 1094–1098. doi:10.1080/15476286.2015.1063770. PMID:26177256.

61. Sofia Quinodoz and Mitchell Guttman, "Long noncoding RNAs: an emerging link between gene regulation and nuclear organization," *Trends in Cell Biology* 24 (2014): 651–663. doi:10.1016/j.tcb.2014.08.009. PMID:25441720.

62. Ezgi Hacisuleyman, Loyal A. Goff, Cole Trapnell, Adam Williams, Jorge Henao-Mejia, Lei Sun, Patrick McClanahan, David G. Hendrickson, Martin Sauvageau, David R. Kelley, Michael Morse, Jesse Engreitz, Eric S. Lander, Mitchell Guttman, Harvey F. Lodish, Richard Flavell, Arjun Raj, and John L. Rinn, "Topological organization of multichromosomal regions by the long intergenic noncoding RNA Firre," *Nature Structural and Molecular Biology* 21 (2014): 198–206. doi:10.1038/nsmb.2764. PMID:24463464.

63. Zheng Chen, "Progress and prospects of long noncoding RNAs in lipid homeostasis," *Molecular Metabolism* 5 (2015): 164–170. doi:10.1016/j.molmet.2015.12.003. PMID:26977388.

64. Shaohai Xu, Peng Chen, and Lei Sun, "Regulatory networks of non-coding RNAs in brown/beige adipogenesis," *Bioscience Reports* 35 (2015): e00262. doi:10.1042/BSR20150155. PMID:26283634.

65. Hong Zan and Paolo Casali, "Epigenetics of peripheral B-cell differentiation and the antibody response," *Frontiers in Immunology* 6 (2015): 631. doi:10.3389/fimmu.2015.00631. PMID:26697022.

66. Jing Ouyang, Jiayue Hu, and Ji-Long Chen, "lncRNAs regulate the innate immune response to viral infection," *Wiley Interdisciplinary Reviews RNA* 7 (2016): 129–143. doi:10.1002/wrna.1321. PMID:26667656.

216   Chapter 6 (Pages 115–130)

67. Wenwen Jia, Wen Chen, and Jiuhong Kang, "The functions of microRNAs and long non-coding RNAs in embryonic and induced pluripotent stem cells," *Genomics Proteomics Bioinformatics* 11 (2013): 275–283. doi:10.1016/j.gpb.2013.09.004. PMID:24096129.

68. Alessandro Rosa and Monica Ballarino, "Long noncoding RNA regulation of pluripotency," *Stem Cells International* 2016 (2016): 1797692. doi:10.1155/2016/1797692. PMID:26697072.

69. Thomas C. Roberts, Kevin V. Morris, and Matthew J. A. Wood, "The role of long non-coding RNAs in neurodevelopment, brain function and neurological disease," *Philosophical Transactions of the Royal Society of London B* 369 (2014): 20130507. doi:10.1098/rstb.2013.0507. PMID:25135968.

70. Laura Stappert, Beate Roese-Koerner, and Oliver Brüstle, "The role of microRNAs in human neural stem cells, neuronal differentiation and subtype specification," *Cell and Tissue Research* 359 (2015): 47–64. doi:10.1007/s00441-014-1981-y. PMID:25172833.

71. Mohammad Q. Hassan, Coralee E. Tye, Gary S. Stein, and Jane B. Lian, "Non-coding RNAs: Epigenetic regulators of bone development and homeostasis," *Bone* 81 (2015): 746–756. doi:10.1016/j.bone.2015.05.026. PMID:26039869.

72. Nguyen P. T. Huynh, Britta Anderson, Farshid Guilak, and Audrey McAlinden, "Emerging roles for long non-coding RNAs in skeletal biology and disease," *Connective Tissue Research* (June 2, 2016): 1–26. doi:10.1080/03008207.2016.1194406. PMID:27254479.

73. Mao Nie, Zhong-Liang Deng, Jianming Liu, and Da-Zhi Wang, "Noncoding RNAs, emerging regulators of skeletal muscle development and diseases," *Biomed Research International* 2015 (2015): 676575. doi:10.1155/2015/676575. PMID:26258142.

74. B. Cardinali, M. Cappella, C. Provenzano, J. M. Garcia-Manteiga, D. Lazarevic, D. Cittaro, F. Martelli, and G. Falcone, "MicroRNA-222 regulates muscle alternative splicing through Rbm24 during differentiation of skeletal muscle cells," *Cell Death and Disease* 7 (2016): e2086. doi:10.1038/cddis.2016.10. PMID:26844700.

75. Alexander F. Palazzo and T. Ryan Gregory, "The case for junk DNA," *PLoS Genetics* 10 (2014): e1004351. doi:10.1371/journal.pgen.1004351. PMID:24809441.

76. Olga A. Vakhrusheva, Georgii A. Bazykin, and Alexey S. Kondrashov, "Genome-level analysis of selective constraint without apparent sequence conservation," *Genome Biology and Evolution* 5 (2013): 532–541. doi:10.1093/gbe/evt023. PMID:23418180.

77. Ken C. Pang, Martin C. Frith, and John S. Mattick, "Rapid evolution of noncoding RNAs: Lack of conservation does not mean lack of function," *Trends in Genetics* 22 (2006): 1–5. doi:10.1016/j.tig.2005.10.003. PMID:16290135.

78. W. Ford Doolittle, "Is junk DNA bunk? A critique of ENCODE," *Proceedings of the National Academy of Sciences USA* 110 (2013): 5294–5300. doi:10.1073/pnas.1221376110. PMID:23479647.

79. Manolis Kellis, Barbara Wold, Michael P. Snyder, Bradley E. Bernstein, Anshul Kundaje, Georgi K. Marinovc, Lucas D. Ward, Ewan Birney, Gregory E. Crawford, Job Dekker, Ian Dunham, Laura L. Elnitski, Peggy J. Farnham, Elise A. Feingold, Mark Gerstein, Morgan C. Giddings, David M. Gilbert, Thomas R. Gingeras, Eric D. Green, Roderic Guigo, Tim Hubbard, Jim Kent, Jason D. Lieb, Richard M. Myers, Michael J. Pazin, Bing Ren, John A. Stamatoyannopoulos, Zhiping Weng, Kevin P. White, and Ross C. Hardison, "Defining functional DNA elements in the human genome,"

Proceedings of the National Academy of Sciences USA 111 (2014): 6131–6138. doi:10.1073/pnas.1318948111. PMID:24753594.

80. Tyler D. P. Brunet and W. Ford Doolittle, "Getting 'function' right," *Proceedings of the National Academy of Sciences USA* 111 (2014): E3365. doi:10.1073/pnas.1409762111. PMID:25107292.

81. Dan Graur, Yichen Zheng, Nicholas Price, Ricardo B.R. Azevedo, Rebecca A. Zufall, and Eran Elhaik, "On the immortality of television sets: 'Function' in the human genome according to the evolution-free gospel of ENCODE," *Genome Biology and Evolution* 5 (2013): 578–90. doi:10.1093/gbe/evt028. PMID:23431001.

82. Dan Graur, "How to assemble a human genome," lecture at the University of Houston (December 2013), slides 16, 19. http://www.slideshare.net/dangraur1953/update-version-of-the-smbesesbe-lecture-on-encode-junk-dna-graur-december-2013.

83. Arthur Keith, "The functional nature of the caecum and appendix," *British Medical Journal* 2 (1912): 1599–1602. PMID:20766420.

CHAPTER 7 (PAGES 131–148)

1. Charles Darwin, *On the Origin of Species by Means of Natural Selection*, 1st ed. (London: John Murray, 1859), 186–187.

2. Dan-Erik Nilsson, Lars Gislén, Melissa M. Coates, Charlotta Skogh, and Anders Garm, "Advanced optics in a jellyfish eye," *Nature* 435 (2005): 201–205. doi:10.1038/nature03484. PMID:15889091.

3. Stephen R. Wilk, "The eye in the spiral: Animals with pinhole visual systems," *Optics & Photonics* (June, 2008). http://www.osa-opn.org/Content/ViewFile.aspx?id=11013.

4. Luitfried von Salvini-Plawen and Ernst Mayr, "On the evolution of photoreceptors and eyes," *Evolutionary Biology* 10 (1977): 207–263. doi:10.1007/978-1-4615-6953-4_4.

5. Euan Clarkson, Riccardo Levi-Setti, and Gabor Horváth, "The eyes of trilobites: The oldest preserved visual system," *Arthropod Structure & Development* 35 (2006): 247–259. doi:10.1016/j.asd.2006.08.002. PMID:18089074.

6. Riccardo Levi-Setti, *Trilobites*, 2nd ed. (Chicago: The University of Chicago Press, 1993), 29.

7. Michael S. Y. Lee, James B. Jago, Diego C. García-Bellido, Gregory D. Edgecombe, James G. Gehling, and John R. Paterson, "Modern optics in exceptionally preserved eyes of Early Cambrian arthropods from Australia," *Nature* 474 (2011): 631–634. doi:10.1038/nature10097. PMID:21720369.

8. Fangchen Zhao, David J. Bottjer, Shixue Hu, Zongjun Yin, and Maoyan Zhu, "Complexity and diversity of eyes in Early Cambrian ecosystems," *Scientific Reports* 3 (2013): 2751. doi:10.1038/srep02751. PMID:24067397.

9. Jun-Yuan Chen, David J. Bottjer, Paola Oliveri, Stephen Q. Dornbos, Feng Gao, Seth Ruffins, Huimei Chi, Chia-Wei Li, and Eric H. Davidson, "Small bilaterian fossils from 40 to 55 million years before the Cambrian," *Science* 305 (2004): 218–222. doi:10.1126/science.1099213. PMID:15178752.

10. Dan-Eric Nilsson, "Eye evolution: a question of genetic promiscuity," *Current Opinion in Neurobiology* 14 (2004): 407–414. doi:10.1016/j.conb.2004.07.004. PMID:15321060.

11. Stefan Bengtson, John A. Cunningham, Chongyu Yin, and Philip C. J. Donoghue, "A merciful death for the 'earliest bilaterian,' *Vernanimalcula*," *Evolution and Development* 14 (2012): 421–427. doi:10.1111/j.1525-142X.2012.00562.x. PMID:22947315.

12. Rebecca Quiring, Uwe Walldorf, Urs Kloter, and Walter J. Gehring, "Homology of the *eyeless* gene of *Drosophila* to the *Small eye* gene in mice and *Aniridia* in humans," *Science* 265 (1994): 785–789. doi:10.1126/science.7914031. PMID:7914031.

13. Georg Halder, Patrick Callaerts, and Walter J. Gehring, "Induction of ectopic eyes by targeted expression of the *eyeless* gene in *Drosophila*," *Science* 267 (1995): 1788–1792. doi:10.1126/science.7892602. PMID:7892602.

14. Stanislav I. Tomarev, Patrick Callaerts, Lidia Kos, Rina Zinovieva, Georg Halder, Walter J. Gehring, and Joram Piatigorsky, "Squid Pax-6 and eye development," *Proceedings of the National Academy of Sciences USA* 94 (1997): 2421–2426. doi:10.1073/pnas.94.6.2421. PMID:9122210.

15. Yasuko Onuma, Shuji Takahashi, Makoto Asashima, Shoichiro Kurata, and Walter J. Gehring, "Conservation of Pax 6 function and upstream activation by *Notch* signaling in eye development of frogs and flies," *Proceedings of the National Academy of Sciences USA* 99 (2002): 2020–2025. doi:10.1073/pnas.022626999. PMID:11842182.

16. Halder, Callaerts, and Gehring, "Induction of ectopic eyes," 1788.

17. Walter J. Gehring and Kazuho Ikeo, "*Pax6*: mastering eye morphogenesis and eye evolution," *Trends in Genetics* 15 (1999): 371–377. doi:10.1016/S0168-9525(99)01776-X. PMID:10461206.

18. Dan-Eric Nilsson and Susanne Pelger, "A pessimistic estimate of the time required for an eye to evolve," *Proceedings of the Royal Society of London B* 256 (1994): 53–58. doi:10.1098/rspb.1994.0048. PMID:8008757.

19. Richard Dawkins, "Climbing Mount Improbable," lecture at the Royal Institution of London (1991), starting at 31:50. http://richannel.org/christmas-lectures/1991/richard-dawkins#/christmas-lectures-1991-richard-dawkins--climbing-mount-improbable.

20. Dawkins, "Climbing Mount Improbable," 32:26–33:11.

21. Richard Dawkins, *River out of Eden* (New York: Basic Books, 1995), 79–80.

22. Vincent Torley, "Could the eye have evolved by natural selection in a geological blink?" *Uncommon Descent* (March 18, 2013). http://www.uncommondescent.com/intelligent-design/could-the-eye-have-evolved-by-natural-selection-in-a-geological-blink/.

23. Nilsson and Pelger, "A pessimistic estimate," 56.

24. Ibid., 58.

25. David Berlinski, "A Scientific Scandal," Discovery Institute (2003). http://www.discovery.org/a/1509.

26. Mark Ridley, *Evolution*, 3rd ed. (Chichester, UK: Wiley-Blackwell Publishing, 2004). https://www.blackwellpublishing.com/ridley/a-z/Evolution_of_the_eye.asp.

27. Zbynek Kozmik, Jana Ruzickova, Kristyna Jonasova, Yoshifumi Matsumoto, Pavel Vopalensky, Iryna Kozmikova, Hynek Strnad, Shoji Kawamura, Joram Piatigorsky, Vaclav Paces, and Cestmir Vlcek, "Assembly of the cnidarian camera-type eye from vertebrate-like components," *Proceedings of the National Academy of Sciences USA* 105 (2008): 8989–8993. doi:10.1073/pnas.0800388105. PMID:18577593.

28. Fangchen Zhao, David J. Bottjer, Shixue Hu, Zongjun Yin, and Maoyan Zhu, "Complexity and diversity of eyes in early Cambrian ecosystems," *Scientific Reports* 3 (2013): 2751. doi:10.1038/srep02751. PMID:24067397.

29. Akihisa Terakita, "The opsins," *Genome Biology* 6 (2005): 213. doi:10.1186/gb-2005-6-3-213. PMID:15774036.

30. Mineo Iseki, Shigeru Matsunaga, Akio Murakami, Kaoru Ohno, Kiyoshi Shiga, Kazuichi Yoshida, Michizo Sugai, Tetsuo Takahashis, Terumitsu Hori, and Masakatsu Watanabe, "A blue-light-activated adenylyl cyclase mediates photoavoidance in *Euglena gracilis*," *Nature* 415 (2002): 1047–1051. doi:10.1038/4151047a. PMID:11875575.

31. Michael J. Behe, *Darwin's Black Box* (New York: The Free Press, 1996), 39.

32. Gehring and Ikeo, "*Pax6*," 376.

33. Behe, *Darwin's Black Box*, 176.

34. Todd H. Oakley and M. Sabrina Pankey, "Opening the "Black Box": The genetic and biochemical basis of eye evolution," *Evolution: Education and Outreach* 1 (2008): 390–402. doi:10.1007/s12052-008-0090-3.

35. Yoshinori Shichida and Take Matsuyama, "Evolution of opsins and phototransduction," *Philosophical Transactions of the Royal Society of London B* 364 (2009): 2881–2895. doi:10.1098/rstb.2009.0051. PMID:19720651.

36. David C. Plachetzki, Caitlin R. Fong, and Todd H. Oakley, "The evolution of phototransduction from an ancestral cyclic nucleotide gated pathway," *Proceedings of the Royal Society of London B* 277 (2010): 1963–1969. doi:10.1098/rspb.2009.1797. PMID:20219739.

37. Roberto Feuda, Sinead C. Hamilton, James O. McInerney, and Davide Pisani, "Metazoan opsin evolution reveals a simple route to animal vision," *Proceedings of the National Academy of Sciences USA* 109 (2012): 18868–18872. doi:10.1073/pnas.1204609109. PMID:23112152.

38. Oakley and Pankey, "Opening the Black Box," 396.

39. Yoshinori Shichida and Take Matsuyama, "Evolution of opsins," 2892.

40. Plachetzki, Fong, and Oakley, "Evolution of phototransduction," 1967.

41. Feuda, Hamilton, McInerney, and Pisani, "Metazoan opsin evolution," 18868.

42. Richard Dawkins, *The Blind Watchmaker* (New York: W.W. Norton, 1986), 93.

43. George C. Williams, *Natural Selection: Domains, Levels, and Challenges* (New York: Oxford University Press, 1992), 73.

44. Kenneth R. Miller, "Life's Grand Design," *Technology Review* 97 (February–March, 1994): 24–32. http://www.millerandlevine.com/km/evol/lgd/.

45. Douglas J. Futuyma, *Evolution* (Sunderland, MA: Sinauer Associates, 2005), 49.

46. Jerry A. Coyne, "The faith that dare not speak its name: The case against intelligent design," *The New Republic* (August 22 & 29, 2005): 21–33. http://pondside.uchicago.edu/ee/faculty/Coyne/pdf/New_Republic_ID.pdf.

47. Jonathan N. Tinsley, Maxim I. Molodtsov, Robert Prevedel, David Wartmann, Jofre Espigulé-Pons, Mattias Lauwers, and Alipasha Vaziri, "Direct detection of a single photon by humans," *Nature Communications* 7 (2016): 12172. doi:10.1038/ncomms12172. PMID:27434854.

48. Gordon Lynn Walls, *The Vertebrate Eye* (New York: Hafner, 1963), 652.

49. Sidney Futterman, "Metabolism and photochemistry in the retina," pp. 406–419 in *Adler's Physiology of the Eye*, ed. Robert A. Moses, 6th ed. (St. Louis: C. V. Mosby, 1975), 406.

50. Albert Alm and Anders Bill, "Ocular and optic nerve blood flow at normal and increased intraocular pressures in monkeys (*Macaca irus*): A study with radioactively labeled microspheres including flow determinations in brain and some other tissues," *Experimental Eye Research* 15 (1973): 15–29. doi:10.1016/0014-4835(73)90185-1. PMID:4630581.

51. Paul Henkind, Richard I. Hansen, and Jeanne Szalay, "Ocular circulation," pp. 98–155 in *Physiology of the Human Eye and the Visual System*, ed. Raymond E. Records (Hagerstown, MD: Harper & Row, 1979), 139–140.

52. Roy H. Steinberg, "Interactions between the retinal pigment epithelium and the neural retina," *Documenta Ophthalmologica* 60 (1985): 327–346. doi:10.1007/BF00158922. PMID:3905312.

53. Michael J. Denton, "The inverted retina: Maladaptation or preadaptation?" *Origins & Design* 19:2 (1999), issue 37. http://www.arn.org/docs/odesign/od192/invertedretina192.htm.

54. Richard W. Young, "The renewal of photoreceptor cell outer segments," *Journal of Cell Biology* 33 (1967): 61–72. doi:10.1083/jcb.33.1.61. PMID:6033942.

55. Richard W. Young and Dean Bok, "Participation of the retinal pigment epithelium in the rod outer segment renewal process," *Journal of Cell Biology* 42 (1969): 392–403. doi:10.1083/jcb.42.2.392. PMID:5792328.

56. Steinberg, "Interactions," 328.

57. Kristian Franze, Jens Grosche, Serguei N. Skatchkov, Stefan Schinkinger, Christian Foja, Detlev Schild, Ortrud Uckermann, Kort Travis, Andreas Reichenbach, and Jochen Guck, "Müller cells are living optical fibers in the vertebrate retina," *Proceedings of the National Academy of Sciences USA* 104 (2007): 8287–8292. doi:10.1073/pnas.0611180104. PMID:17485670.

58. Amichai M. Labin and Erez N. Ribak, "Retinal glial cells enhance human vision acuity," *Physical Review Letters* 104 (2010): 158102. doi:10.1103/PhysRevLett.104.158102. PMID:20482021.

59. Kate McAlpine, "Evolution gave flawed eye better vision," *New Scientist* (May 6, 2010). http://www.newscientist.com/article/mg20627594.000-optical-fibre-cells-transform-our-weird-retinas.html.

60. Editorial, "The eye was evolution's great invention," *New Scientist* (May 6, 2010. https://www.newscientist.com/article/mg20627592.400-the-eye-was-evolutions-great-invention/.

61. Kenneth A. Mason, Jonathan B. Losos, and Susan R. Singer, *Raven and Johnson's Biology*, 10th ed. (New York: McGraw-Hill, 2014), 428–429.

62. Alberto Wirth, Giuliano Cavallacci, and Frederic Genovesi-Ebert, "The advantages of an inverted retina," *Developments in Ophthalmology* 9 (1984): 20–28. doi:10.1159/000409800. PMID:6098490.

63. Ronald H. H. Kröger and Oliver Biehlmaier, "Space-saving advantage of an inverted retina," *Vision Research* 49 (2009): 2318–2321. doi:10.1016/j.visres.2009.07.001. PMID:19591859.

64. Nathan H. Lents, "The poor design of the human eye," *Human Evolution Blog* (January 12, 2015). http://thehumanevolutionblog.com/2015/01/12/the-poor-design-of-the-human-eye/.

CHAPTER 8 (PAGES 149–168)

1. George C. Williams and Randolph M. Nesse, "The dawn of Darwinian medicine," *Quarterly Review of Biology* 66 (1991): 1–22. doi:10.1086/417048. PMID:2052670.

2. Ibid., 11–14.

3. Peter M. Small, Martin G. Täuber, Corinne J. Hackbarth, and Merle A. Sande, "Influence of body temperature on bacterial growth rates in experimental pneumococcal meningitis in rabbits," *Infection and Immunity* 52 (1986): 484–487. PMID:3699893.

4. Neil M. H. Graham, Christopher J. Burrell, Robert M. Douglas, Pamela Debelle, and Lorraine Davies, "Adverse effects of aspirin, acetaminophen, and ibuprofen on immune function, viral shedding, and clinical status in rhinovirus-infected volunteers," *Journal of Infectious Diseases* 162 (1990): 1277–1282. doi:10.1093/infdis/162.6.1277. PMID:2172402.

5. Paul W. Ewald, "Cultural vectors, virulence, and the emergence of evolutionary epidemiology," *Oxford Surveys in Evolutionary Biology* 5 (1988): 215–245.

6. Paul W. Ewald, "Infectious disease and the evolution of virulence," *Evolution* (Boston: WGBH Educational Foundation, 2001). http://www.pbs.org/wgbh/evolution/library/01/6/text_pop/l_016_06.html.

7. John Snow, "On the mode of communication of cholera," *Edinburgh Medical Journal* 1 (1856): 668–670. http://www.ph.ucla.edu/epi/snow/lettermodecommcholera.html.

8. Thomas McKeown, *The Role of Medicine* (Princeton: Princeton University Press, 1979).

9. K. Codell Carter, "Review of Sherwin B. Nuland, *The Doctors' Plague: Germs, Childbed Fever, and the Strange Story of Ignác Semmelweis* (New York: W. W. Norton, 2003)," *Bulletin of the History of Medicine* 78 (2004): 898–899. http://www.indiana.edu/~koertge/H205SciReas/SciReasCarterSemmelweis.pdf.

10. "Smallpox," *World Health Organization* (2016). http://www.who.int/csr/disease/smallpox/en/.

11. Kul Gautam, "A history of global polio eradication," UNICEF (2005). http://www.unicef.org/immunization/files/the_history_of_polio.pdf.

12. Alexander Fleming, "On the antibacterial action of cultures of a Penicillium, with special reference to their use in the isolation of *B. influenzae*," *British Journal of Experimental Pathology* 10 (1929): 226–236. http://www.asm.org/ccLibraryFiles/FILENAME/0000000263/21-3flemingchainabraham.pdf.

13. Ernst Chain, Howard W. Florey, Arthur D. Gardner, Norman G. Heatley, Margaret A. Jennings, Jean Orr-Ewing, and A. G. Sanders, "Penicillin as a chemotherapeutic agent," *The Lancet* 239 (1940): 226–228. http://www.asm.org/ccLibraryFiles/FILENAME/0000000263/21-3flemingchainabraham.pdf.

14. Albert Schatz, Elizabeth Bugie, and Selman A. Waksman, "Streptomycin, a substance exhibiting antibiotic activity against gram-positive and gram-negative bacteria," *Proceedings of the Society for Experimental Biology and Medicine* 55 (1944): 66–69.

15. J. C. Walker, *Benjamin Minge Duggar, 1872–1956: A Biographical Memoir* (Washington, DC: National Academy of Sciences, 1958). http://www.nasonline.org/publications/biographical-memoirs/memoir-pdfs/duggar-benjamin.pdf.

16. Benjamin M. Duggar, "Aureomycin; a product of the continuing search for new antibiotics," *Annals of the New York Academy of Sciences* 51 (1948): 177–181. PMID:18112227.

17. Alexander Fleming, "Banquet Speech," *Nobel Prizes and Laureates* (December 10, 1945). http://nobelprize.org/medicine/laureates/1945/fleming-speech.html.

18. Ernst Chain, "Social responsibility and the scientist in modern western society," *Perspectives in Biology and Medicine* 14:3 (1971): 347–369. doi:10.1353/pbm.1971.0028. PMID:5103428.

19. Selman A. Waksman, "The role of antibiotics in natural processes," *Giornale di Microbiologia* 2 (1956): 1–14.

20. Philip S. Skell, "Why Do We Invoke Darwin?" *The Scientist* 19:16 (August 29, 2005): 10. http://www.the-scientist.com/?articles.view/articleNo/16649/title/Why-Do-We-Invoke-Darwin-/.

21. Edward P. Abraham and Ernst Chain, "An enzyme from bacteria able to destroy penicillin," *Nature* 146 (1940): 837. doi:10.1038/146837a0.

22. Heather K. Allen, Justin Donato, Helena Huimi Wang, Karen A. Cloud-Hansen, Julian Davies, and Jo Handelsman, "Call of the wild: Antibiotic resistance genes in natural environments," *Nature Reviews Microbiology* (2010): 251–259. doi:10.1038/nrmicro2312. PMID:20190823.

23. Vanessa M. D'Costa, Christine E. King, Lindsay Kalan, Mariya Morar, Wilson W. L. Sung, Carsten Schwarz, Duane Froese, Grant Zazula, Fabrice Calmels, Regis Debruyne, G. Brian Golding, Hendrik N. Poinar, and Gerard D. Wright, "Antibiotic resistance is ancient," *Nature* 477 (2011): 457-61. doi:10.1038/nature10388. PMID:21881561.

24. Eugenie C. Scott, "Dealing with anti-evolutionism," *Reports of the National Center for Science Education* 17 (July–August 1997): 24–30. http://www.ucmp.berkeley.edu/fosrec/Scott1.html, and http://www.ucmp.berkeley.edu/fosrec/Scott2.html.

25. Carl Zimmer, *Evolution: The Triumph of an Idea* (New York: Harper Collins, 2001), 336.

26. Jim O'Neill, "Tackling drug-resistant infections globally: Final report and recommendations," *Wellcome Trust and U.K. Government* (May 2016), 4–5. https://amr-review.org/sites/default/files/160518_Final%20paper_with%20cover.pdf.

27. Ibid.

28. Mark P. Brynildsen, Jonathan A. Winkler, Catherine S. Spina, I. Cody MacDonald, and James J. Collins, "Potentiating antibacterial activity by predictably enhancing endogenous microbial ROS production," *Nature Biotechnology* 31 (2013): 160–165. doi:10.1038/nbt.2458. PMID:23292609.

29. Alexander J. Meeske, Eammon P. Riley, William P. Robins, Tsuyoshi Uehara, John J. Mekalanos, Daniel Kahne, Suzanne Walker, Andrew C. Kruse, Thomas G. Bernhardt, and David Z. Rudner, "SEDS proteins are a widespread family of bacterial cell wall polymerases," *Nature* 537 (2016): 634–638. doi:10.1038/nature19331. PMID:27525505.

30. Zuzanna Kaźmierczak, Andrzej Górski, and Krystyna Dąbrowska, "Facing antibiotic resistance: *Staphylococcus aureus* phages as a medical tool," *Viruses* 6 (2014): 2551–2570. doi:10.3390/v6072551. PMID:24988520.

31. Tom Parfitt, "Georgia: An unlikely stronghold for bacteriophage therapy," *The Lancet* 365 (2005): 2166–2167. doi:10.1016/S0140-6736(05)66759-1. PMID:15986542.

32. Andrzej Górski, "Clinical phage therapy 2015," Ludwik Hirszfeld Institute of Immunology and Experimental Therapy, Polish Academy of Sciences, Wrocław, Poland. http://www.iitd.pan.wroc.pl/en/clinphage2015.

33. Anthony Wright, Catherine H. Hawkins, Erik E. Änggård, and David R. Harper, "A controlled clinical trial of a therapeutic bacteriophage preparation in chronic otitis due to antibiotic-resistant *Pseudomonas aeruginosa*: A preliminary report of efficacy," *Clinical Otolaryngology* 34 (2009): 349–357. doi:10.1111/j.1749-4486.2009.01973.x. PMID:19673983.

34. Daniel E. Kadouri, Kevin To, Robert M. Q. Shanks, Yohei Doi, "Predatory bacteria: a potential ally against multidrug-resistant Gram-negative pathogens," *PLoS One* 8 (2013): e63397. doi:10.1371/journal.pone.0063397. PMID:23650563.

35. Shilpi Gupta, Chi Tang, Michael Tran, and Daniel E. Kadouri, "Effect of predatory bacteria on human cell lines," *PLoS One* 11 (2016): e0161242. doi:10.1371/journal. pone.0161242. PMID:27579919.

36. Julian Davies and Dorothy Davies, "Origins and evolution of antibiotic resistance," *Microbiology and Molecular Biology Reviews* 74 (2010): 417–433. doi:10.1128/ MMBR.00016-10. PMID:20805405.

37. Gautam Dantas and Morten O. A. Sommer, "How to fight back against antibiotic resistance," *American Scientist* 102 (2014): 42–51. doi.org/10.1511/2014.106.42.

38. Dominica Nichols, N. Cahoon, E. M. Trakhtenberg, L. Pham, Alka Mehta, A. Belanger, Tanya S. Kanigan, Kim Lewis, and Slava S. Epstein, "Use of ichip for high-throughput in situ cultivation of 'uncultivable' microbial species," *Applied and Environmental Microbiology* 76 (2010): 2445–2450. doi:10.1128/AEM.01754-09. PMID:20173072.

39. Losee L. Ling, Tanja Schneider, Aaron J. Peoples, Amy L. Spoering, Ina Engels, Brian P. Conlon, Anna Mueller, Till F. Schäberle, Dallas E. Hughes, Slava Epstein, Michael Jones, Linos Lazarides, Victoria A. Steadman, Douglas R. Cohen, Cintia R. Felix, K. Ashley Fetterman, William P. Millett, Anthony G. Nitti, Ashley M. Zullo, Chao Chen, and Kim Lewis, "A new antibiotic kills pathogens without detectable resistance," *Nature* 517 (2015): 455–459. doi:10.1038/nature14098. PMID:25561178.

40. Mark G. Charest, Christian D. Lerner, Jason D. Brubaker, Dionicio R. Siegel, and Andrew G. Myers, "A convergent enantioselective route to structurally diverse 6-deoxytetracycline antibiotics," *Science* 308 (2005): 395–398. doi:10.1126/ science.1109755. PMID:15831754.

41. Ian B. Seiple, Ziyang Zhang, Pavol Jakubec, Audrey Langlois-Mercier, Peter M. Wright, Daniel T. Hog, Kazuo Yabu, Senkara Rao Allu, Takehiro Fukuzaki, Peter N. Carlsen, Yoshiaki Kitamura, Xiang Zhou, Matthew L. Condakes, Filip T. Szczypiński, William D. Green, and Andrew G. Myers, "A platform for the discovery of new macrolide antibiotics," *Nature* 533 (2016): 338–345. doi:10.1038/nature17967. PMID:27193679.

42. Fan Liu and Andrew G. Myers, "Development of a platform for the discovery and practical synthesis of new tetracycline antibiotics," *Current Opinion in Chemical Biology* 32 (2016): 48–57. doi:10.1016/j.cbpa.2016.03.011. PMID:27043373.

43. Robert J. Woods and Andrew F. Read, "Clinical management of resistance evolution in a bacterial infection: A case study," *Evolution, Medicine, and Public Health* 2015 (2015): 281–288. doi:10.1093/emph/eov025. PMID:26454762.

44. Michael Baym, Tami D. Lieberman, Eric D. Kelsic, Remy Chait, Rotem Gross, Idan Yelin, and Roy Kishony, "Spatiotemporal microbial evolution on antibiotic landscapes," *Science* 353 (2016): 1147–1151. doi:10.1126/science.aag0822. PMID:27609891.

45. Harvard Medical School, "The evolution of bacteria on a 'Mega-Plate' Petri dish," September 2016. https://vimeo.com/180908160.

46. Ed Yong, "Stunning videos of evolution in action," *The Atlantic* (September 8, 2016). http://www.theatlantic.com/science/archive/2016/09/stunning-videos-of-evolution-in-action/499136/.

47. Baym, "Spatiotemporal microbial evolution," 1151.

48. Randolph M. Nesse and Joshua D. Shiffman, "Evolutionary biology in the medical school curriculum," *BioScience* 53 (2003): 585–587. doi:10.1641/0006-3568(2003)053[0585:EBITMS]2.0.CO;2.

49. Randolph M. Nesse, Stephen C. Stearns, and Gilbert S. Omenn, "Medicine needs evolution," *Science* 311 (2006): 1171. doi:10.1126/science.1125956. PMID:16497889.

50. Ajit Varki, "Nothing in medicine makes sense, except in the light of evolution," *Journal of Molecular Medicine (Berlin)* 90 (2012): 481–494. doi:10.1007/s00109-012-0900-5. PMID:22538272.

51. Michael F. Antolin, Kristin P. Jenkins, Carl T. Bergstrom, Bernard J. Crespi Subhajyoti De, Angela Hancock, Kathryn A. Hanley, Thomas R. Meagher, Andres Moreno-Estrada, Randolph M. Nesse, Gilbert S. Omenn, and Stephen C. Stearns, "Evolution and medicine in undergraduate education: A prescription for all biology students," *Evolution* 66 (2012): 1991–2006. doi:10.1111/j.1558-5646.2011.01552.x. PMID:22671563.

52. Eugene E. Harris and Avelin A. Malyango, "Evolutionary explanations in medical and health profession courses: Are you answering your students' 'why' questions?" *BMC Medical Education* 5 (2005): 16. doi:10.1186/1472-6920-5-16. PMID:15885137.

53. Brandon H. Hidaka, Anila Asghar, C. Athena Aktipis, Randolph M. Nesse, Terry M. Wolpaw, Nicole K. Skursky, Katelyn J. Bennett, Matthew W. Beyrouty, and Mark D. Schwartz, "The status of evolutionary medicine education in North American medical schools," *BMC Medical Education* 15 (2015): 38. doi:10.1186/s12909-015-0322-5. PMID:25884843.

54. Paola Palanza and Stefano Parmigiani, "Why human evolution should be a basic science for medicine and psychology students," *Journal of Anthropological Sciences* 94 (2016): 183–192. PMID:27101590.

55. "Cancer Statistics," *National Cancer Institute* (March 14, 2016). https://www.cancer.gov/about-cancer/understanding/statistics.

56. Julian S. Huxley, *Biological Aspects of Cancer* (London: Allen & Unwin, 1958), 15.

57. Leigh M. Van Valen and Virginia C. Maiorana, "HeLa, a new microbial species," *Evolutionary Theory & Review* 10 (1991): 71–74. http://leighvanvalen.com/evolutionary-theory/.

58. Mark D. Vincent, "The animal within: Carcinogenesis and the clonal evolution of cancer cells are speciation events sensu stricto," *Evolution* 64 (2010): 1173–1183. doi:10.1111/j.1558-5646.2009.00942.x. PMID:20059538.

59. Peter Duesberg, Daniele Mandrioli, Amanda McCormack, and Joshua M. Nicholson, "Is carcinogenesis a form of speciation?" *Cell Cycle* 10 (2011): 2100–2114. doi:10.4161/cc.10.13.16352. PMID:21666415.

60. Arne Müntzing, "Cytogenetic investigations on synthetic *Galeopsis tetrahit*," Hereditas 16 (1932): 105–154. doi:10.1111/j.1601-5223.1932.tb02564.x.

61. Georgii D. Karpechenko, "The production of polyploid gametes in hybrids," *Hereditas* 9 (1927): 349–368. http://onlinelibrary.wiley.com/doi/10.1111/j.1601-5223.1927. tb03536.x/epdf.

62. S. Joshua Swamidass, "Cancer and evolutionary theory," *The BioLogos Forum* (September 12–14, 2016). https://discourse.biologos.org/t/cancer-and-evolutionary-theory/5673.

63. Peter C. Nowell, "The clonal evolution of tumor cell populations," *Science* 194 (1976): 23–28. PMID:959840.

64. Mohammad Ilyas and Ian P. M. Tomlinson, "Genetic pathways in colorectal cancer," *Histopathology* 28 (1996): 389–399. doi:10.1046/j.1365-2559.1996.339381.x. PMID:8735714.

65. Robert A. Gatenby and Thomas L. Vincent, "An evolutionary model of carcinogenesis," *Cancer Research* 63 (2003): 6212–6220. PMID:14559806.

66. Mel Greaves and Carlo C. Maley, "Clonal evolution in cancer," *Nature* 481 (2012): 306–313. doi:10.1038/nature10762. PMID:22258609.

67. David S. Goodsell, "The molecular perspective: The ras oncogene," *The Oncologist* 4 (1999): 263–264. PMID:10394594.

68. Celia R. Berkers, Oliver D.K. Maddocks, Eric C. Cheung, Inbal Mor, and Karen H. Vousden, "Metabolic regulation by p53 family members," *Cell Metabolism* 18 (2013): 617–633. doi:10.1016/j.cmet.2013.06.019. PMID:23954639.

69. Varda Rotter, "p53, a transformation-related cellular-encoded protein, can be used as a biochemical marker for the detection of primary mouse tumor cells," *Proceedings of the National Academy of Sciences USA* 80 (1983): 2613–2617. doi:10.1073/pnas.80.9.2613. PMID:6189126.

70. Moshe Oren and Varda Rotter, "Mutant p53 gain-of-function in cancer," *Cold Spring Harbor Perspectives in Biology* 2 (2010): a001107. doi:10.1101/cshperspect.a001107. PMID:20182618.

71. Pierre-Luc Germain, "Cancer cells and adaptive explanations," *Biology and Philosophy* 27 (2012): 785–810. doi:10.1007/s10539-012-9334-2.

72. Pedro M. Enriquez-Navas, Yoonseok Kam, Tuhin Das, Sabrina Hassan, Ariosto Silva, Parastou Foroutan, Epifanio Ruiz, Gary Martinez, Susan Minton, Robert J. Gillies, and Robert A. Gatenby, "Exploiting evolutionary principles to prolong tumor control in preclinical models of breast cancer," *Science Translational Medicine* 8 (2016): 327ra24. doi:10.1126/scitranslmed.aad7842. PMID:26912903.

73. Robert A. Gatenby, Ariosto S. Silva, Robert J. Gillies, and B. Roy Frieden, "Adaptive therapy," *Cancer Research* (2009): 4894–4903. doi:10.1158/0008-5472.CAN-08-3658. PMID:19487300.

Chapter 9 (Pages 169–187)

1. Richard C. Lewontin, "Billions and billions of demons," *The New York Review of Books* 44 (January 9, 1997): 28. http://www.nybooks.com/articles/1997/01/09/billions-and-billions-of-demons/.

2. "Why sex?" *PBS Evolution*, Public Broadcasting System (November 2001), starting at 50:10. https://www.youtube.com/watch?v=f8Nn-MNC1ik.

3. Daniel C. Dennett, *Darwin's Dangerous Idea* (New York: Simon & Schuster, 1995), 18, 63.

4. James R. Moore, *The Post-Darwinian Controversies* (Cambridge: Cambridge University Press, 1979).

5. David C. Lindberg and Ronald L. Numbers, *God and Nature: Historical Essays on the Encounter between Christianity and Science* (Berkeley: University of California Press, 1986).

6. Tobin Grant, "Graphs: 5 signs of the 'Great Decline' of religion in America," *Religion News Service* (August 1, 2014). http://religionnews.com/2014/08/01/five-signs-great-decline-religion-america-gallup-graphs-church/.

7. Michael Lipka, "Why America's 'nones' left religion behind," *Pew Research Center*, accessed August 24, 2016. http://www.pewresearch.org/fact-tank/2016/08/24/why-americas-nones-left-religion-behind/.

8. Michael Zimmerman, "Background," *The Clergy Letter Project*, accessed September 12, 2016. http://www.theclergyletterproject.org/Backgd_info.htm.

9. Michael Zimmerman, "The Clergy Letter – from American Christian Clergy," *The Clergy Letter Project*, accessed September 12, 2016. http://www.theclergyletterproject.org/Christian_Clergy/ChrClergyLtr.htm.

10. Stephen Jay Gould, "Nonoverlapping Magisteria," *Natural History* 106 (March 1997): 16–22. http://www.stephenjaygould.org/library/gould_noma.html.

11. Eugenie C. Scott, quoted in Thomas J. Oord and Eric Stark, "A conversation with Eugenie Scott," *Science and Theology News* (April 1, 2002). http://web.archive.org/web/20050309214648/http://www.stnews.org/archives/2002/Apr_features.html#2.

12. Neela Banerjee and Anne Berryman, "At churches nationwide, good words for evolution," *The New York Times* (February 13, 2006). http://www.nytimes.com/2006/02/13/us/at-churches-nationwide-good-words-for-evolution.html.

13. Michael Zimmerman, "Evolution Weekend," *The Clergy Letter Project*, accessed September 12, 2016. http://theclergyletterproject.org/rel_evolution_weekend_2016.html.

14. United Methodist Church, "Book of resolutions: God's creation and the church," *United Methodist Communications* (2008). http://www.umc.org/Evolution_weekend/2008_evol_weekend.htm.

15. Southwestern Washington Synod Assembly, "Resolution on Faith and Science" (2009). http://www.theclergyletterproject.org/pdf/Southwestern%20WA%20ELCA.pdf.

16. General Assembly of the Presbyterian Church (U.S.A.), "Regarding endorsing the Clergy Letter Project," *PC Biz* (June 2016). https://www.pc-biz.org/#/search/6304.

17. David P. Barash, "God, Darwin and my college biology class," *The New York Times Sunday Review* (September 27, 2014). https://www.nytimes.com/2014/09/28/opinion/sunday/god-darwin-and-my-college-biology-class.html.

18. Deborah Kelemen, "Are children 'intuitive theists'?" *Psychological Science* 15 (2004): 295–301. doi:10.1111/j.0956-7976.2004.00672.x. PMID:15102137.

19. Deborah Kelemen, Natalie A. Emmons, Rebecca Seston Schillaci, and Patricia A. Ganea, "Young children can be taught basic natural selection using a picture-storybook intervention," *Psychological Science* 25 (2014): 893–902. doi:10.1177/0956797613516009. PMID:24503874.

20. Michael B. Berkman and Eric Plutzer, "Enablers of doubt: How future teachers learn to negotiate the evolution wars in their classrooms," *Annals of the American Academy of Political and Social Science* 658 (2015): 253–270. doi:10.1177/0002716214557783.

21. Michael B. Berkman and Eric Plutzer, "Defeating creationism in the courtroom, but not in the classroom," *Science* 331 (2011): 404–405. doi:10.1126/science.1198902. PMID:21273472.

22. Quoted in Matt Swayne, "Biology teachers: Understanding faith, teaching evolution not mutually exclusive," *ScienceDaily* (February 25, 2015). http://www.sciencedaily.com/releases/2015/02/150225114425.htm.

23. Eugenie C. Scott and Glenn Branch, "Evolution: what's wrong with 'teaching the controversy'," *Trends in Ecology and Evolution* 18 (2003): 499–502. doi:10.1016/S0169-5347(03)00218-0. http://d43fweuh3sg51.cloudfront.net/media/assets/wgbh/evol07/evol07_doc_teachcontr/evol07_doc_teachcontr.pdf.

24. John G. West, *Darwin Day in America: How our politics and culture have been dehumanized in the name of science* (Wilmington, DE: Intercollegiate Studies Institute, 2015), 231–268.

25. Linus Pauling, *No More War!* (New York: Dodd, Mead & Company, 1958), 209.

26. Bruce Alberts, "Science and human needs," 137th Annual Meeting of the National Academy of Sciences, Washington, DC, May 1, 2000. https://brucealberts.ucsf.edu/publications/NAS2000.pdf.

27. Donald D. Hoffman and Chetan Prakash, "Objects of consciousness," *Frontiers in Psychology* 5 (2014): 577. doi:10.3389/fpsyg.2014.00577. PMID:24987382.

28. Ajit Varki and Danny Brower, *Denial: Self-deception, false beliefs, and the origins of the human mind* (New York: Twelve, 2013), 172.

29. Ibid., 27, 144–149.

30. C. S. Lewis, *Miracles* (London: G. Bles, 1947), 21–22.

31. Thomas Nagel, *Mind and Cosmos: Why the materialist neo-Darwinian conception of nature is almost certainly false* (New York: Oxford University Press, 2012), 16, 27.

32. Ibid., 50, 66.

33. Ibid., 128.

34. Richard Van Noorden, "Science publishing: The trouble with retractions," *Nature* 478 (2011): 26–28. doi:10.1038/478026a. PMID:21979026.

35. Paul Voosen, "Amid a sea of false findings, the NIH tries reform," *Chronicle of Higher Education* (March 16, 2015). http://www.bc.edu/content/dam/files/research/pdf/RSI-Erickson-False%20Findings-Reform-Article.pdf.

36. Paul E. Smaldino and Richard McElreath, "The natural selection of bad science," *Royal Society Open Science* 3 (2016): 160348. doi:10.1098/rsos.160384. PMID:27703703.

37. Ferric C. Fang, R. Grant Steen, and Arturo Casadevall, "Misconduct accounts for the majority of retracted scientific publications," *Proceedings of the National Academy of Sciences USA* 109 (2012): 17028–17033. doi:10.1073/pnas.1212247109. PMID:23027971.

38. "Questions about intelligent design," Discovery Institute, accessed September 2016. http://www.discovery.org/id/faqs/#questionsAboutIntelligentDesign.

39. Michael J. Behe, *Darwin's Black Box* (New York: The Free Press, 1996).

40. Stephen C. Meyer, "DNA by design: An inference to the best explanation for the origin of biological information," *Rhetoric & Public Affairs* 1 (1998): 519–556. doi:10.1353/rap.2010.0105. http://www.discovery.org/f/100.

41. William A. Dembski, *The Design Revolution: Answering the Toughest Questions about Intelligent Design* (Downers Grove, IL: Intervarsity Press, 2004).

42. Pam Belluck, "Board for Kansas deletes evolution from the curriculum," *The New York Times* (August 12, 1999). http://www.nytimes.com/1999/08/12/us/board-for-kansas-deletes-evolution-from-curriculum.html.

43. Scott C. Todd, "A view from Kansas on that evolution debate," *Nature* 401 (1999): 423. doi:10.1038/46661. PMID:10519534.

44. Massimo Pigliucci, *Denying Evolution: Creationism, Scientism, and the Nature of Science* (Sunderland, MA: Sinauer Associates, 2002), 2–3.

45. Pat Shipman, "Being stalked by intelligent design," *American Scientist* 93 (2005): 500–502. doi:10.1511/2005.56.3471. http://www.americanscientist.org/libraries/documents/2005103135553_646.pdf.

46. Gerald Weissmann, "The facts of evolution: fighting the Endarkenment," *FASEB Journal* 19 (2005): 1581–1582. doi:10.1096/fj.05-1001ufm. PMID:16195364.

47. Marshall Berman, "Intelligent Design: The new creationism threatens all of science and society," *APS News* 14:9 (October 2005). https://www.aps.org/publications/apsnews/200510/backpage.cfm.

48. Robyn Williams, *Unintelligent Design* (Crows Nest, Australia: Allen & Unwin, 2006), 2.

49. Niall Shanks, *God, the Devil, and Darwin* (Oxford: Oxford University Press, 2006), xi–xii.

50. Ibid., 246.

51. Kenneth R. Miller, *Only a Theory: Evolution and the Battle for America's Soul* (New York: Viking Press, 2008), 190–191.

52. Ibid., 16.

53. George Harrison, "Here comes the sun" (The Beatles, *Abbey Road*, 1969). https://www.youtube.com/watch?v=bgiQD56eWDk.

54. James A. Shapiro, "A third way," *Boston Review* (February/March 1997). http://bostonreview.net/archives/BR22.1/shapiro.html.

55. Massimo Pigliucci, "Do we need an extended evolutionary synthesis?" *Evolution* 61 (2007): 2743–2749. doi:10.1111/j.1558-5646.2007.00246.x. PMID:17924956.

56. Elizabeth Pennisi, "Modernizing the modern synthesis," *Science* 321 (2008): 196–197. doi:10.1126/science.321.5886.196. PMID:18621652.

57. Suzan Mazur, *The Altenberg 16: An Exposé of the Evolution Industry* (Wellington, New Zealand: Scoop Media, 2009), v.

58. Massimo Pigliucci and Gerd B. Müller, *Evolution: The Extended Synthesis* (Cambridge, MA: MIT Press, 2010).

59. Jerry Fodor and Massimo Piattelli-Palmarini, "Survival of the fittest theory: Darwinism's limits," *New Scientist* (February 3, 2010). http://dingo.sbs.arizona.edu/~massimo/publications/PDF/JF_MPP_darwinisms_limits.pdf.

60. James A. Shapiro, *Evolution: A View from the 21st Century* (Upper Saddle River, NJ: FT Press Science, 2011), 134–137.

61. The Third Way: Evolution in the Era of Genomics and Epigenomics. http://www. thethirdwayofevolution.com.

62. Suzan Mazur, *The Paradigm Shifters: Overthrowing 'the Hegemony of the Culture of Darwin'* (New York: Caswell Books, 2015), 1.

63. Kevin Laland, Tobias Uller, Marc Feldman, Kim Sterelny, Gerd B. Müller, Armin Moczek, Eva Jablonka, John Odling-Smee, Gregory A. Wray, Hopi E. Hoekstra, Douglas J. Futuyma, Richard E. Lenski, Trudy F. C. Mackay, Dolph Schluter, and Joan E. Strassmann, "Does evolutionary theory need a rethink?" *Nature* 514 (2014): 161–164. doi:10.1038/514161a. PMID:25297418.

64. Kevin N. Laland, Tobias Uller, Marcus W. Feldman, Kim Sterelny, Gerd B. Müller, Armin Moczek, Eva Jablonka, and John Odling-Smee, "The extended evolutionary synthesis: its structure, assumptions and predictions," *Proceedings of the Royal Society of London B* 282 (2015): 20151019. doi:10.1098/rspb.2015.1019. PMID:26246559.

65. Denis Noble, "Evolution beyond neo-Darwinism: A new conceptual framework," *Journal of Experimental Biology* 218 (2015): 7–13. doi:10.1242/jeb.106310. PMID:25568446.

66. Clarence A. Williams, "Neo-Darwinism is just fine," *Journal of Experimental Biology* 218 (2015): 2658–2659. doi:10.1242/jeb.125088. PMID:26290594.

67. Denis Noble, "Central tenets of neo-Darwinism broken. Response to 'Neo-Darwinism is just fine'," *Journal of Experimental Biology* 218 (2015): 2659. doi:10.1242/jeb.125526. PMID:26290595.

68. "New trends in evolutionary biology: Biological, philosophical and social science perspectives," Royal Society of London (November 7–9, 2016). https://royalsociety.org/ science-events-and-lectures/2016/11/evolutionary-biology/.

69. Suzan Mazur, *Royal Society: The Public Evolution Summit* (New York: Caswell Books, 2016).

70. Paul A. Nelson, "Specter of intelligent design emerges at the Royal Society meeting," *Evolution News & Views* (November 8, 2016). http://www.evolutionnews.org/2016/11/ specter_of_inte103270.html.

71. Paul A. Nelson and David Klinghoffer, "Scientists confirm: Darwinism is broken," *CNS News* (December 13, 2016). http://www.cnsnews.com/commentary/david-klinghoffer/ scientists-confirm-darwinism-broken.

72. Thomas S. Kuhn, *The Structure of Scientific Revolutions*, 2nd ed. (Chicago: University of Chicago Press, 1970), 103–105, 163.

73. Ibid., 159.

74. William A. Dembski, *The Design Inference* (Cambridge: Cambridge University Press, 1998).

75. William A. Dembski, *No Free Lunch: Why Specified Complexity Cannot Be Purchased without Intelligence* (Lanham, MD: Rowman & Littlefield, 2002).

76. Casey Luskin, "The Evolutionary Informatics Lab: Putting intelligent design predictions to the test," *Evolution News & Views* (February 7, 2012). http://www.evolutionnews. org/2012/02/the_evolutionar056061.html.

77. "Publications," *The Evolutionary Informatics Lab* (2016). http://www.evoinfo.org/ publications/.

78. Robert J. Marks II, Michael J. Behe, William A. Dembski, Bruce L. Gordon, and John C. Sanford (editors), *Biological Information: New Perspectives* (Singapore: World Scientific, 2013). http://www.worldscientific.com/worldscibooks/10.1142/8818#t=toc.

79. Kuhn, *Structure of Scientific Revolutions*, 157–158.

80. David Snoke, "Systems biology as a research program for intelligent design," *Bio-Complexity* 2014:3 (2014): 1–11. doi:10.5048/BIO-C.2014.3.

81. "About," *Biologic Institute* (2016). http://www.biologicinstitute.org/about.

82. Mariclair A. Reeves, Ann K. Gauger, and Douglas D. Axe, "Enzyme families—shared evolutionary history or shared design? A study of the GABA-aminotransferase family," *Bio-Complexity* 4 (2014): 1–16. http://bio-complexity.org/ojs/index.php/main/article/view/BIO-C.2014.4.

83. Paul A. Nelson, "'A few years ago, we couldn't have filled a Kombi': The Brazilian intelligent design adventure," *Evolution News & Views* (November 21, 2014). http://www.evolutionnews.org/2014/11/a_few_years_ago091381.html.

INDEX

Made in United States
Orlando, FL
22 January 2022

13886265R00146